KT-219-719

Digital Engineering with Minecraft™

Copyright © 2016 by Que Publishing

ISBN-13: 978-0-7897-5547-6
ISBN-10: 0-7897-5547-5

Library of Congress Control Number: 2015944478

Printed in the United States of America

First Printing: September 2015

Trademarks

All terms mentioned in this book that are known to be trademarks or
service marks have been appropriately capitalized. Que Publishing cannot
attest to the accuracy of this information. Use of a term in this book should
not be regarded as affecting the validity of any trademark or service mark.

Minecraft ®/™ & © 2009-2013 Mojang / Notch

Minecraft is a trademark of Mojang Synergies / Notch Development AB.
This book is not affiliated with or sponsored by Mojang Synergies/Notch
Development AB.

Warning and Disclaimer

Special Sales

For information about buying this title in bulk quantities, or for special
sales opportunities (which may include electronic versions; custom
cover designs; and content particular to your business, training goals,
marketing focus, or branding interests), please contact our corporate sales
department at corpsales@pearsoned.com or (800) 382-3419.

For government sales inquiries, please contact
governmentsales@pearsoned.com.

For questions about sales outside the U.S., please contact
international@pearsoned.com.

Editor-in-Chief
Greg Wiegand

Executive Editor
Rick Kughen

Development Editor
Greg Kettell

Managing Editor
Sandra Schroeder

Project Editor
Seth Kerney

Copy Editor
Kitty Wilson

Indexer
Heather McNeill

Proofreader
Jess DeGabriele

Technical Editor
Timothy L. Warner

**Publishing
Coordinator**
Kristen Watterson

Book Designer
Mark Shirar

Compositor
Mary Sudul

DIGITAL ENGINEERING WITH MINECRAFT™

James Floyd Kelly

Contents at a Glance

Table of Contents

About the Author

James Floyd Kelly is a writer from Atlanta, Georgia. He has degrees in industrial engineering and English and has written technology books on a number of subjects, including CNC machines, 3D printing, open source software, LEGO robotics, and electronics.

Dedication

For Decker and Sawyer, my Minecraft maniacs.

Acknowledgments

If you'll take a look a few pages back, you'll see the list of Que staff who were responsible for making this book a reality. I'd like to thank each and every one of them for doing such a great job in making this book shine.

I'd like to call out one particular person for being this book's champion and pushing it along so readers would have access to some of the fun and unusual things I do with Minecraft. That person is Executive Editor Rick Kughen. Rick is always enthusiastic about my book proposals, and this one just seemed to grab his attention and required very little persuasion to get approval to start writing. If you like this book, drop Rick an email and tell him thank you for making it happen.

My wife, Ashley, will always have my thanks for any book I write—but this time I have two very young people to also thank: my boys, Decker and Sawyer. They discovered Minecraft and dragged me along for the ride. As I discovered their fascination and enjoyment with the game, I jumped in to see what the fuss was all about...and I'm glad I did! I continue to enjoy exploring worlds with them, and many of the projects in this book came about because of something they asked for or observed or wanted, but couldn't quite figure out how to make it happen. I put on the Dad-hat and figured out some things so they could extend their fun, never knowing a book would come out of the experience. So, thank you boys!

We Want to Hear from You!

As the reader of this book, *you* are our most important critic and commentator. We value your opinion and want to know what we're doing right, what we could do better, what areas you'd like to see us publish in, and any other words of wisdom you're willing to pass our way.

We welcome your comments. You can email or write to let us know what you did or didn't like about this book—as well as what we can do to make our books better.

Please note that we cannot help you with technical problems related to the topic of this book.

When you write, please be sure to include this book's title and author as well as your name and email address. We will carefully review your comments and share them with the author and editors who worked on the book.

Email: feedback@quepublishing.com

Mail: Que Publishing
  ATTN: Reader Feedback
  800 East 96th Street
  Indianapolis, IN 46240 USA

Reader Services

Visit our website and register this book at quepublishing.com/register for convenient access to any updates, downloads, or errata that might be available for this book.

Introduction

Minecraft. This single word can make kids grin a mile wide and parents scratch their heads. It's both phenomenon and mystery. Mojang (pronounced Moe-Yang, rhymes with Joe-Sang), the company that created Minecraft, made a fortune in game sales, merchandise, and Minecraft-related books—and then turned another fortune by selling the company. (And sales continue, with thousands of copies being sold every day as new fans discover the game.) Computer games come and go, but Minecraft survives; I am having a difficult time thinking of another game that continues to be played by so many fans, year after year, and continues to grow in popularity.

Game designer Markus Persson, known as Notch to his fans, released an early version of Minecraft in May 2009; the final version (with new features and fixed bugs) showed up in November 2011. Minecraft quickly became available on a variety of platforms, including Windows, Mac, Android, iOS devices such as the iPad, and even game consoles such as the Xbox and PlayStation. With sales of more than 60 million games (and climbing) and well over 100 million players, it's not hard to understand why in 2014 Microsoft made an offer to purchase Mojang. In November 2014, three years after the full version of the game was released, Microsoft bought Mojang and its Minecraft game for $2,500,000,000.00. Yes, you read that right: $2.5 billion.

Mojang did sell a few other games, but let's be honest: Microsoft bought Mojang because of the incredible popularity of one game and one game only—Minecraft. (Microsoft has even dropped a bit of news that it fully intends to make Minecraft 2, but they chose (wisely) not to share a release date.)

Ask Minecraft fans what they like best about the game, and you'll get dozens and dozens of different responses. The game was designed first as a sandbox-style platform—which still exists in the Creative mode of the game—allowing players to build whatever they could imagine (within limits, of course). Another mode, called Survival mode, was added; in it, players are pitted against enemies and must scavenge for food and build shelter, among other activities. The Multiplayer mode allows more than one player to exist in the same play area (called a World); players can work together or compete. Additional modes and features have been added over the years, helping ensure that new players can find at least one mode that suits their style of play.

I prefer Survival mode. I like being dropped into a new game with no weapons, no food, and no shelter. It's a fun challenge to survive that first night (and the creatures that magically appear when the sun goes down). My two young boys prefer Creative mode and Multiplayer. They love building tall houses with secret rooms, laying down miles of track for a custom-made roller-coaster, and creating traps to snare the bad guys. If you're a Minecraft player, you've probably got your favorite things to do in the game as well.

Never played Minecraft? Well, I've got some good news and some bad news. The good news is that dozens of books and hundreds of websites are available to help turn you into a Minecraft expert. Trust me: It won't take long for you to learn your way around the Minecraft interface and all the various tools you can use in the game. The bad news is that the book you're holding in your hands is not going to teach you how to play Minecraft.

NOTE

Books on Minecraft

Fellow writer and Minecraft fan, Stephen O'Brien, has a number of Minecraft books out that can teach you all sorts of tricks and tips for playing Minecraft. You can find more information here: http://www.quepublishing.com/authors/bio/2cfac6df-79ea-4e90-bbc3-01c2bb6cad6b

But even if you're not already a Minecraft player, this book is for you—not only will you discover the Minecraft game and just how much fun it is to play, but you'll also learn some new skills that are useful outside of Minecraft. In it you'll use a lot of non-Minecraft software to perform some amazing tasks. You'll still be spending some time in Minecraft, too, if you follow along with this book's projects, but as you'll learn next, there are some interesting things you can do (and learn) outside of Minecraft to create some jaw-dropping creations inside the game.

NOTE

Using different versions of Minecraft

It doesn't matter if you use a PC or Mac version of Minecraft or even the Pocket Edition that's available for mobile devices such as iPad and Android tablets. Most of the software I use in this book is available for multiple platforms, but I'll point out alternatives for you when a software tool might not be available for a particular operating system or version of Minecraft.

Minecraft Can Make You Money

I imagine there are a lot of Minecraft fans who just read the above subhead and sat up a bit straighter! I can almost hear you now: "Are you kidding? I can get paid to play Minecraft?"

Well...no. I don't know anyone who gets paid to play Minecraft except for maybe Mojang's employees. While there are people in the real world who get paid to play video games, that group is very small. (And most of them are playing ultra-competitive shoot-em-up-style games like Counter-Strike.)

When I say that Minecraft can make you money, I mean the skills you learn while inside the game are skills that many companies find useful. Companies that design physical products are often in need of employees who can visualize objects in three dimensions as well as create new and unique objects. Think about any modern-day electronic device you own; chances are it was first designed in software. Mobile phones, tablets, and game controllers are all objects that started out as ideas; someone thought up each one and then created it as a digital object on a screen for someone else to approve or reject. These designers use special software to create 3D digital objects, and they often get paid very well for their work.

MONEY FROM MINECRAFT SERVERS

You can find a new book, *The Ultimate Guide to Minecraft Server*, from Timothy Warner that will teach you to setup your own Minecraft servers. More information on this book can be found here: http://www.quepublishing.com/store/ultimate-guide-to-minecraft-server-9780789754578

And the same goes for software companies, especially game developers. Pretty much any video game today requires in-game objects (such as characters, weapons, or vehicles) to be created as three-dimensional objects that can be rotated around and viewed from any angle. Someone has to create those objects that are used in games, and game developers (such as Mojang) hire people who are skilled in designing 3D objects. Oh yeah...they, too, get paid very well for their work.

The software that these 3D digital designers use is special. While the software can be learned by just about anyone, it takes time to learn all the tools and capabilities the software has to offer and put them together to create advanced designs. Digital designers who dive deep into this special software and become skilled in its use are often sought out (and then paid handsomely) by companies needing those skills.

Throughout this book, you're going to be learning about this special software, called CAD, which stands for computer-aided design, software. If you work through the book's projects, you'll gain some basic skills with the software. If you continue to dig deeper into the software when you're done with the book, you can move from being a novice to having the skills of an expert. And, as you just read, those expert skills could come in handy one day.

Becoming a Minecraft Engineer

I like the term *Minecrafter*. If you've ever designed anything in the game—a house, a castle, or something as simple as a chest to store stuff—then you're a Minecrafter. But I've got bigger goals for you. My plan is to turn you into a *Minecraft engineer*.

Engineers design things—big things, little things, complicated things, and crazy things. Engineers also tend to use some of the most amazing tools on the planet, and that's exactly what you'll be doing by the time you finish this book. You'll be pushing the limits of the Minecraft game, and you'll also be pushing your creative skills to the max!

TIP

Engineering Career Gameplan

Want to know more about what engineers do and how to study to become one? One of the best places to start is the Wikipedia page on engineering. This page provides links that can tell you about the different types of engineers, what they study, and what kinds of work they perform. Open a web browser and visit http://en.wikipedia.org/wiki/Engineering to learn more.

Trust me: If you enjoy playing and designing inside Minecraft, you'll find the software I'm going to introduce to you just as enjoyable. You'll also be spending more time playing and enjoying Minecraft once you've learned how to create the things you need much faster than you do now.

Getting Started

Throughout this book, I'm going to make one large assumption: that you've installed Minecraft (any version) and understand the basics of playing the game and using the crafting tools. If this isn't you, then get your hands on some of the books I mentioned earlier by Tim Warner or Stephen O'Brien. Turn to those books if you need help, have a parent help you search for "Minecraft Tutorials" on Google or YouTube, and prepare to be blown away by just how many how-to videos and guides are out there. Be aware that many YouTube videos on Minecraft contain unsuitable language and content, so ask a parent or teacher before you go looking on the Internet for help.

Throughout the book, as I introduce you to other specialty software, I'll tell you where to find it, how to download and install it, and how to use it.

With a lot of books, you first learn some (boring) theory and do a lot of (boring) reading before you get to the fun stuff, right? Well, not with this book. I'm going to be doing things a little out of order. I've got a lot of projects to show you, and with each project I'm first going to show you the fun, cool, awesome stuff and how it actually works in Minecraft.

Then I'll get to the nitty-gritty details about the software needed, how to install that software, and how to use it. Why am I introducing projects in this order? Because once you see a special project actually implemented in Minecraft, I think you'll be more curious and more energized to learn the ins and outs of the new software so you can modify the projects and make them your own. If you like my projects, you're going to be going crazy creating your own with the tools I'll be showing you!

Are you ready to make the jump from Minecrafter to Minecraft engineer? Of course you are! And I can't think of a better way to start your journey as a Minecraft engineer than by creating the ultimate home for yourself: a castle that will protect your from enemies and make your friends green with envy. I'll see you in Chapter 1, "Taking Over a Castle."

Taking Over a Castle

What You'll Be Doing

- Meet Coolcrafter10, a budding Minecraft engineer
- Become a friend to digital shortcuts
- Find a suitable (and sizable) place to call home with Thingiverse
- Use Tinkercad to make a new home Minecraft compatible
- Import a castle into a world with MCEdit
- Move in!

"Not too bad," said Coolcrafter10 to the only other moving creature in his vision, a sheep grazing randomly around the clearing. "My new house. What do you think?" The sheep looked up for a moment and then returned its attention to the nearby grass. "Uh, thanks."

Coolcrafter10 had spent almost two hours building a small two-story house, complete with three rooms, five beds (for his friends DoubleDecker8, SuperSawSaw, ZombieFighterZ, and GreenFingers), a few chests to store his armor and weapons, and plenty of torches to discourage unfriendly night-time visitors. Coolcrafter10 opened the front door, walked into his new home, and closed the door behind himself. A grin spread across his face as he examined his work. He already had some ideas for adding a few more rooms and maybe a basement, but for now he was content to take a rest.

The sunlight was fading, and Coolcrafter10 knew what that meant: skeletons, zombies, spiders, and the worst of the bunch...creepers. As an afterthought, Coolcrafter10 quickly ran outside and added four more torches to the outside of his house, one at each corner. He ran back inside, closed the door, and for added security dropped a big block of diorite behind the door—a block that he'd recently collected during one of his explorations. "That should keep 'em out," he said.

Coolcrafter10 yawned. Building your own home is a lot of work, he thought. He began walking to the stairs, ready to head up to his bedroom and take a well-deserved rest in his new bed, when he heard a loud knock on the front door.

Stay quiet, thought Coolcrafter10. Don't make a sound. Don't let them know you're in here.

"Hey, you inside!" Coolcrafter10 didn't recognize the voice. "Please let me in! I wasn't able to get back to my house in time. Please hurry! I'm a friend!"

Coolcrafter10 thought for a moment. It doesn't sound like a monster, and I know I'd hate to be caught outside at night. He nodded. "Hang on! I'm coming!"

Coolcrafter10 quickly removed the diorite block and opened the door. "Hurry, hurry! Get in!"

Coolcrafter10 slammed the door shut and added another block of diorite before turning to the new arrival.

A young woman dressed in diamond armor smiled back at Coolcrafter10. "Thank you so much," she said. "I lost track of time and was being chased by a mob of zombies. You really saved the day!" She looked around the room and smiled. "Nice work. You're new here, aren't you? I'm Didgee-Engie. All my friends just call me Didgee. Nice to meet you." She stuck out her hand.

Coolcrafter10 shook her hand and smiled. "I'm Coolcrafter10. And yeah, I just moved here. Do you live nearby?"

"No," replied Didgee. "My castle is a good three days' travel from here, although I have a few small cabins scattered around the world for when I get too far from home. The mob that was chasing me cut me off from the nearest cabin, but I saw your torches and ran this way."

"You have a castle?" asked Coolcrafter10. "A real castle? With turrets and towers? That must have taken forever to build! Maybe one day I'll be lucky enough to have one."

"Well, Coolcrafter10," said Didgee. "Today's your lucky day. It looks like I'll be needing to stay here tonight, but because you were so trusting and helped me, I'm going to help you out. You've got a nice big piece of land out here—plenty of room for a castle of your own. Would you like me to help you build one?"

Coolcrafter10 grinned. "Of course, but it'll take forever. I only have a few other friends who can help me, and the kind of castle I'm thinking about will take weeks, maybe even months, for us to build!"

Didgee smiled and laughed. "Well, not really. I know a few tricks, if you're interested. Why don't you create a desk and a computer over in the corner? We have a long night ahead of us, and since we can't go outside, how about I show you the steps you'll need to create your own castle that you'll be sleeping in tomorrow night?"

Coolcrafter10 shook his head in disbelief. "Are you serious?" he asked, as he quickly created a small desktop and a computer on its flat surface.

"Oh, yeah," replied Didgee. "You're going to be the envy of your friends tomorrow."

Digital Tools Make Great Shortcuts

When it comes to Minecraft, there's nothing wrong with starting small. Most Minecrafters start out crafting small structures, such as a small house with a bed and a door for a place to hide and sleep at night while the monsters are roaming.

But if you've got to hide for a while, why not hide in style? A house is great, but nothing beats a castle. Nothing.

But building a castle is obviously going to take more time than building a simple four-walled house with a single door, right? Not necessarily. If you choose to use the basic tools of Minecraft to build a castle block-by-block-by-block-by-block-by-block...it's going to take a while. There's nothing wrong with putting in that kind of hard work and then enjoying the fruits of your labor. But remember that you live in a digital world, and you can take full advantage of an array of digital tools that can make your life easier and get your work done faster.

In this book, you're going to learn how to use a number of digital tools that you can pair with Minecraft to create some amazing in-game surprises for other Minecrafters. These tools are not difficult to use, but you're still going to have to learn their controls and how they work in order to get results. But don't worry about that right now.

For now let's skip the block-by-block-by-block assembly of a castle and take a shortcut—a big shortcut. And it all starts with a visit to a sort-of digital library that contains thousands and thousands of objects that you may want to put into your world—objects such as one seriously kick-butt castle.

NOTE

See an example and then do it for yourself

In the Introduction to this book, I explained that I'd be initially skipping over the training and lessons and drop you right into the fun stuff and showing you many things you can do in Minecraft. My goal is to show you something really really cool in one chapter and then explain in more detail how you can do it yourself in the next chapter. I'll be following this pattern throughout the rest of the book, so don't get worried as you read this chapter (and Chapters 3, "Crafting a Super Maze," 5, "Modifying a 3D World," and so on) if you aren't seeing specific details about how to duplicate what you're reading. That information will be provided in Chapter 2, "Creating Your Own Castle" (and Chapters 4, "Getting Lost (in a Maze)," 6, "Creating Your Own Monster Island," and so on). Just keep reading and see what amazingly fun stuff you can do and make with Minecraft...and then keep reading if you want to learn the steps to do it yourself in your own Minecraft world.

Finding a Castle with Thingiverse

You could easily browse the Internet or consult some books for castle designs to help shorten the time it takes to build one. This might save you the trial-and-error of placing blocks in the wrong place or learning that a staircase just won't work with a particular tower. But how much better would it be to just find an existing picture of a castle and convert it quickly to a digital castle in your Minecraft world? Yeah, I thought you'd like that idea.

TIP

Outside exploration

Would you like to know the names of various areas of a castle or gain a better understanding of how real castles were built? If so, visit http://history.howstuffworks.com/historical-figures/castle.htm or http://www.exploring-castles.com/medieval_castle_layout.html to read more.

My search for the perfect castle begins with a web browser and a trip to Thingiverse.com. Figure 1.1 shows the opening screen for Thingiverse, but keep in mind that the home page sometimes changes its look, so don't worry if it doesn't look exactly like the image shown in Figure 1.1 when you visit.

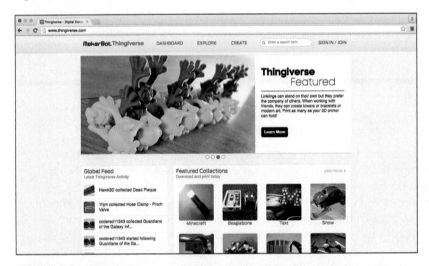

FIGURE 1.1   My castle is somewhere on Thingiverse.com.

CAUTION

The Chrome web browser

You can use any web browser to visit Thingiverse.com, but some websites I'll be visiting in this book will only work with certain ones. For this reason, I tend to favor Chrome. Most of the figures in this book that involve a web browser use Chrome. You can download and install the Chrome web browser by visiting chrome.google.com. If you're a student, you may need to ask a parent or teacher if it's okay before installing Chrome on a computer.

The secret to finding what you need on Thingiverse.com is using the Search bar found in the upper-right corner of the screen. Figure 1.2 shows that I've entered the word "castle" in the Search bar.

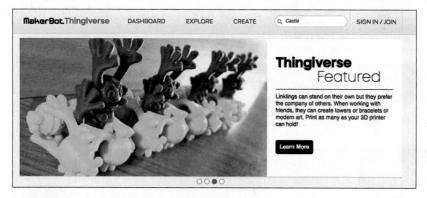

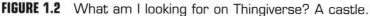

FIGURE 1.2   What am I looking for on Thingiverse? A castle.

After entering a search term, I press the Enter key, and the browser's screen changes. Instead of the Thingiverse home page, I see a scrolling window with small boxes containing photos of examples of the object I want to find.

In Figure 1.3, I've scrolled down a little bit to see what Thingiverse is offering in the way of castles today.

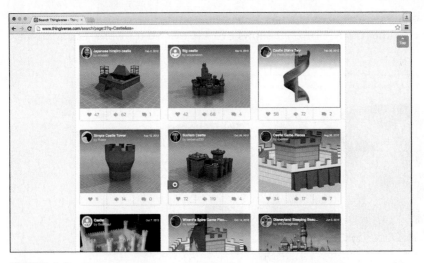

FIGURE 1.3 Searching through Thingiverse for the perfect castle.

After spending a few minutes scrolling through the results, I think I've found a castle I'd be proud to call home. I click on the box containing the image I want, and the page changes to show me this particular castle's information, as shown in Figure 1.4.

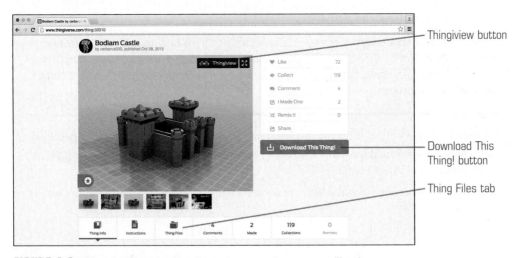

Thingiview button

Download This Thing! button

Thing Files tab

FIGURE 1.4 That's my castle—but you can have one like it, too.

Before downloading this castle file so I can use it with Minecraft, I'd like to look at it from all sides. Thingiverse makes it easy to do this: Just click the Thingiview button.

When I click the Thingiview button, the image of the castle turns into an image I can rotate around and view from different angles. To rotate the castle, I click and hold the left mouse button anywhere on the castle while moving the mouse around. When I do this with the castle shown in Figure 1.4, I can see that one side of the castle has a large door, and the back (rear) of the castle is a solid wall, as shown in Figure 1.5. Yep, this is the castle I want!

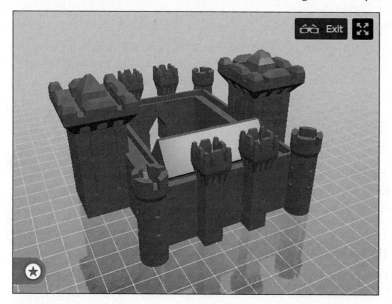

FIGURE 1.5   Making certain the castle only has one door.

Now that I've picked my castle, it's time to download the castle file I'll need in order to move this castle into my Minecraft world. To do that, I click the big blue Download This Thing! button. (It's hard to miss but labeled in Figure 1.4 just in case.) When you click this button, the page jumps to the Thing Files tab, as shown in Figure 1.6.

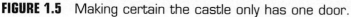

Thing Info	Instructions	Thing Files	4 Comments	2 Made	124 Collections	0 Remixes

File Name	Downloads	Size	
castbod5.stl Last updated: 10-28-12	999	2mb	Bodiam Castle by cerberus333 is licensed under the Creative Commons - Attribution - Non-Commercial license.
castbod6.stl Last updated: 10-29-12	1367	4mb	By downloading this thing, you agree to abide by the license: Creative Commons - Attribution - Non-Commercial

Download All Files

(506 kb zip file)

FIGURE 1.6   The Thing Files tab is where the digital castle file is located.

TIP

Dealing with multiple digital files

Some objects you find on Thingiverse.com will have multiple files listed (such as the two shown in Figure 1.6: castbod5.stl and castbod6.stl). If you're not sure which one to download, consult the Instructions tab (to the left of the Thing Files tab), which will usually tell you the differences between multiple files. In this case, castbod5 is an older version, with "rougher" edges. The instructions state to use the castbod6.stl file for better results.

When I click on the castbod6.stl file, it downloads to my computer. I'll save that file in a folder that I can easily find later. For now, I'm done with Thingiverse.com, so I close down the browser and get ready for the next part of the process.

Preparing the Castle with Tinkercad

Now I've got the digital castle file stored on my computer, but it's not a digital file that will automatically work with Minecraft. There are methods for taking objects from Thingiverse (such as my castle) into Minecraft, but before I do that, I need to transform this digital file. I'll cover this transformation process in more detail in Chapter 2, but for now I'm going to move somewhat quickly so you'll see how fun and easy it is to move Thingiverse objects into Minecraft.

The next step involves another website, Tinkercad.com. You'll learn much more about Tinkercad throughout this book, but right now I just want you to follow along as I prepare my castle for use in my Minecraft world.

TIP

Tinkercad requires a compatible web browser

Tinkercad.com requires a web browser that supports what's called OpenGL. OpenGL is required for three-dimensional objects to be properly displayed on a screen, and it also allows for rotation of objects (as shown with the castle earlier). If you're uncertain whether your web browser will work, simply open it and visit Tinkercad.com. When you click the Start Tinkering Now button, you'll get an alert from Tinkercad if your browser won't work. Chrome works great because OpenGL is already built into the browser, so visit chrome.google.com to download it if you need it.

Figure 1.7 shows Tinkercad.com. You need to create a user account to use it. It's free, but do ask a parent or teacher for help (and permission) if you're under age 13. Once you have an account, you can click the Sign In button to log in with your username and password.

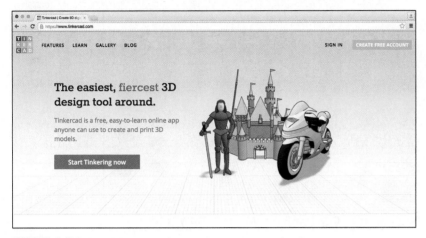

FIGURE 1.7 The Tinkercad.com home page is the next stop.

I've used Tinkercad for some time now, so my login screen will show a lot of different projects. If you've never used Tinkercad, you won't have any projects yet, but that will change fast!

To get my castle prepared for Minecraft, I need to first create a new project. To do that, I click the Create New Design button shown in Figure 1.8.

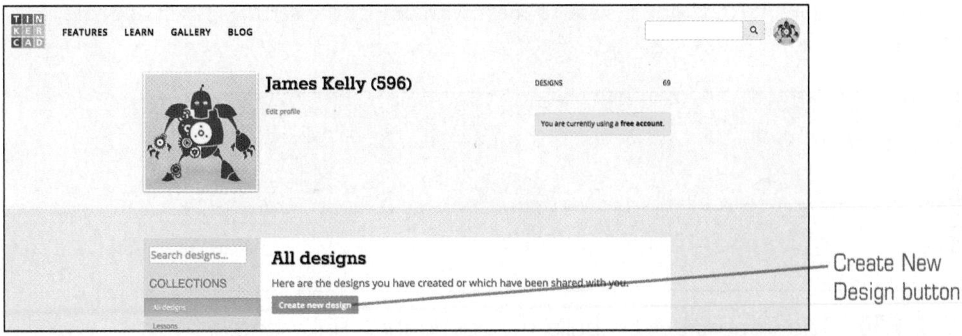

Create New
Design button

FIGURE 1.8 The Create New Design button helps me prepare my castle.

When you open a new project, you see the odd screen shown in Figure 1.9. Notice the blue grid in the center of the screen and the buttons running down the right side of the screen.

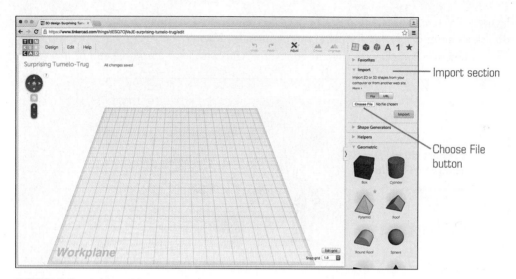

Import section

Choose File button

FIGURE 1.9   A new Tinkercad project shows an empty grid.

Tinkercad always gives a new project a really crazy name. The one in Figure 1.9 is called Surprising Tumelo-Trug. I have no idea what that means, and you probably don't either. But don't worry. You can easily change the name of the project later to something more useful and easier to decipher.

Right now, I need to bring that digital castle file I downloaded into Tinkercad. To do that, I'll click the Choose File button in the Import section. This is where I'll need to browse and find the folder where I stored my digital castle file. After selecting it, I click the Import button shown in Figure 1.10. (I don't want to mess with any of the settings, such as Scale or Unit, at this point.)

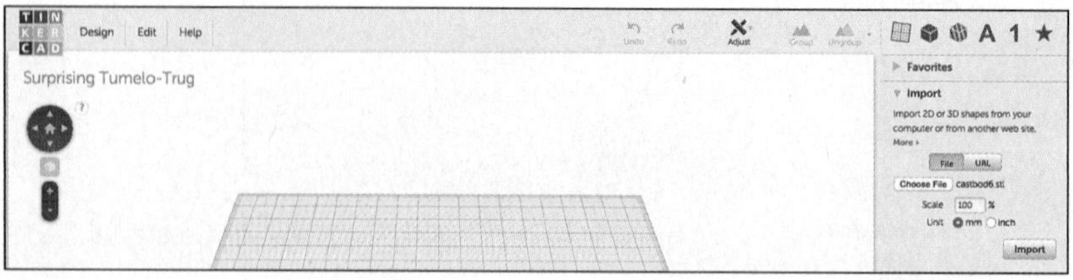

FIGURE 1.10   The Import button pulls my castle into Tinkercad.

After about 20 seconds, that empty grid is no longer empty. Figure 1.11 shows that the digital castle sitting on Tinkercad's grid.

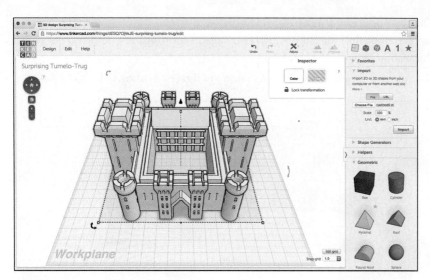

FIGURE 1.11   That is one nice-looking castle!

There are all kinds of tools in Tinkercad that I could use to do things like make it taller or shorter, add another door or tower, flip it upside down, or even cut it in half. I'll explain how to use many of them later in this book.

But for now I just want to prepare this castle so it can be imported into Minecraft. And to do that, I click the Design menu to get the options shown in Figure 1.12.

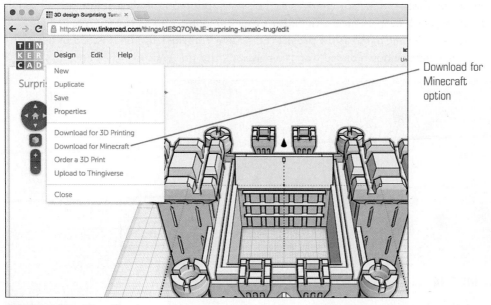

FIGURE 1.12   The Design menu has many options, including one very special feature.

Look at that! The sixth option from the top is Download for Minecraft. How cool is that? Tinkercad has an actual option for converting (also called exporting) an imported 3D object to something that will work with Minecraft!

When I select that option, a new window appears on my screen, as shown in Figure 1.13.

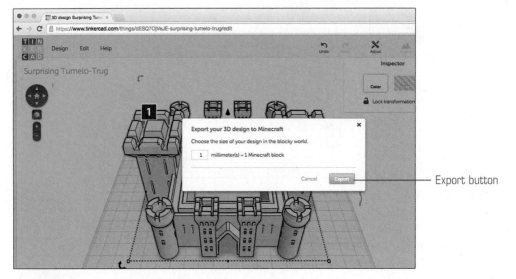

FIGURE 1.13   Exporting to Minecraft is so easy!

Once again, I won't make any changes to the single option on the screen. Instead, I'll simply click the Export button. A file downloads to your computer, and as you can see in Figure 1.14, it has the same name as my project (Surprising Tumelo-Trug) but instead of being an .stl file (like the one downloaded from Thingiverse), this one ends in .schematic.

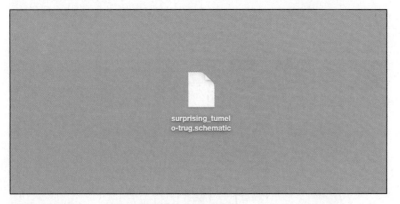

FIGURE 1.14   A special file is saved to my computer.

Guess what? Files ending in .schematic can be imported into Minecraft. I'm almost done!

Importing the Castle into Minecraft

All that's left to do is find a way to import the .schematic file into Minecraft. Unfortunately, Minecraft can't do the import by itself. Fortunately, though, there's a free application that can. It's called MCEdit, and not only can it import a file into a Minecraft world, but it also has many more uses that you'll learn about later in the book.

I've got a world called EngineerLand that will be a suitable home for this new castle. To move the castle into Minecraft, I'll open MCEdit—but only after I close down Minecraft.

CAUTION

Close Minecraft when using MCEdit

When using MCEdit to import an object into a world, it is super-important that you not have that world open at the same time in Minecraft. If you have your world open in Minecraft and then open that same world with MCEdit, you will likely lose that world and everything you've ever created or mined in it. The safest thing to do is to simply close down Minecraft altogether before you use MCEdit. Then open the Minecraft world again only after you've closed down MCEdit.

When I open MCEdit, I'm greeted with a very simple screen like the one in Figure 1.15.

FIGURE 1.15 Using MCEdit to put the castle into a Minecraft world.

I'll show you additional uses for MCEdit later in the book, but right now all I want to do is get my castle into EngineerLand. To do this, I'll click the Open button. When I do, I'm provided with a list of folders that contain names of the various worlds I have saved in Minecraft. Figure 1.16 shows just one world created right now (EngineerLand), but if I had multiple worlds, they would appear in this window as well.

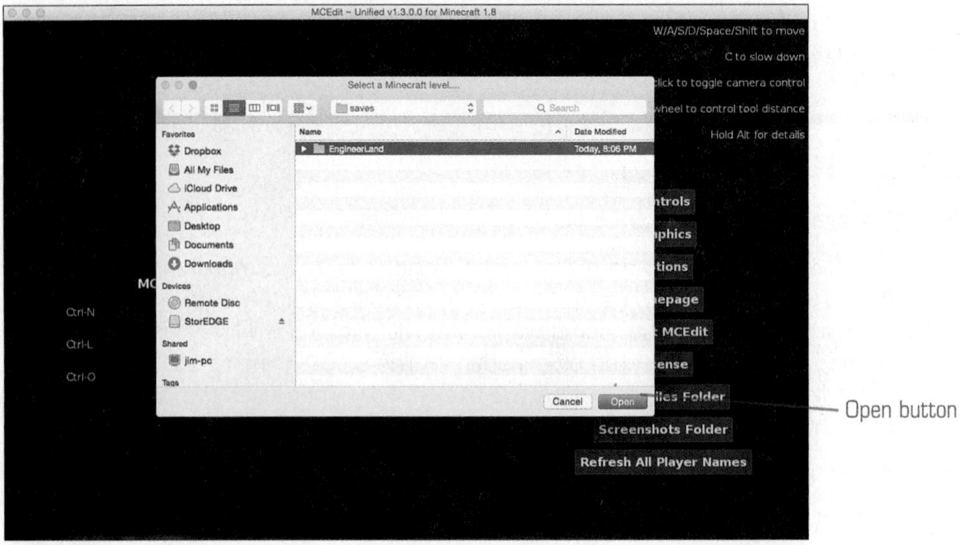

Open button

FIGURE 1.16 Selecting EngineerLand as the world for the castle.

Double-clicking the EngineerLand folder opens it and displays various other folders and files related to my EngineerLand world. The one I'm interested in is called level.dat, so I'll select that file, as shown in Figure 1.17, and click the Open button.

level.dat file

FIGURE 1.17   Selecting the level.dat file for my EngineerLand world.

When MCEdit opens my world, it looks a lot like Minecraft. But notice that there are some buttons running along the bottom and top edges of the screen, as shown in Figure 1.18.

FIGURE 1.18   My world opened in MCEdit looks similar to how it looks in Minecraft.

I need to find a spot to place my castle, so I use the WASD keys on my keyboard to move around my world until I find a suitable spot, such as the one in Figure 1.19. Note that I'm "floating" above my world a bit so I can see more of it. (In Chapter 2 I'll explain the controls shown in this screen.)

Import button

FIGURE 1.19   This looks like a good spot for a giant castle!

I click the Import button—the sixth button from the left on the bottom toolbar. (You can hover your mouse pointer over a button to see the name of each button.) A window like the one in Figure 1.20 appears.

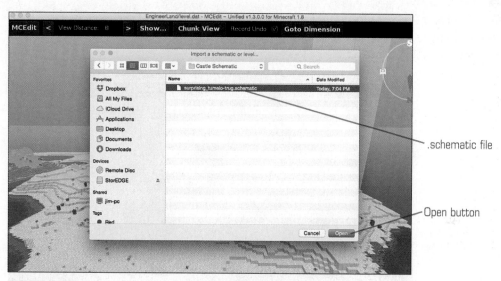

FIGURE 1.20 Now it's time for that .schematic file!

I now select the .schematic file (the file that was created using Tinkercad) and click the Open button. A green box appears (in this case a very large green box) that I can move around on the screen by using the mouse pointer. If I stop moving the green box, the shape of the castle appears, as shown in Figure 1.21.

FIGURE 1.21 Finding a good place to put the castle.

When I'm happy with the location, I simply left-click the mouse, and the green box is "locked" in place on the map. The Import button that's visible on the left side of the screen becomes solid yellow (instead of gray), as shown in Figure 1.22.

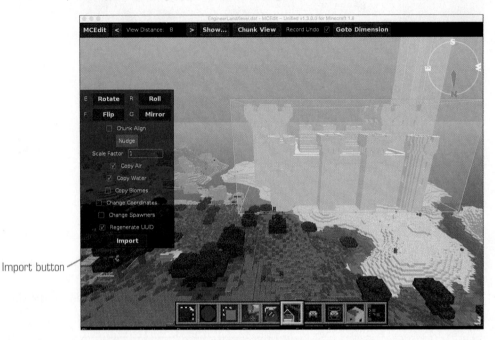

Import button

FIGURE 1.22 The castle's resting spot is selected.

I click that yellow Import button and BOOM! The new castle becomes a permanent structure in EngineerLand, as shown in Figure 1.23.

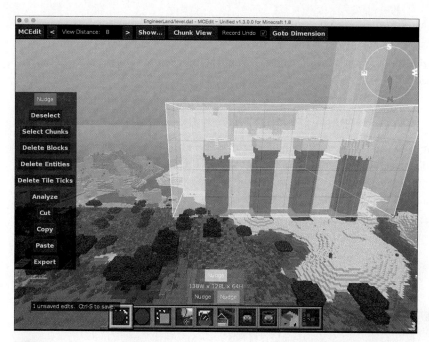

FIGURE 1.23   The castle is now a permanent part of EngineerLand!

All that's left to do is save my work and exit out of MCEdit. To do this, I click on the MCEdit menu in the upper-left corner of the screen, as shown in Figure 1.24, and select Save.

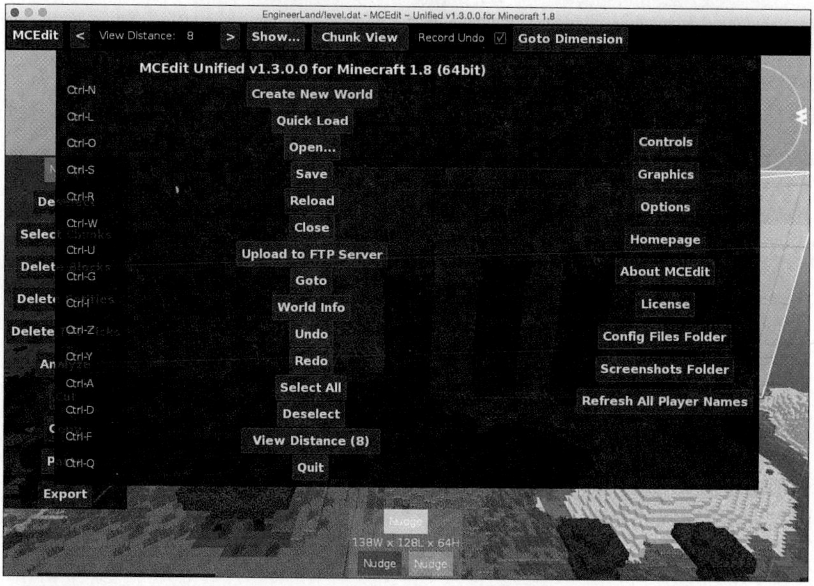

FIGURE 1.24   A special file is saved to my computer.

Next, I click the MCEdit menu again and choose Quit to close down MCEdit.

MCEdit is a powerful application with lots of special features, and you'll learn about many of them later in the book. Right now, however, I want to go check out my new castle by opening up Minecraft.

Exploring the New Castle

It's time to open up Minecraft and the EngineerLand world and see how my castle looks. After opening up EngineerLand, it didn't take long to find the castle! I climbed to the top of the nearest hill/mountain, and even before I got to the top, I spotted one of the towers. As I climbed over the hill, the castle was waiting for me, as shown in Figure 1.25.

FIGURE 1.25   The castle wasn't hard to find once I got near the top of the hill.

I raced down the hill, swam across a small river, and ran around to the front of the castle. (Remember that there's only one door.) Figure 1.26 shows that my castle was open and ready for me to move in.

FIGURE 1.26   Now THAT'S a front door!

The inside of the castle is completely empty, as you can see in Figure 1.27.

FIGURE 1.27   The castle doesn't have anything on the inside...yet.

When I'm ready to start adding rooms, I'll have a couple choices. I can do it block by block by block.... Or I can once again use Thingiverse to find a bunch of rooms, Tinkercad to convert them to .schematic files, and MCEdit to stick them inside the walls of the new castle. (Or maybe I can just find a smaller castle and tuck that one inside my larger castle!)

I have lots of options for my castle, and I'll explore some of them in Chapter 2. For example, I can change the type of blocks that make up the castle. I can rotate the castle so the front door is facing away from the water. I can even raise it up so it's a floating castle! You'll be able to do these things and many more once you begin to explore the MCEdit application.

But right now I just want to enjoy my new home. I'll have to add a door (a very big door) at some point, but right now I can just block it up if I want to keep critters out. It's also going to need some torches because it gets really dark at night.

Up Next...

In this chapter, I've introduced three different tools to you: Thingiverse, Tinkercad, and MCEdit. I didn't get too deep into their use because I wanted you to see something fun that can be done using these tools. In Chapter 2, I'm going to go into more detail about MCEdit, including showing you where to find the software, how to install it, and how to use it. You'll learn to do more with MCEdit than simply place a castle or some other object, and you'll discover just how much fun MCEdit can be when it comes to modifying your worlds. (I'll also touch on a few basics of Tinkercad with more of Tinkercad's features in Chapter 4.)

So read Chapter 2, learn as much as you can, and then I'll show you in Chapter 3 how to add a fun (and useful) feature to your castle that I know you're going to love.

Creating Your Own Castle

What You'll Be Doing

- Find and install MCEdit
- Find your own structure on Thingiverse
- Log in to Tinkercad and explore some of its features
- Import your own castle with MCEdit
- Explore more MCEdit features

I hope you enjoyed following along in Chapter 1, "Taking Over a Castle," as I found a castle and brought it into my Minecraft world. I moved quickly in that chapter because I had a lot to cover, but in this chapter I'm going to slow things down a bit and go into a little more detail about the tools I used.

This chapter gives you a chance to mimic what I showed you in Chapter 1 and create your very own castle—or any other object you like. Along the way, you're going to get a little more experience in using MCEdit and Tinkercad, two very important (and free) tools that are pure gold to a Minecraft engineer.

This is a hands-on chapter, so you should have it with you as you sit in front of your Mac or Windows computer. I'm going to ask you to actually perform the steps I describe as I do them. Hopefully you'll like what you discover in this book and will be repeating the steps over and over again to grow your own Minecraft worlds. At some point, you won't need to reference the book any longer because you'll know the proper steps and their correct order to make fun things happen.

NOTE

Minecraft Pocket Edition works fine

If you're a Minecraft Pocket Edition user running the game on an iPad or Android tablet, don't worry. You, too, can have a castle in your world—but you are going to need access to a Mac or Windows computer because MCEdit doesn't work on tablets (at least not yet). You'll also need another piece of software installed on your Mac or Windows computer (also free) that will allow MCEdit to access your world's level.dat file. I cover accessing world files on tablets and phones in Appendix A, "Using MCEdit with Minecraft Pocket Edition."

For this chapter, you'll need the following:

- Minecraft or Minecraft Pocket Edition installed on a computer or tablet
- A web browser (such as my favorite, Chrome) that supports OpenGL
- A (free) user account with Tinkercad.com
- MCEdit installed on your computer

I think it's probably a safe bet that you already have Minecraft or Minecraft Pocket Edition installed on a computer or tablet, and most computers have a web browser installed for accessing Thingiverse.com and Tinkercad.com. But you probably do not have MCEdit installed. Next, I'll show you where to get that application and how to install it.

Downloading and Opening MCEdit

MCEdit is one amazingly powerful tool for Minecraft that provides mind-blowing features and options. It seems to be continually updated, so you'll want to keep your eyes open when using it. You never know what new superpower it will grant you for modifying your worlds.

But before you can use it, you've got to download and install it. Fortunately, both tasks are extremely simple. Start by opening a web browser and pointing it to mcedit.net, as shown in Figure 2.1. (Be careful to only download MCEdit from the official site as there are versions of MCEdit that are infected with viruses and malware that you can download from other websites.)

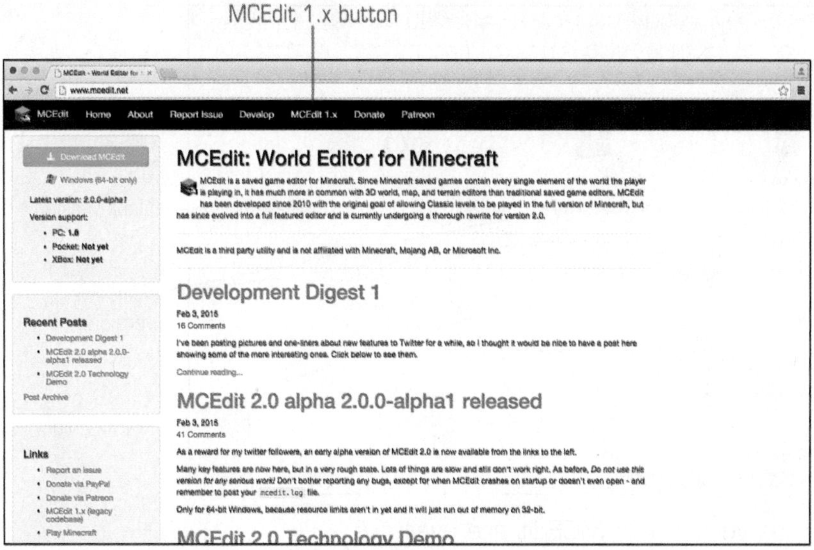

MCEdit 1.x button

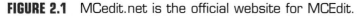

FIGURE 2.1   MCedit.net is the official website for MCEdit.

CAUTION

MCEdit Version 1.0 Versus 2.0

Currently MCEdit is going through a major revision from version 1.0 to version 2.0, so you'll probably find notes and updates regarding how this update is proceeding. If you're a Windows user, feel free to download the 2.0 beta version if you like. Many of the features found in version 1.0 and covered in this book will work just fine in version 2.0, although you may have to do a little digging around and testing because some tool buttons and features may have been moved around a bit.

On the mcedit.net home page, click on the MCEdit 1.x button near the top of the screen. This will take you to a new page that looks like the one in Figure 2.2.

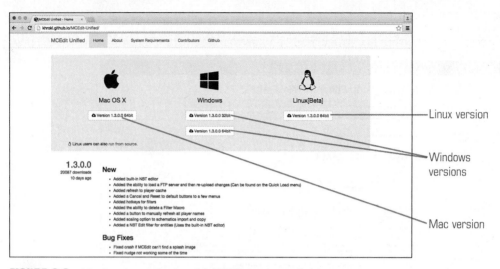

Linux version

Windows versions

Mac version

FIGURE 2.2 Various versions of MCEdit are available.

At this point, you need to download the version that corresponds to your computer's operating system. (At the time I'm writing this, the most recent version is 1.3.0.0 for Mac, Windows, and Linux users.) If you're a Mac user, click on the single button just below the Mac OSX icon, if you're a Windows user click the appropriate button (32-bit or 64-bit) to download the version you need, and if you're a Linux user click your one button choice.

NOTE

MCEdit 32-bit version or 64-bit?

If you're a Windows user and aren't sure whether to download the 32-bit or 64-bit version, find your Computer icon (usually under the Start button) and right-click that icon and choose Properties. Somewhere on the window that appears, you should see a section for operating system; see if that section says 32-bit or 64-bit.

I haven't been able to find any visual differences between the different operating system versions of MCEdit. I use both a Mac laptop and a Windows desktop. Throughout the book, I'll mostly be using my Mac laptop, so don't worry if your screen doesn't look exactly like mine. Just keep in mind that MCEdit will work the same for Mac, Linux, and Windows users.

After you click the appropriate version button, the application will download to your computer. There isn't an installation process for Mac users but for Windows users you'll need to double-click the downloaded file that creates an MCEdit folder—inside that folder you'll find the MCEdit icon. When the download completes, you just double-click that icon to open and run MCEdit. Figure 2.3 shows the MCEdit icon on the far left and the MCEdit application open and ready to go.

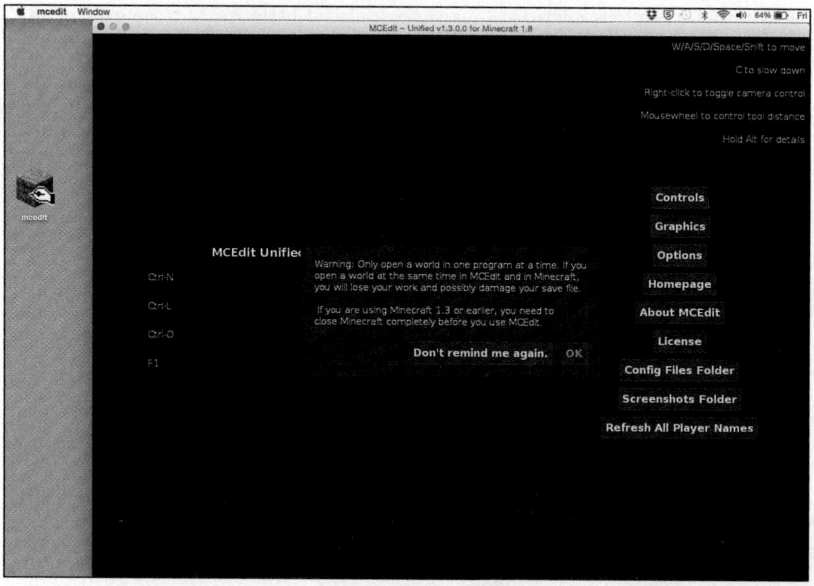

FIGURE 2.3 Double-click the MCEdit icon to open and run the application.

CAUTION

A warning from MCEdit

The first time you open MCEdit, you'll get a warning like the one shown in Figure 2.3. This basically tells you to *never* open a world in Minecraft and MCEdit simultaneously. Doing so can result in damage to the file that holds all of your world's information. Click the OK button to make the warning go away. I prefer not to click the Don't Remind Me Again button because I always want MCEdit to remind me to close down Minecraft before I open any worlds. Feel free to click that button, but keep in mind that from that point forward, MCEdit will open a world without worrying if it's also open in Minecraft. You've been warned!

Once you've downloaded MCEdit and opened it up, you can leave it open or close it down. You'll return to MCEdit a bit later in this chapter, but right now it's time for you to find your own castle or other suitably large building.

Discover Your Own Castle...or Something Else!

In Chapter 1, I gave you a quick glimpse of how I used the website Thingiverse.com to find a castle and then download it. In this section, I want to spend a little more time exploring Thingiverse and explain the files that Thingiverse offers in a little more detail.

TIP

Follow along for best results

I'd like you to actually follow along and perform the steps as I describe them. This is the easiest way for you to begin to remember the steps so you can use them over and over again without consulting the book every time.

Open a web browser and point it to Thingiverse.com, as shown in Figure 2.4.

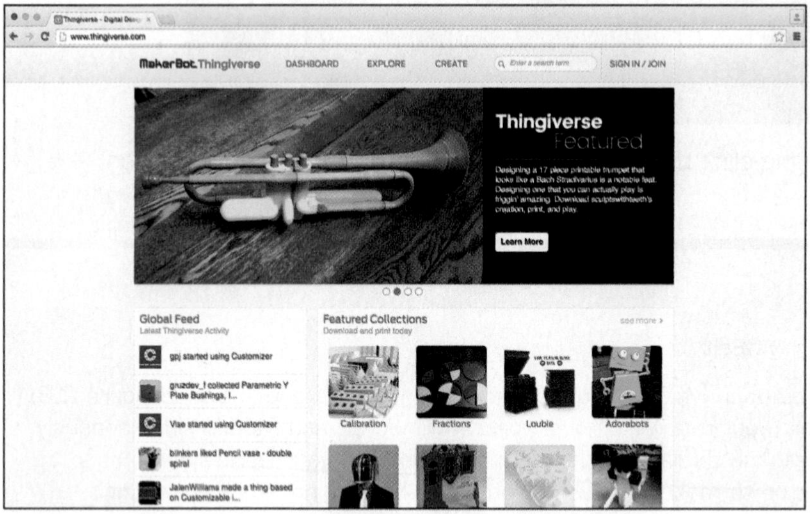

FIGURE 2.4 Thingiverse is like a library of fun stuff.

Think about Thingiverse as a library. With most libraries, you can go in and check out books (for a period of time), read them, and then return them. Most public libraries are free, so there's no charge to check out books.

Well, Thingiverse doesn't hold books. Instead, it holds digital files that represent physical objects in the real world. These digital files go by a bunch of names: 3D models, digital models, .stl files, and more. I prefer the term *3D model*. A 3D model is a three-dimensional representation of an object, but it doesn't have to represent a real-life object. There are 3D models for dragons and fairies, for example. You've already seen a 3D model of a castle.

The important thing to remember is that Thingiverse is filled with digital files of 3D objects that Thingiverse users have created and uploaded for other people to use.

One of the most popular uses for 3D files is for 3D printing. The "old-fashioned" type of printer that you're probably already familiar with prints using ink on paper. A 3D printer such as the one in Figure 2.5 melts plastic and then "prints" out 3D model files to create small plastic representations of digital objects.

FIGURE 2.5 A 3D printer prints out a 3D model file in plastic.

NOTE

Outside exploration

The subject of 3D printers and 3D printing is a fun topic to explore, but it's much too large to cover in this chapter. If you're interested, check out my book *3D Printing: Build Your Own 3D Printer and Print Your Own 3D Objects*, which explains how to build a 3D printer from a kit and also covers how to download files from Thingiverse and print those 3D models using a 3D printer. You can find more information about this book by visiting http://www.quepublishing.com/store/3d-printing-build-your-own-3d-printer-and-print-your-9780789752352.

Thankfully, you don't need a 3D printer to use the 3D model files with Minecraft. But you do need to convert a 3D model file that you download from Thingiverse before you can import it into Minecraft. (You can use Tinkercad.com to do this, as described in detail later in this chapter.) Before you perform this conversion, however, you need something to convert.

It's time for you to find a castle or other object that you'd like to transfer into one of your Minecraft worlds, and the easiest way to do this is to use the Search bar in Thingiverse.

Type in "castle" or "tower" or "house" or anything else you're thinking about using in Minecraft. You can also be very specific, such as searching for "Eiffel Tower" or "White House." How would you like a copy of the Eiffel Tower in your world? Figure 2.6 shows a search for 3D versions of the Eiffel Tower, but you can search for whatever you want. Whatever object you choose, just keep following my instructions, and you'll soon have it imported into a Minecraft world of your choice.

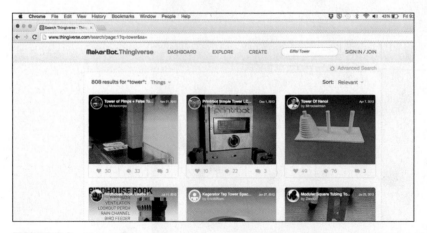

FIGURE 2.6 I've always wanted to visit the Eiffel Tower...in Minecraft.

TIP

The Minecraft Effect–Blocky-looking structures

Remember that buildings and objects in Minecraft are a bit "blocky" rather than smooth. Any 3D models you import into Minecraft will retain their basic shape, but smooth surfaces are impossible in Minecraft. For this reason, you shouldn't bother trying to find 3D models with intricate patterns. Sometimes the most basic 3D models without any fancy embellishments work best for imports—as you'll soon see.

There are a *bunch* of 3D models of the Eiffel Tower. Some are very intricate and are so detailed that they even show bolts and rivets. Figure 2.7 shows two versions of an Eiffel Tower 3D model. One has the basic shape and the other is extremely detailed. Your choice of basic versus detailed is based to some degree on the size you're going to make the object in your Minecraft world. For example, if I'm going to put a really big Eiffel Tower in my world, so I'm going to choose a more intricate one, but if I wanted to place a small Eiffel Tower, I'd go for a less detailed one. Whatever object you choose, you'll have a chance to decide how big (or small) it will be in your own Minecraft world a bit later in the chapter.

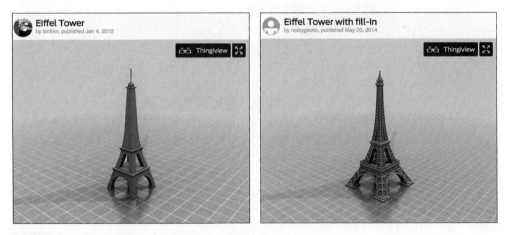

FIGURE 2.7 Two 3D models of the Eiffel Tower.

TIP

Give credit where it's due

In Figure 2.7, notice that the images include the Thingiverse usernames for the two creators of these 3D models. It's always a good idea to give credit to a 3D model designer, especially if you modify someone's existing 3D model. If you modify it (using an application such as Tinkercad.com) and then upload it to Thingiverse for other users to use, always include the name of the original 3D model file and its creator. Don't take credit for someone else's hard work.

Once you've found a 3D model that you like, click on it to open its information page. Figure 2.8 shows the information page for the detailed Eiffel Tower created by Thingiverse user noisygecko.

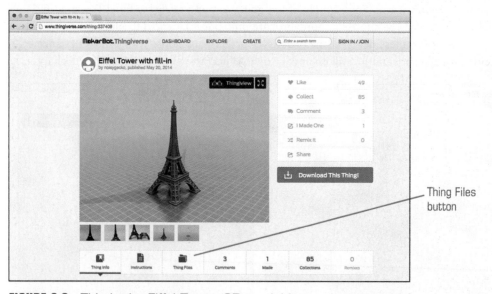

Thing Files button

FIGURE 2.8   This is the Eiffel Tower 3D model I want in my world.

You can click on the Instructions button to read any information the 3D model designer has included about the design. Sometimes you will see multiple files that can be downloaded, and the Instructions page will often tell you the differences between files.

The button you're interested in now, however, is the Thing Files button. Click on that button to view a list of files available for download. Figure 2.9 shows three different files available for download. In this case, I'm only going to be downloading one of them: EiffelTower_fixed2.stl.

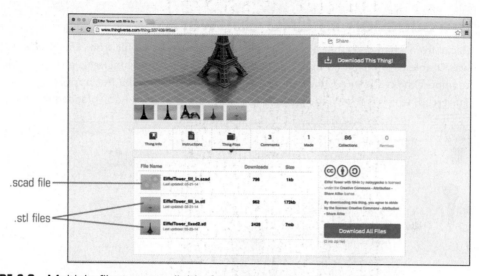

.scad file

.stl files

FIGURE 2.9 Multiple files are available for download.

Thingiverse supports a variety of different types of files, but when you're exporting files for Minecraft use, you always want to be on the lookout for .stl files. If you don't see an .stl file for the object you've selected, you're going to need to go back and find another Thingiverse object.

CAUTION

So many types of files from one source

The various file types that Thingiverse supports include .stl, .obj, .thing, .scad, .amf, .dae, .3ds, .x3d, .blend, .ply, .dxf, .ai, .svg, .cdr, .ps, .eps, .epsi, .sch, and .brd. The only file type that you will be downloading for use in this book is .stl.

Once you find an .stl file for a suitable object, click on it to download it to your computer. Then grab that downloaded file and place it on your desktop or in a folder—and remember the location where you saved it because you're going to need it for the next set of steps.

Before moving on to those next steps, however, think about what you've done for a moment. You've used a repository (Thingiverse) to browse thousands and thousands of user-created objects (3D models) and downloaded a specific file (with the .stl extension) for free. F-R-E-E. Hundreds of thousands of objects have been downloaded for free from Thingiverse over the years. Most of them have been printed (in plastic) using 3D printers. But this repository isn't useful just to owners of 3D printers. As you're about to see, .stl files can be used in many ways, including for creating your own modifications.

Introduction to CAD Software

Recall from Chapter 1, that after I downloaded my castle's .stl file from Thingiverse, I wasn't able to immediately import it into Minecraft. Between Thingiverse and using MCEdit to import the castle into Minecraft, I took a middle step: I used a free application called Tinkercad, which is shown in Figure 2.10, along with the castle I downloaded in Chapter 1.

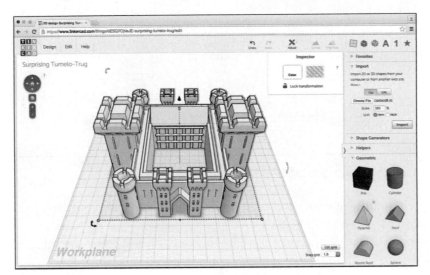

FIGURE 2.10   Tinkercad is the perfect CAD application for Minecraft engineers.

I'll be covering many of Tinkercad's features in Chapters 3 and 4, but right now I just want to explain it in a little more detail so you'll start to understand just how important this application (and others like it) really is to Minecraft engineers.

Tinkercad is a type of tool called a CAD (rhymes with mad and sad, although using a CAD application is fun and shouldn't make you either of those things) application. CAD stands for *computer-aided design*, and it's pretty easy to understand despite the complicated name. The first part, *computer*, says it all: When CAD applications were first being developed, they were created for use on computers. Today, CAD applications still run on desktop and laptop computers, but they can also run on small computers such as tablets (such as an iPad) and even mobile phones! As you'll soon see, however, using a CAD app on a phone isn't always easy because of the small screen. Tablets are a little more useful with CAD apps, and you can see one called 123D Design running on an iPad in Figure 2.11. But you may find as I have that when using a CAD application, the bigger the screen the better!

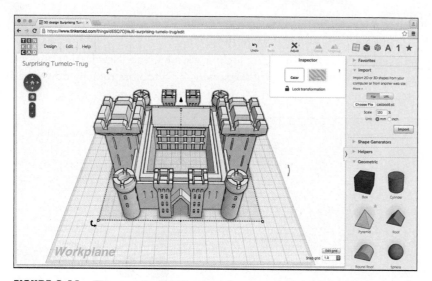

FIGURE 2.11   There are CAD apps that run on tablets and even mobile phones.

The next part of the name, *aided*, simply means that the software helps you do some of the complicated stuff. Can you hand-draw a perfect circle or pyramid? I can't either, but with a CAD application can help you draw a shape such as a circle and ensure that it's perfect in every way. The software can even help you draw the circle with a specific diameter. CAD software can do many more things besides draw perfect shapes—all of the functions that humans often find difficult or tedious. (You'll soon see some example of how CAD software aids a human user.)

Finally, the last part of the name, *design*, should be obvious to you. The software allows you, the user, to design some amazing things—and not just castles. Companies today use CAD apps to design all sorts of products, from the cases that go around mobile phones to the shape of a hood on a prototype car. As a Minecraft player, you design in-game things using the built-in tools and blocks available to you. A CAD application allows you to design anything your imagination can come up with, using dozens (and sometimes hundreds) of tools to get the job done.

CAD software can move you from Minecrafter to Minecraft engineer, and the best part is how fun CAD apps are to use.

Do you have your 3D model downloaded and ready? If so, it's time for you to open up a CAD application and try it out. If not, get that done first and meet me in the next section.

Using Tinkercad to Prepare Your 3D Model

Tinkercad will only work in a web browser that supports OpenGL—a special bit of software that lets a web browser display 3D objects on a screen, where they can be rotated around and viewed from different angles, such as from above or underneath. Without OpenGL, browser-based CAD apps such as Tinkercad won't be able to operate.

I highly recommend using Chrome for Tinkercad; login, click the Create New Design button, and you should see a blank grid in the center of the screen and a toolbar running down the right side of the screen, as shown in Figure 2.12.

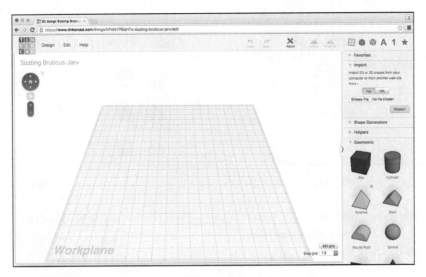

FIGURE 2.12   Tinkercad is a 3D model design tool.

I'm going to go into more features of Tinkercad in Chapter 3, "Crafting a Super Maze," but right now I just want to give you some hands-on time using the visual controls of Tinkercad. This includes zooming in and out and rotating an object around to view it from different angles.

Imagine for a moment that you are in a room with a square table sitting in front of you and a remote-controlled airplane resting on its surface. You could walk around the table to see the airplane from the sides and rear. You could squat down and look underneath the wings. If the table's surface were made of glass, you could even get underneath the table and view the underside of the airplane.

Think of the workplane in Tinkercad as a digital glass table. Anything that's placed on it can be viewed from different angles, including from straight above or underneath. And just as you could get your face close to the airplane to see details of the cockpit, you can also zoom in and out on the workplane to see details on an object or get a complete view of a larger object.

To understand this better, it's time to take that digital .stl file you downloaded earlier and pull it into Tinkercad. To do that, click on the Import section on the right to open it up so it looks as shown in Figure 2.13.

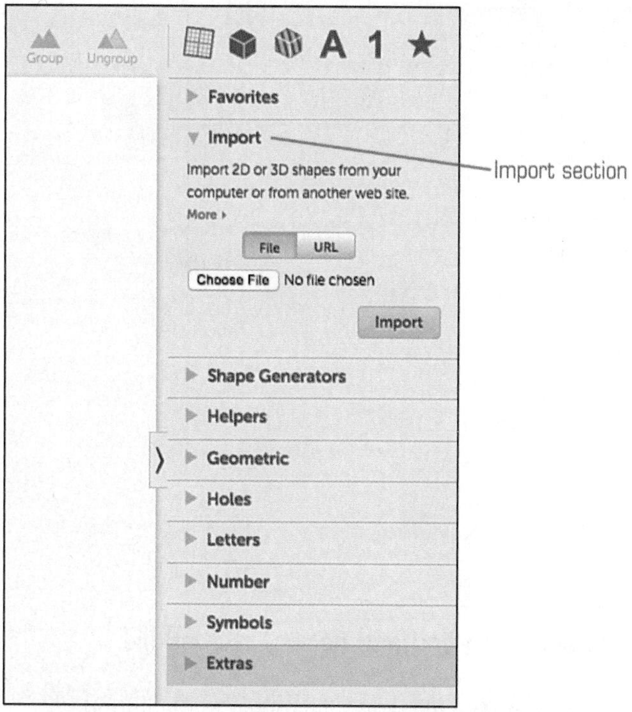

FIGURE 2.13 Use the Import section to pull in an .stl file.

NOTE

Expand a section and explore all the options

The Import section is just one of many sections on the toolbar. The toolbar also has Shape Generators, Helpers, Geometric, Holes, Letters, Number, Symbols, and Extras sections. You click on a triangle next to a section name to open or close it. If the triangle next to a section name is pointing down, the section is open. If the triangle is pointing left (toward the section name), that section is closed.

Click on the Choose File button, and a window like the one in Figure 2.14 appears. You use this window to find the .stl file you downloaded.

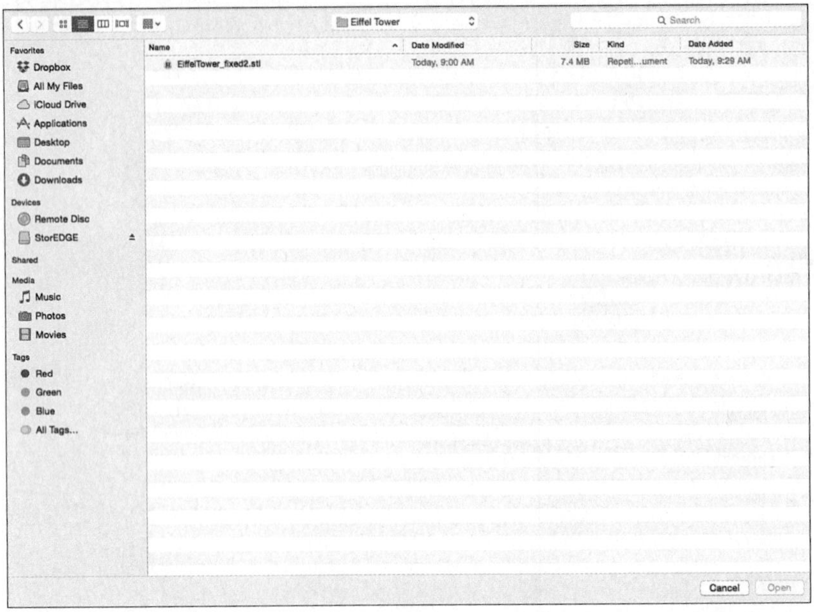

FIGURE 2.14   Use the Choose File button to find and select your .stl file.

Select your .stl file and click the Open button. The filename will appear in the Import section, as shown in Figure 2.15.

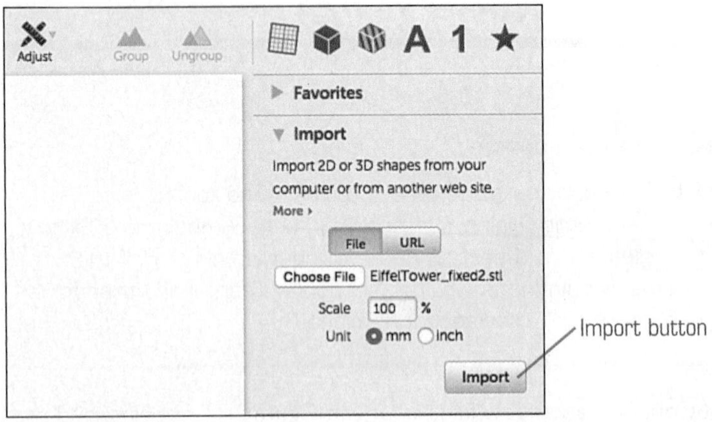

FIGURE 2.15   Your file is almost ready for import into Tinkercad.

Make certain that millimeters (mm) is the Unit option, but you shouldn't fiddle with the Scale setting at this point. Then click on the Import button to star the import of your file. This could take anywhere from 30 seconds to a minute, depending on the complexity of the 3D model you selected and your Internet speed.

When the import process is completed, you should see your 3D model sitting on the workplane, as shown in Figure 2.16.

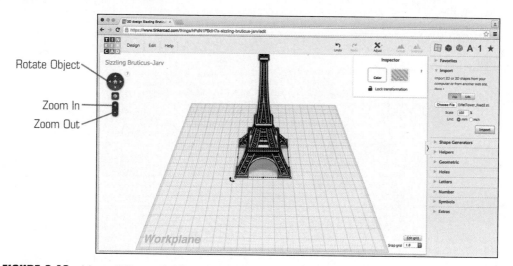

Rotate Object

Zoom In

Zoom Out

FIGURE 2.16 Your 3D model is now sitting on the workplane.

Notice in Figure 2.16 that the top part of the Eiffel Tower isn't visible. The entire object is too tall to be completely displayed on the screen. Maybe your 3D model is also extending beyond the viewable edges of the screen, too. This is easy to fix. All you need to do is zoom out a bit.

TIP

Exploring

You don't have to wait for later chapters to dive deeper into Tinkercad. Once you're logged in, feel free to click on the Learn button (which is on the menu bar at the top of the screen) and follow along with some of the free lessons that the Tinkercad crew have created to help you become familiar with more of Tinkercad's tools. You can also check out a book I wrote that covers 90% or more of Tinkercad's features (not 100% because the application is always being updated with new features). It's called *Learn 3D Modeling Basics with Tinkercad*. For more details, head to http://www.quepublishing.com/articles/article.aspx?p=2222099.

There are different ways to zoom in and out on a 3D model: You can use a mouse (with a wheel button on top), a touchpad, or onscreen controls. Let's start with the onscreen controls. Move your mouse pointer to the Zoom Out button (it's the one with the – sign in the upper-left corner of the workplane window; refer to Figure 2.16) and click it once or twice. You should see your object shrink a little, as though you were walking further away from the object. Figure 2.17 shows that I've zoomed out a bit, and the entire Eiffel Tower is now visible.

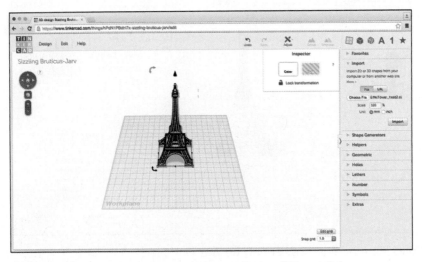

FIGURE 2.17 Zoom out to see more of your 3D model.

Click on the Zoom In button (the one with the + sign) a few times. This is similar to moving closer to an object on a table so you can get your face super-close for a good look. Figure 2.18 shows that I've zoomed in close to the tower.

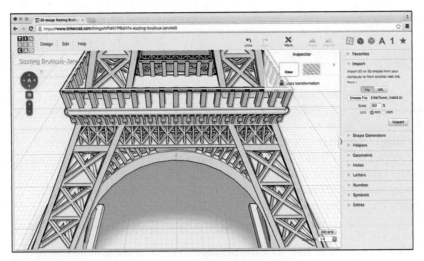

FIGURE 2.18 Zoom in to see details in your 3D model.

You can also use a mouse or touchpad to zoom in and out. With a mouse you use the wheel button (on top): Roll the button forward to zoom in the screen, and roll the button backward to zoom out the screen. Easy!

Zooming with a touchpad is a little different and may take some practice to get it right:

- On a Mac, place two fingers on the touchpad. Swiping your fingers forward (to the top edge of the touchpad) simultaneously zooms in, and swiping your fingers backward (to the bottom edge of the touchpad) zooms out.

- On a Windows touchpad, you'll need to consult your documentation to determine the method for zooming in and out—it will probably be similar to the Mac version of pinching to zoom, but could be different.

After you're comfortable using the Zoom In and Zoom Out features of Tinkercad, you're ready to learn to rotate an object so you can view it from different sides (including above and below). Once again, there are different ways to do this.

Just above the Zoom In and Zoom Out buttons, you'll see a small icon of a house with four triangles pointing in different directions. This is the Rotate Object tool (refer to Figure 2.16).

Click on the triangle pointing to the right, and the object automatically rotates 45 degrees clockwise (along with the workplane). Figure 2.19 shows the Eiffel Tower rotated 45 degrees so it is visible from a slightly different angle.

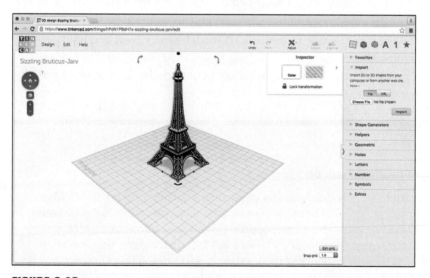

FIGURE 2.19 Use the Rotate Object buttons to rotate an onscreen 3D model.

Click on the left triangle, and the object rotates counterclockwise 45 degrees (and again, the workplane also rotates). Clicking the arrow pointing up rotates the object back toward you (allowing you to view more of the top of an object), and clicking the arrow pointing down rotates the object away from you. Go ahead and try it so you can get really familiar with how the tool works. Figure 2.20 shows the object rotated so from the underside is visible.

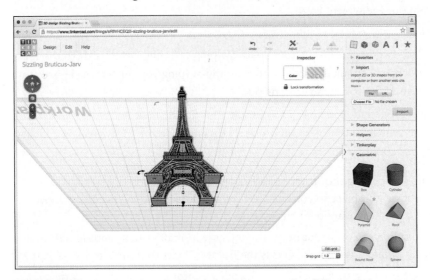

FIGURE 2.20   It's easy to look at the bottom of a 3D model.

You can also rotate a 3D model by using a touchpad or mouse, but the rotations are in much smaller degree increments, giving you a smooth rotation instead of 15- or 45-degree turns.

With a standard (two-button) mouse, to rotate a 3D model, simply press and hold both buttons down and move the mouse around. As long as you hold the two buttons down, you can move the mouse left, right, forward, and back to change the orientation of the 3D model you are viewing.

NOTE

Rotation using a touchpad can be tricky

Rotating with a touchpad is a little different depending on whether you're on a Mac or a Windows machine, so you'll need to consult your documentation, but just experimenting a bit will usually allow you to find out the proper way to rotate objects on the screen. For example, most Mac touchpad users will find that moving the pointer to any blank portion of the workplane and then pressing and holding two fingers down on the touchpad will work. Likewise, many Windows touchpad users will find that pressing and holding both fingers to rotate does the job. Try a few combinations of tapping and holding one or both fingres while moving the pointer around around and you'll be able to figure out what works for your computer.

When you're rotating your object, you can click on the little house icon in the center of the Rotate Object tool, and your 3D model returns to a more upright position.

The final feature you need to try for now is using Tinkercad controls to determine the height, width, and length of your 3D models. To do this, click once on your 3D model on the workplane to select it. How do you know it's selected? If the object appears with a small black cone near the tip of the model, as shown in Figure 2.21, it's selected.

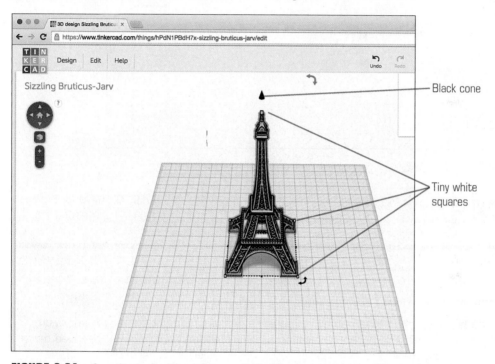

FIGURE 2.21   A selected object has a little black cone above it.

When an object is selected, look closely, and you should also see tiny white squares in various locations around your model. Don't fiddle with them right now; instead, move your mouse pointer over the little white square near the top of your 3D model (and just below the black cone). Don't click on it; just move your mouse pointer over the block, and a value should appear, as shown in Figure 2.22.

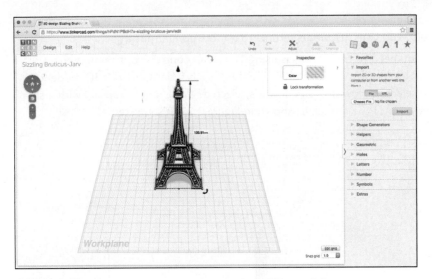

FIGURE 2.22   Discover the height of your 3D model.

The value that appears is the height (in millimeters) of your 3D model. As shown in Figure 2.22, my Eiffel Tower is 120.91mm tall. Your 3D model will most likely be a different height.

CAUTION

Checking your model's dimensions

If you hover over the other tiny white squares, you can find out the length and width of your object. Be careful not to click on a square and move it, though, because doing so can modify the look of your object by making it wider or longer. (Clicking on the little white box at the top and dragging up will stretch your object and make it taller, for example.) Feel free to play with the squares if you like, but you'll get more practice with them later in the book.

In just a moment, you'll learn why knowing the height of your object is important. Once you've determined the height (you might want to write it down), move your mouse pointer away from your object so you don't accidentally modify it.

Throughout the book, I'll introduce more tools and features in Tinkercad, but now it's time to take this 3D model in Tinkercad and prepare it so MCEdit can place it in one of your Minecraft worlds.

Preparing Your Model For Importing With MCEdit

Preparing a Tinkercad 3D model for MCEdit couldn't be any easier. You simply click on the Design menu shown in Figure 2.23 and select the Download for Minecraft option.

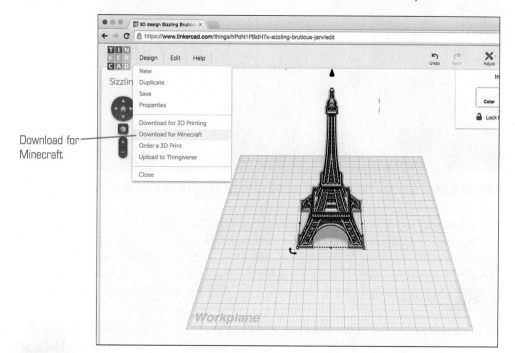

FIGURE 2.23   Download a Minecraft-compatible version of your 3D model.

After clicking the Download for Minecraft option, a window like the one in Figure 2.24 appears.

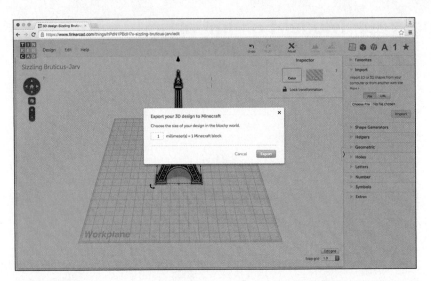

FIGURE 2.24   You can adjust the scale of your model before downloading.

Remember that earlier in this chapter, when you were importing your .stl file, to leave the Unit setting at millimeters (mm)? I hope you listened because that's important. When you download a 3D model for Minecraft, you define the height of your 3D model by using a ratio of Minecraft blocks to millimeters. My Eiffel Tower is 120.91 millimeters tall, and according to this pop-up window, when I import the tower into Minecraft, it will be 120 blocks tall—which means it'll extend into the clouds. Very cool!

If I don't want my Eiffel Tower to be that tall, I can change the value in the small box shown in Figure 2.24. Right now, it's set to download the Eiffel Tower so that 1mm = 1 block. If I change the 1 to a 5 (that is, 5mm = 1 block), I divide the height of my 3D model by 5 and get 24 so that the Eiffel Tower will import into Minecraft with a height of 24 blocks.

In this case, I want to create a slightly shorter-than-original version of the Eiffel Tower by setting the value to 2. This will give me a Minecraft version of the Eiffel Tower with a height of 60 blocks (every 2mm = 1 block, so 120mm = 60 blocks).

Once you've decided on a value for your object, click on the Export button. The file that downloads is no longer an .stl file. Now it is a .schematic file, as you can see in Figure 2.25. (Notice that I renamed the file from the silly name Sizzling Bruticus-Jarv that Tinkercad gave it to EiffelTower.schematic.)

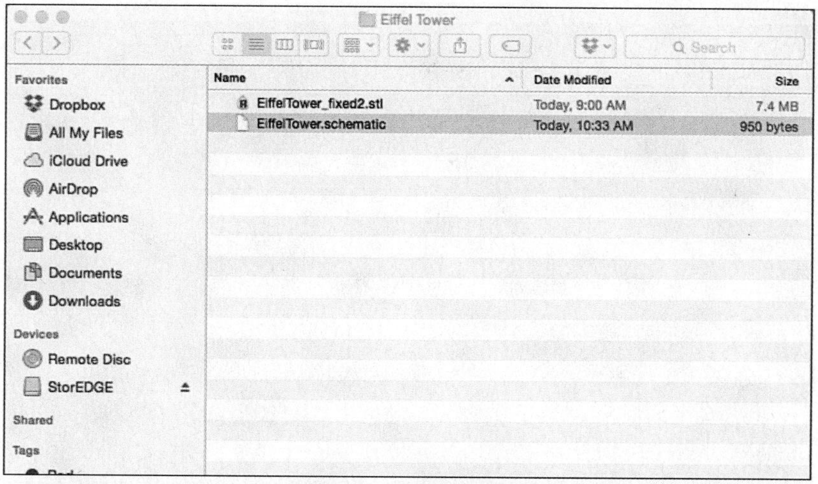

FIGURE 2.25   My 3D model is downloaded and ready for MCEdit.

TIP

Rename your model

You can rename your 3D model inside Tinkercad by clicking on the Design menu (shown in Figure 2.24), selecting the Properties option, and changing the name in the window that appears.

With your new .schematic file, you are now ready to bring the 3D model you selected earlier in this chapter into your Minecraft world.

Using MCEdit with Your 3D Model

Are you excited? You're about to add to your Minecraft world a 3D object that may very well have taken you hours, days, or even weeks to create block-by-block. Once you get the hang of downloading objects from Thingiverse and pulling them into Tinkercad (so you can use the Download to Minecraft option to create a .schematic file), you'll be quickly adding all sorts of craziness to your Minecraft worlds.

If you haven't already downloaded and installed MCEdit to your computer, do that now. (Refer to the beginning of the chapter for instructions.) Also, make certain that Minecraft is closed on your computer; if it's open, you'll at least want to make certain that whatever world you have open in Minecraft isn't the world you'll be opening with MCEdit. (I sternly warned you about this in Chapter 1.)

Double-click the MCEdit icon, and the tool opens as shown in Figure 2.26

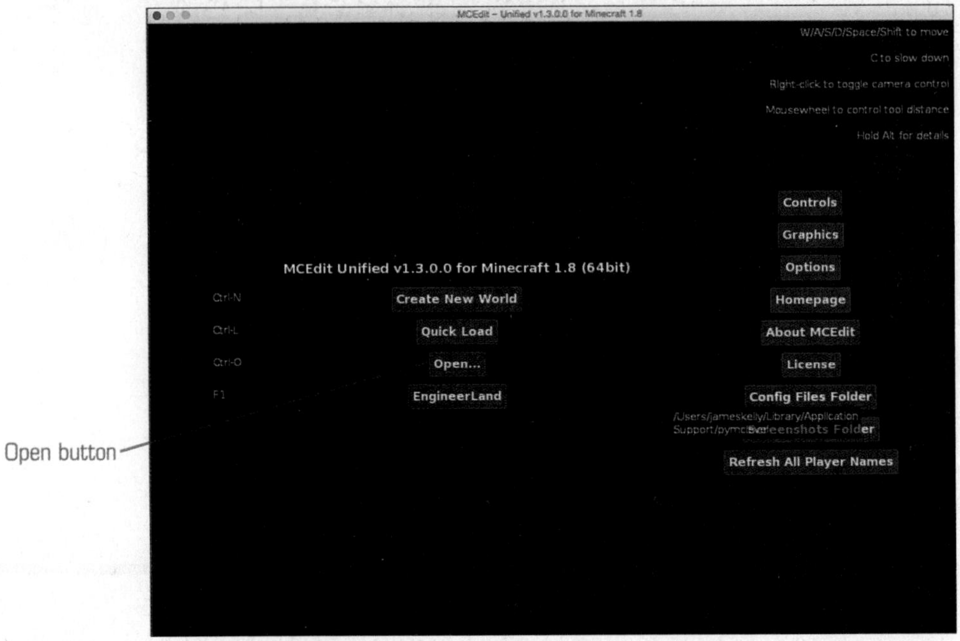

Open button

FIGURE 2.26   The MCEdit start screen.

The MCEdit start screen may not look fancy, but this is one powerful tool. I'll show you some of its features shortly, but I think you've waited long enough to import your 3D model, so I'll let you do that right now.

On the MCEdit start screen, click on the Open button. MCEdit automatically checks the default folder where Minecraft stores its game files, including those that are related to your worlds. Figure 2.27 shows the window that MCEdit opens, where you should see a list of folders that have the names you've given your Minecraft worlds. (The list will be empty, of course, if you haven't yet created a world.)

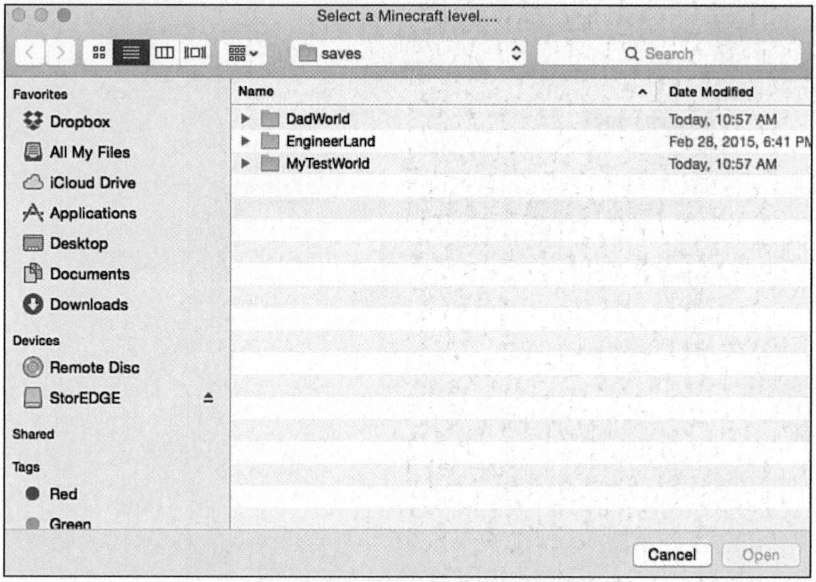

FIGURE 2.27 Find one of your worlds to open.

I have three Minecraft worlds here. EngineerLand is the world I'm using for many of the projects in this book, DadWorld is the world I play in with my sons, and MyTestWorld is what I use when I want to test a new tool (such as Tinkercad) to make certain it works before I use it with one of my other worlds.

Click on a folder, and it will open and display a bunch of files, as shown in Figure 2.28.

CAUTION

Do not delete files

Be very careful here *not* to delete any files or move them to other locations, or you might find that a world no longer works.

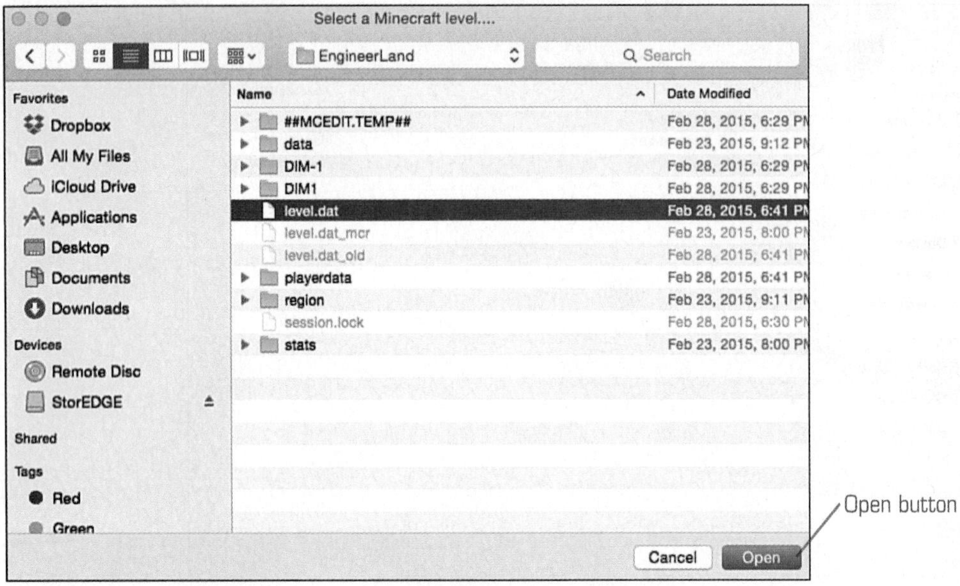

FIGURE 2.28   You can open a world folder to explore its contents.

The file you need to find is called level.dat. Click on this file one time to select it and then click the Open button. MCEdit then opens the world. Be patient, as it can sometimes take a minute or longer for it to open. Once the world is open, you see a screen like the one in Figure 2.29.

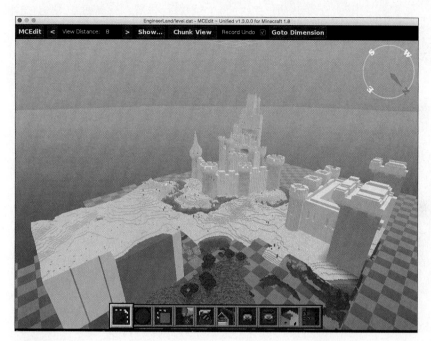

FIGURE 2.29   Your Minecraft world, open in MCEdit.

NOTE

It doesn't matter if your world is pristine or filled with structures

As you can see in Figure 2.30, I've already pulled a couple of castles into EngineerLand. You may have a pristine landscape with no structures, or you may see other elements that you've built in your world.

Movement controls in MCEdit may be somewhat familiar to you. You use the WASD keys for left, right, forward, and backward movement. Note that if you're not careful moving forward or backward, you could find yourself sinking quickly below the surface, as shown in Figure 2.30.

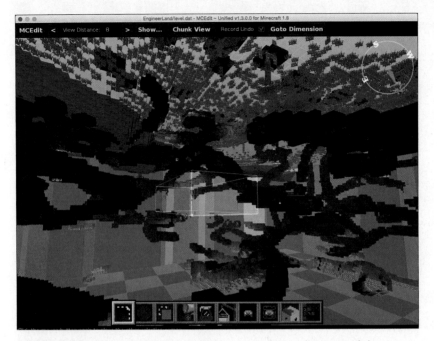

FIGURE 2.30 With MCEdit, moving around can be surprising.

While using MCEdit, think of yourself as a ghost. You can pass through solid objects easily, including the ground. Instead of tunneling down into the ground or having to locate the front door into a castle, MCEdit lets you just zoom around and through objects that would normally be treated as solid and require you to dig or mine through.

The other set of controls you'll need to practice with right now is the IJKL keys on your keyboard. Pressing J keeps you in place but turning to the left. (In contrast, pressing the A key moves "you" to the left while continuing to look forward.) The L key rotates you so you can look to the right. Press I, and it's like you're turning your head to look up. And the K key turns your digital head so you're looking down. Keep in mind that you can customize your key selections in MCEdit if you don't like using WASD or IJKL keys, but if you've not done this, these are the default settings.

It takes some practice to get used to these controls, but you'll be a pro at it with just a few minutes of playing around with them. Try using the IJKL keys with your right hand as you use the WASD keys with your left hand and practice flying around your world a bit.

Once you've got the WASD and IJKL keys figured out, go search for a suitable place to put your 3D model. I've found a spot to the left of the large castle shown in Figure 2.31.

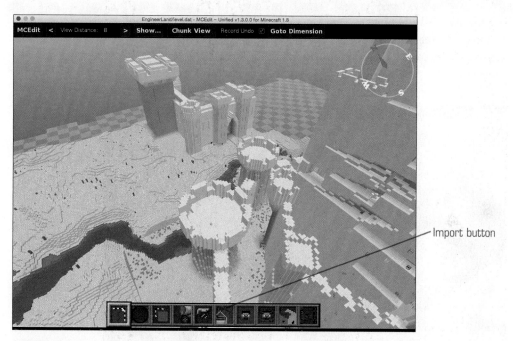

FIGURE 2.31 Find a suitable location for your imported model.

Next, click the Import button, and a window like the one in Figure 2.32 appears. Browse to the .schematic file you downloaded from Tinkercad, click on it once, and click the Open button.

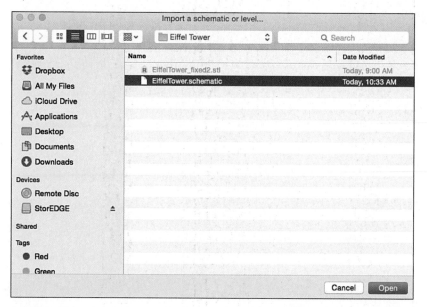

FIGURE 2.32 Find the .schematic file you downloaded from Tinkercad.

Use the WASD and IJKL keys to move the view if needed. Then use your mouse or touchpad to move the green box that appears onscreen and contains the size and shape of your 3D model (see Figure 2.33). The green box could be small, large, or gigantic. You may need to zoom out (using the WASD and IJKL keys) in order to see the entire box.

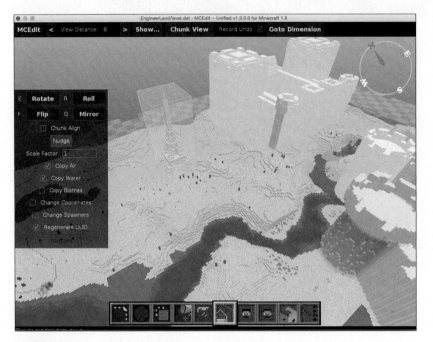

FIGURE 2.33 Move the green box to a suitable location.

When you're happy with the location of the green box, left-click to lock the green box in place. Once the box is locked, you can use some of the tools that appear on the left side of the screen in Figure 2.34, including the Import button.

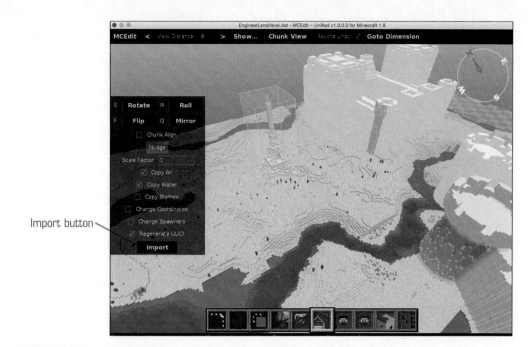

Import button

FIGURE 2.34 Lock in the location of your 3D model with a single click.

Now you can click on the Import button to start the process, which doesn't take long. When the import is done, your 3D model will be sitting pretty in the location you selected, as shown in Figure 2.35.

FIGURE 2.35 Your 3D model is now a real object in your Minecraft world.

You may have noticed that the imported Eiffel Tower doesn't look like the nice smooth version I downloaded from Thingiverse. Remember that this is Minecraft! Everything in Minecraft is made of blocks, so smooth surfaces aren't normal. Still, it does really look like a Minecraft version of the Eiffel Tower, right?

I can use the WASD and IJKL keys to zoom in and inspect the object. Figure 2.36 shows that I've zoomed in to check out my new tower.

FIGURE 2.36 A close-up with my new Minecraft Eiffel Tower.

In later projects, I'll introduce you to other useful features that MCEdit offers. Before you finish this chapter, however, I'd like to show you how to use MEdit to quickly change a block (or collection of blocks) of one type to a completely different block type. For example, if you have a large lake of water blocks, you can easily change all the water blocks to iron blocks, or even lava. This technique is even useful for changing buildings from one material to another. For example, I like that my Eiffel Tower is made of stone blocks, but you might want to change it to all brick blocks.

To do this, use the WASD and IJKL keys to zoom out a bit and then use your mouse pointer to select the object you want to change. To do this, move your mouse pointer to a piece of ground that's near a corner of your object. In Figure 2.37, you can see that a small white box appears near the lower-left corner of the Eiffel Tower.

FIGURE 2.37   Select a point near a corner of your object.

Next, click and hold the left mouse button (or press and hold a single finger on a touchpad) and drag that small white box to the left (or right) of the object and then drag to the rear of the object. This will create a white square that surrounds the base of your 3D model, as shown in Figure 2.38.

FIGURE 2.38   Surround your object with a white selection square.

Now click and hold on top of the white box and drag up. This way, you create a 3D box that will completely surround your 3D model, as shown in Figure 2.39.

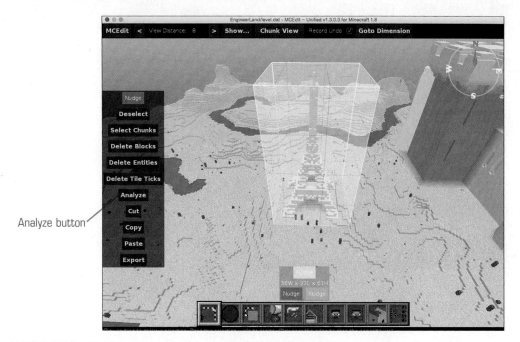

Analyze button

FIGURE 2.39   Surround your object with a white box.

Now that the object is selected, you need to know what material it is made of at the moment. Sometimes you can guess, but it's really better to know for sure. To figure it out, after selecting your object, click on the Analyze button on the left side of the screen. A new window like the one in Figure 2.40 appears.

FIGURE 2.40 Analyze a selection to discover its material.

In Figure 2.40, you can see that inside my selection box are a mix of materials: air, sand, and even a cactus. Air has the most blocks (77091 blocks), and there are quite a few sand blocks (1257 blocks), but it's the block of quartz that is the material making up the Eiffel Tower, with 2136 blocks in all. Make note of the material of your object (write it down as it is written on the screen) because you'll need it for the next step. Click the OK button to make the Analyze screen disappear.

Your object should still be surrounded by the selection box. Click on the Fill and Replace button on the toolbar that runs along the bottom of the screen. (This button is fourth from the left. Remember that you can hover your mouse pointer over a button briefly, and the name of the tool will appear.)

Two new windows appear, as shown in Figure 2.41.

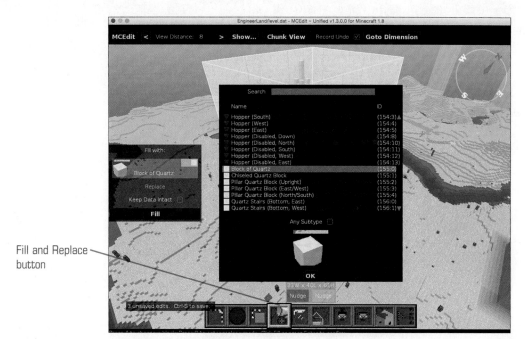

Fill and Replace button

FIGURE 2.41   Click on the Fill and Replace button.

On the smaller window, click the Replace button, and the smaller window changes again and look like the one in Figure 2.42.

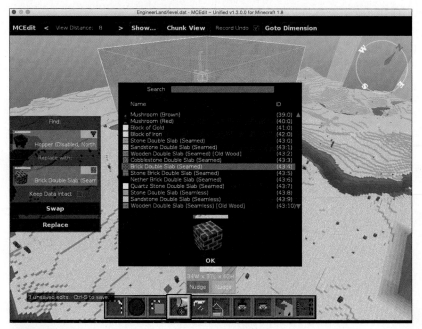

FIGURE 2.42   The Find and Replace With window.

Click on whatever material is visible in the top part of this small window. (In Figure 2.42, it's Hopper (Disabled North), but that's not important.) When you click this, a scrolling list of materials appears to the right, as shown in Figure 2.43.

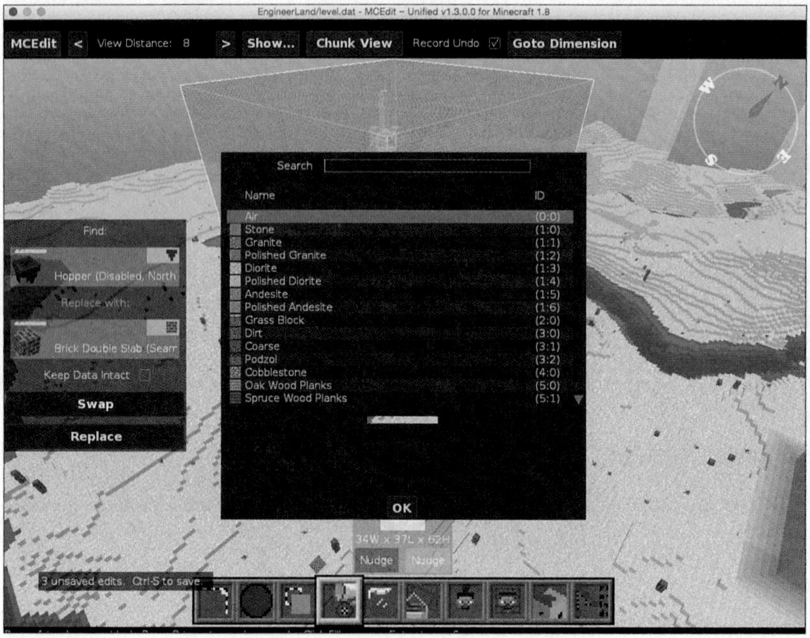

FIGURE 2.43 Scroll through the list and find your model's material.

You can scroll through this list to find the material that currently makes up your object. If you know the exact wording, you can instead just type it into the top Search bar, as shown in Figure 2.44.

FIGURE 2.44 Use the search bar to specify a particular material.

Once you've found the material by using the *exact* name you discovered with the Analyze tool, click the OK button.

Next, click on the material beneath the Replace With section in the smaller window and once again scroll through the list to find the material you wish to use as a replacement. If you know the exact name or a part of it, type it into the Search box at the top, as I've done with Brick in Figure 2.45.

FIGURE 2.45 A window with a list of every brick block type in Minecraft.

Click the OK button, and you should now see that the smaller window contains two materials: On top is the current material of your object, and beneath it is the material to use as a replacement (see Figure 2.46).

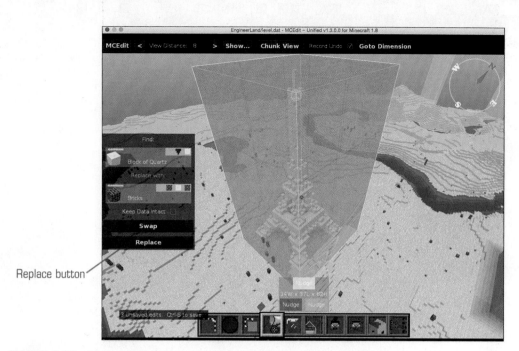

Replace button

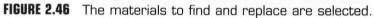

FIGURE 2.46   The materials to find and replace are selected.

Click the Replace button, wait 10 to 30 seconds, and the replacement should be done, as shown in Figure 2.47. (Click the Deselect button on the right toolbar to turn off the selection box or just click anywhere else on the screen.)

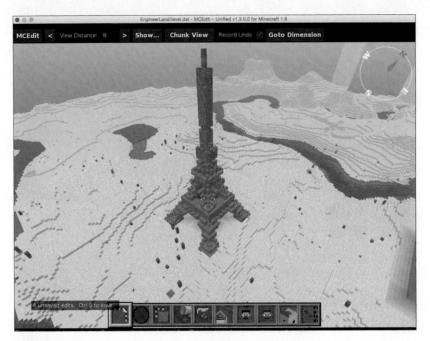

FIGURE 2.47   My new brick-blocked Eiffel Tower.

Slick, huh? I could easily go and select one of my castles and turn its walls into the super-tough obsidian or maybe just dirt. It's my world, and I can do as I please...just like you can with your worlds!

MCEdit is a Minecraft engineer's dream. There are so many fun things you can do with this app, and you'll be learning a few more throughout the remaining chapters. But for now enjoy your new model. You didn't have to build it block-by-block, which could have taken hours, days, or even weeks.

Feel free to go back to Thingiverse and find a few other fun objects. Practice what you've learned in this chapter: downloading an .stl file, importing the .stl file into Tinkercad, saving the 3D model in Tinkercad to a Minecraft-compatible file, and then using MCEdit to send that .schematic file into one of your worlds. After doing this a few times, you'll have the process memorized and will be able to start really building your worlds with dozens or hundreds of amazing objects.

TIP

Save your work!

Be sure to click the MCEdit button in the upper-left corner of the screen and click the Save button to save your world followed by the Quit button. Then you can open up Minecraft, open up the world you just modified with MCEdit, and check out your work as a player in the game. Invite your friends!

Up Next...

Tinkercad is sort of the middle step to getting a lot of things done, and in the next couple chapters, you're going to see me use some more of Tinkercad's tools and get some hands-on time for yourself.

Now that you know about Thingiverse, you know where to find ready-made objects that can be imported into Minecraft. But what if you'd like to create something that's not available on Thingiverse? Up next, in Chapter 3, I'm going to show you a tool (that's free to use) that allows you to do some more amazing things and create even crazier constructions for your Minecraft worlds.

3

Crafting a Super Maze

What You'll Be Doing

- Watch Didgee and Coolcrafter10 plan additional security
- Create your custom maze
- Use online-convert.com to create your .svg file
- Use Tinkercad to turn your 2D maze into a 3D maze
- Import your maze into Minecraft

"This is unbelievable," said Coolcrafter10. "It's a real castle. On my land!" He turned and smiled at Didgee-Engie. "This would have taken me weeks—no, months—to build!"

The sun was up but hiding behind some rain clouds in the distance, and the temperature had dropped a bit. A storm was coming, but Coolcrafter10 wasn't focused on the weather. In front of him, a new castle rested, its many towers disappearing high into the sky.

Didgee nodded. "These days, I use swords for fighting and shovels and pick axes for mining. When it comes to building, I always look for digital tools like Tinkercad and MCEdit to help me."

"I cannot thank you enough for showing me how to do this," Coolcrafter10 replied. "You are welcome to stay in my castle anytime you're in the neighborhood."

Didgee laughed. "Thank you. I may be taking you up on that if that storm starts moving in this direction." She pointed to the east and frowned.

Coolcrafter10 looked at the sky between the small mountain range to the north and the dense forest to the south. "I was hoping to do some gardening today, but you're right....That sky doesn't look friendly."

"Well, the storm hasn't arrived yet. Why don't we take a look around, and I can make some suggestions for improving your castle?"

"Oh, yeah! That would be great. Where do we start?" asked Coolcrafter10.

"Well, your castle can obviously use some torches right now, but are you familiar with redstone?"

Coolcrafter10 shook his head as he followed Didgee around the inside of his castle. "No. What is redstone?"

Didgee grinned wide. "You're going to have so much fun, I can promise you. Redstone is a special block that you can build with that carries electricity. With electricity, you can add switches to control lights in different parts of your castle. Torches are great, but it's nice to be able to turn on lights when you need them and turn them off when you don't. Oh, and once you get really good with redstone, you can even use it to build weaponry to defend your castles against any baddies that might try to attack."

"Is there a fast way to build with redstone? Something like Tinkercad that can build all these lights and switches for me?" asked Coolcrafter10.

"Unfortunately, no. Redstone is a material and a skill that you can only learn by doing yourself. I'll give you some websites that you can read on your computer to learn how to use it. That should give you plenty to do in the evening."

Coolcrafter10 frowned. "Well, I wish there were a way to defend my castle now while I start to learn about redstone. I think..."

CRAAACK!!!!!

Coolcrafter10 jumped as a lightning bolt hit a tree in the distant forest. The wind had kicked up, and a light rain began to fall.

Didgee scanned the sky. "I suggest we get back to your house while this storm blows over. I wish we could stay in your castle, but it doesn't have any rooms yet, and until you carve a few out and add a large door to that entrance, it's just not safe enough."

CRAAACCKKK!!!! Another lightning bolt popped in the distance.

Coolcrafter10 nodded. "Let's hurry." He ran back to his house and closed and locked the door behind them after Didgee ran in.

Didgee shook the rain off her shoulders and looked over at the computer. "You know, while we're stuck inside, I could show you something we can do right now that can add some extra security to your castle. Are you interested?"

"Are you kidding?" said Coolcrafter10, as he pushed a chair in front of his computer. "Please sit here and show me. Please! And thank you for all your help."

Didgee pulled out the chair from the desk, sat down, and turned on the computer.

"So, what do you have in mind?" asked Coolcrafter10. "A moat filled with giant squids? No! A pit of lava that spills down onto any attacking zombies?"

Didgee laughed. "Those are good ideas, but I've got something better in mind that won't take as long to create. How are you at solving mazes?" she asked with a wink.

"Uh, you mean the kind you solve with a pencil?"

"Not quite," replied Didgee. "Sit down and let me show you."

There's Almost Always a Solution

Back in Chapters 1, "Taking Over a Castle," and 2, "Creating Your Own Castle," you saw two examples of using applications other than Minecraft. Tinkercad and MCEdit are powerful tools, and you're going to get more hands-on time with both of them as the book continues. But there are other applications to explore that also allow you to create things that can be imported into Minecraft.

> **NOTE**
>
> **Reference previous chapters for rusty skills**
>
> Once again, this chapter is going to give you a fast example of another fun project and save the nitty-gritty details for Chapter 4, "Getting Lost (in a Maze)." Now that you've seen examples of Tinkercad and MCEdit, I won't be providing as many screenshots of tasks that you've already learned to do, such as importing an SVG file into Tinkercad or opening up a world in MCEdit. These are tasks that you'll need to know how to do, but if you've forgotten how to perform a task that's already been covered, you can always refer back to earlier chapters for the particular steps.

With today's digital devices—including computers, mobile phones, and tablets—it's easy to move files back and forth between devices. But what hasn't always been easy is changing files from one type to another (such as the change from .stl to .schematic that is done for you by Tinkercad). Fortunately, today you can usually do a simple Google search to find instructions on converting one type of file to another. If you have a need for a conversion, then someone else has probably already come up with a solution. In this chapter, you're going to be introduced to an outstanding online application (that's also free to use) that allows you to do even more amazing things with your Minecraft worlds.

As you work through the various projects in this book, you'll discover that often you need to use more than one application or service to get a job done. If you ever hit a roadblock with a project, just know that there's often a solution out there that's already been created, and you just need to do a little investigation to find it.

Next you'll see an example of another project you can do with Minecraft. In this chapter you'll see what's possible with this example, and then in Chapter 4 you'll get a more detailed walkthrough for your own Minecraft world.

Creating Your Own Hedge Maze

Have you ever been chased by a giant spider or zombie back to your Minecraft house? Or have you ever played a game of hide-and-seek with your friends (in Multiplayer mode) in Minecraft? Wouldn't it be nice to have some method of quickly disappearing from anyone (or anything) chasing you?

One solution is to create a giant maze. Think about it: You can memorize the path through the maze or have a printout of the solution in front of you, and with just a few fast left and right turns, you can quickly throw off any pursuers behind you. What's great about a maze is that if it's designed correctly, you can place it around your house (or castle) for an extra level of defense.

TIP

Outside exploration

Hedge mazes have been around for centuries. They are typically made up of bushes that are carefully trimmed to create the maze walls. If you'd like more information on hedge mazes, here are some links for you to investigate: https://en.wikipedia.org/wiki/Hedge_maze and https://www.youtube.com/watch?v=zAGu2TPt_78.

You can easily draw your own maze and then build it block-by-block inside Minecraft. Another solution is to grab a book of mazes, find a suitable maze in its pages, and then use that as the model. But I've got a different method that's great for creating a maze and saving it in a digital format so I can quickly get it moved into Minecraft and avoid building it block-by-block. Just follow along and rest assured that I'll provide more specific instructions in Chapter 4.

Figure 3.1 shows a maze I created by using a free maze generator (mazegenerator.net, a tool covered in more detail in Chapter 4) on the Internet.

FIGURE 3.1   I've selected to use a circular maze.

What's special about this tool is that you can use it to create circular, rectangular, and many other types of mazes. Even better, you can customize your maze in many ways; with this one, I've enlarged the center area so that a house or tower could be placed inside as a safe retreat.

Once I'm happy with my maze's design, I need to save it as a file. While the maze generator tool can save a maze as an .svg file, there's a problem: The .svg file it saves only retains the outside shape of the maze (circle or square) when imported into Tinkercad, not the pathways that make up the maze. For this reason, one more step is required before moving a maze to Tinkercad.

NOTE

More crazy file extensions

When you work with computers, you'll find there's a neverending list of file types you'll be using. Here are two new ones: .png (Portable Network Graphics) and .svg (Scalable Vector Graphics). Both are related to displaying graphics on a screen, but not every application related to drawing or displaying images is compatible with .png or .svg. Thankfully sites such as online-convert.com will let you convert graphics files from one version to another easily.

Instead of saving as an .svg file, I'll save the maze as a .png file. You can see this file saved on my computer in Figure 3.2.

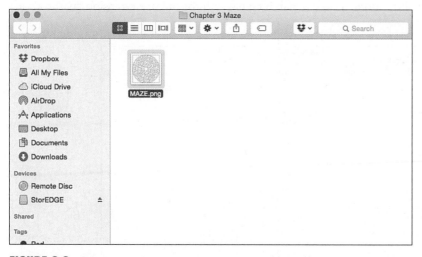

FIGURE 3.2 My maze is saved as a .png image file.

I still need to convert the .png file to .svg (and this conversion will make certain the pathways are retained). To do this, I'll be using a free online tool called online-convert.com, shown in Figure 3.3.

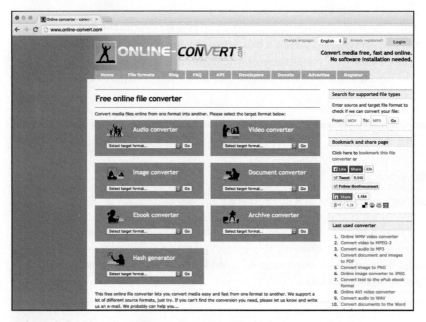

FIGURE 3.3   I'll use online-convert.com to change a .png to .svg.

Once the conversion is done, I have a matching file with the .svg file extension, as shown in Figure 3.4.

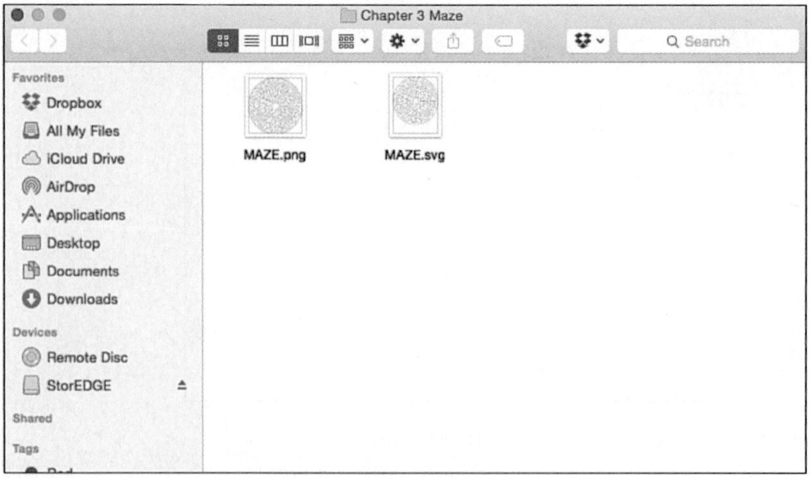

FIGURE 3.4   The .svg file is now ready to import into Tinkercad.

NOTE

Photos of a sketch or printed image will work

If you have a hand-drawn maze (or sketch) or a maze from a book, you can simply take a photo of the sketch. In Chapter 4 I'll show you how to use online-convert.com to convert your photo to an .svg file suitable for use in Tinkercad.

At this point, my maze is only two-dimensional. It has length and width, but no height. But I'm about to change that.

Preparing the Maze with Tinkercad

Back in Chapter 2, you saw how Tinkercad can be used to import an .stl or .svg file and then export it as a .schematic file for use with MCEdit and Minecraft. My maze is now in the .svg format, so I'm going to go ahead and import it into Tinkercad by using the Import tool.

NOTE

Tinkercad only works with .stl and .svg files

Refer to Chapter 2 for complete directions on using the Import tool in Tinkercad to import an .svg or .stl file.

After opening up Tinkercad, I click on the Create New Design button to open up a new project. I use the Import tool and locate the MAZE.svg file. After I click the Open button, the maze appears on the workplane as shown in Figure 3.5.

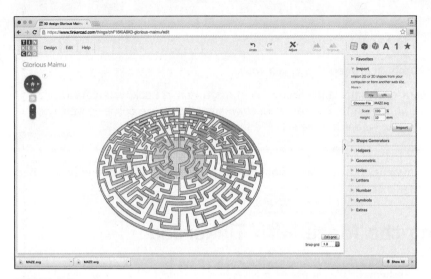

FIGURE 3.5   My maze has now been imported into Tinkercad.

As you can see in Figure 3.5, the maze is much larger than the workplane that is hiding underneath it. I'll shrink the maze down a bit by clicking on it once to select it. In the four corners of the maze, you can see small white boxes (sometimes also called Resize boxes), as indicated in Figure 3.6.

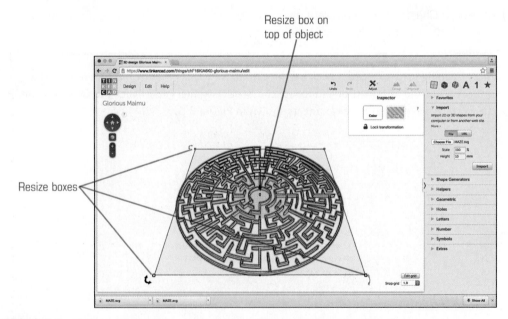

FIGURE 3.6   Select the maze, and small white boxes appear at the corners.

I need to shrink the maze's width and length at the same time and at the same rate. To do this, I hold down the Shift key and then click on one of the four corner white boxes; it doesn't matter which one, as long as it's not the white box on top of the maze.

As I drag a white corner box closer to the center of the maze, the maze shrinks. Figure 3.7 shows that I've shrunk it down to fit inside the workplane. It's not centered over the workplane, but that's okay. I can simply click once and hold on my maze and drag it to center it on the workplane.

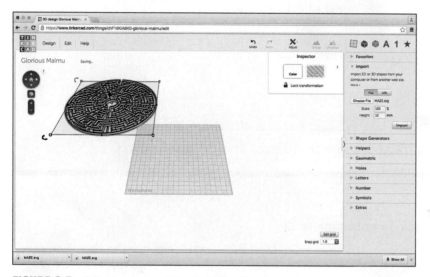

FIGURE 3.7 My maze is shrunk down in size.

Remember from Chapter 2 that when you export an object in Tinkercad to Minecraft, it uses a 1mm = 1 block ratio for the size. As you can see in Figure 3.8, my maze is 192mm in length and width. (Hover your mouse pointer over a corner white box to see the length and width will displayed.)

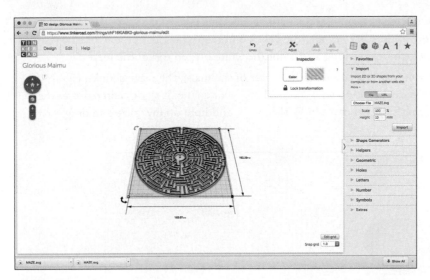

FIGURE 3.8 My maze is currently 192mm in width and length.

TIP

Enlarging a maze takes no time at all

If I find that my maze is too small in my Minecraft world, I just need to open Tinkercad and my maze project. Then I select the maze, hold down the Shift key, and then drag a white box away from the center of the maze to enlarge it.

To see how tall my maze will be, I hover my mouse pointer over the white box in the center of the maze, near the top. As you can see in Figure 3.9, my maze is 3.19mm tall, so it will be three blocks tall.

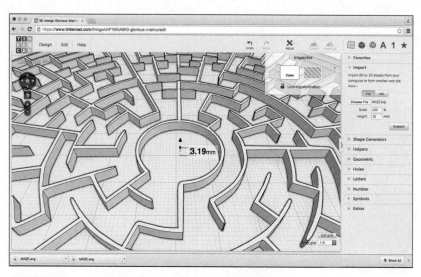

FIGURE 3.9 My maze will be three blocks tall.

What if I want a taller maze? Easy! Click and hold down on that center white block and drag up (slowly) but don't hold down the Shift key. This way you will change only the height of the maze. Figure 3.10 shows that I've resized my maze to be 5mm tall, which means it will be 5 blocks in height once it's imported into Minecraft.

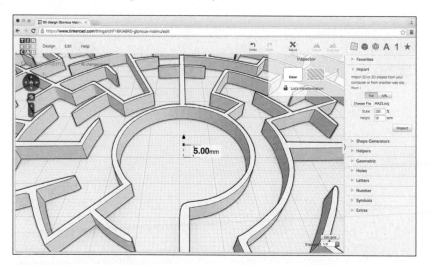

FIGURE 3.10 The maze is resized to be 5 blocks tall.

I've played around with my maze, increasing the inside circle's diameter and the outer diameter until I've ended up with a maze that is 239mm in length and width and 5mm in height. This information will become important shortly, when I find a piece of land to place the maze.

All that's left to do in Tinkercad is to export the maze as a .schematic file. I click on the Design tab and select the Download for Minecraft option, as shown in Figure 3.11.

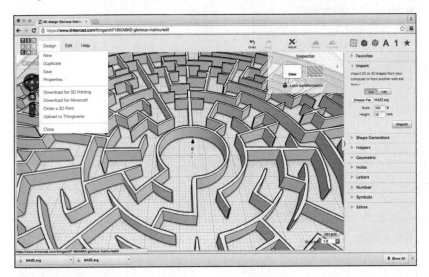

FIGURE 3.11   My maze will be downloaded as a .schematic file.

I've placed this .schematic file in the folder that holds my MAZE.png and MAZE.svg files, as shown in Figure 3.12.

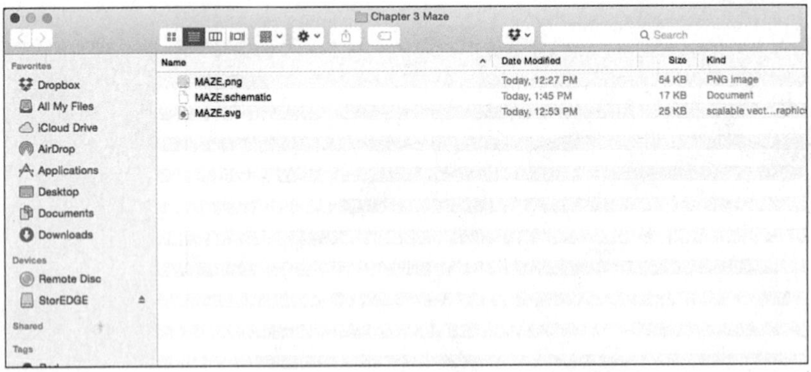

FIGURE 3.12   The MAZE.schematic file is saved to my computer.

Now it's time to open up MCEdit and get this maze imported into a Minecraft world.

Landscaping for Your Minecraft World

Prior to importing my maze, I found a nice medieval tower that I plopped down in my EngineerLand world. You can see it in Figure 3.13, with the Eiffel Tower in the distance.

FIGURE 3.13   A nice little piece of land to place a maze.

I've used MCEdit to import my maze, but as you can see in Figure 3.14, there's a slight problem.

FIGURE 3.14 The maze is imported but not permanently placed.

If you can't see the problem here, take a look at Figure 3.15. Here you can see that I've dropped down (using the WASD and IJKL keys), and you and I can both now see that the maze is floating above the terrain. Not good. What I need is a lot of flat terrain surrounding the tower before I place the maze. Specifically, I need at least 239 blocks by 239 blocks of flat terrain (to fit the length and width of my maze).

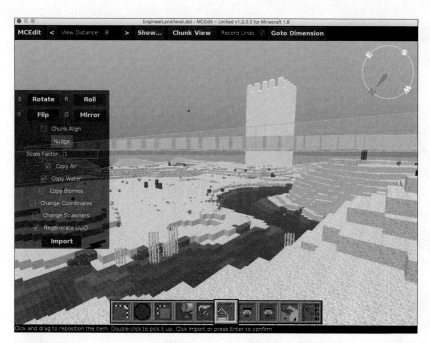

FIGURE 3.15 The maze is floating above the ground.

Normally, you'd have to flatten a piece of land by mining it block by block by block. Yawn. Fortunately, MCEdit can come to my rescue.

There are a lot of things you can do with MCEdit, as you'll discover in this book. One handy help MCEdit gives you is the ability to quickly and easily modify the terrain to suit your needs. In Chapter 2, you saw how easy it is to change one type of block to another; in Chapter 4, I'm going to show you how to use MCEdit to remove large numbers of blocks simultaneously.

I've already done this block removal in Figure 3.16. I'm high up in the air so you can get a good look at the flat terrain that is 250 by 250 blocks of stone—a perfect surface for planting my maze and my tower, although I could have filled it with grass or any other block material.

FIGURE 3.16 This flat terrain will be perfect for my maze.

After placing the maze with a single click (but before clicking the Import button), I can see that it fits well in my 250 × 250-block plot of flat terrain, as shown in Figure 3.17.

FIGURE 3.17 My maze fits well on the flat terrain.

Now it's time to import the tower and place it at the center of the maze. You can see in Figure 3.18 that the tower sits in the center circle. I also converted the rock surface to grass (using the Fill and Replace tool covered in Chapter 2).

FIGURE 3.18   My tower in the middle of the maze.

Before I go explore my maze in Minecraft, I click on the MCEdit menu and choose Save. After the save action is done, I click on MCEdit again and choose Quit. Now I can go check out my maze in Minecraft.

Exploring the Maze

After opening up EngineerLand, it's not hard to find my maze. As you can see in Figure 3.19, it's *gigantic*!

FIGURE 3.19 My maze looks great in Minecraft.

I've circled around and found the maze entrance. I can see that it'll probably be helpful to build some sort of building at the spot shown in Figure 3.20 so that I can easily find the entrance.

Open entrance in maze

FIGURE 3.20 The entrance needs a big ENTER HERE sign.

The real fun begins, however, inside the maze. If I memorize the solution, I'll be able to run through it super-fast, while any enemies chasing me will certainly get lost.

NOTE

Slow players down with some hard walls

Of course, a player can simply dig his way through the walls to the center in Creative mode. If you're planting your maze in Survival mode, however, be sure to select the entire maze and use the Fill and Replace tool to change its material to bedrock. That'll slow them down.

Figure 3.21 shows what it's like to be running through the maze. If you don't know the solution, it can definitely get confusing as you explore.

FIGURE 3.21   Having fun inside my version of a hedge maze.

Before leaving this chapter, think about how long it would take you to build a maze of this size and complexity using simple mining and placement of individual blocks. It would take dozens and dozens of hours...maybe even hundreds.

Guess how long I spent on this entire process? Less than 15 minutes. Here's a breakdown:

- Creating the maze with the maze generator: 2 minutes
- Converting the maze file to .svg with online-convert.com: 1 minute
- Importing into Tinkercad and resizing the maze: 2 minutes

- Exporting the maze to a .schematic file: 1 minute

- Flattening terrain before maze placement: 3 minutes

- Importing the maze and placing it: 2 minutes

- Importing the tower and placing it: 2 minutes

It may take you just a little longer than this because you'll be familiarizing yourself with the various tools, but once you become familiar with Tinkercad, MCEdit, online-convert.com, and other tools, the time it takes you to create these kinds of amazing structures will drop as well.

Up Next...

In this chapter I ran through the process of creating a maze and importing it into Minecraft quickly because I wanted to get you to the end result fast to show you the possibilities. Next, in Chapter 4, I'll slow things down a bit and give you complete step-by-step instructions for every task I covered briefly in this chapter.

Instead of helping you create and add a maze, however, I'll walk you through adding another fun element to a Minecraft world that uses the same tools and procedures you read about in this chapter.

4

Getting Lost (in a Maze)

What You'll Be Doing

- Create your own hedge maze
- Use online-convert.com to turn your maze into an .svg file
- Use Tinkercad to export your maze
- Use MCEdit to import your maze into your Minecraft world

I hope you enjoyed watching me create the maze that surrounds my new tower in my Minecraft world. I moved quickly through Chapter 3, "Crafting a Super Maze," but here in this chapter I'm going to slow things down a bit and walk you through each and every step. I'll also provide more detailed explanation about using MCEdit to mold and shape your Minecraft landscape.

In this chapter, you should actually perform the steps as you read over them. If you do, you will end up with a hedge maze in your world that you and your friends can use to play a game of hide-and-seek or that you can just enjoy as a nice landmark.

To complete this project, you'll first use a free online tool to create your maze. You'll be able to customize the maze a bit, including controlling its complexity—so that you end up with the maze you want, whether it can be solved in a few minutes or an hour or more. You've already seen how easy it is to use Tinkercad to import an .svg file and export it as a .schematic file that you can then use in MCEdit. But to get that .svg file, you'll also be using the online-convert.com tool I briefly showed you in Chapter 3. Finally, you'll need to master the MCEdit Select tool, which is really important for other features that MCEdit offers Minecrafters. Master the Select tool, and you'll be able to do some super-amazing things in your Minecraft worlds that will astound your friends.

Creating Your Maze

Open a web browser to mazegenerator.net, and you see a simple screen, like the one in Figure 4.1.

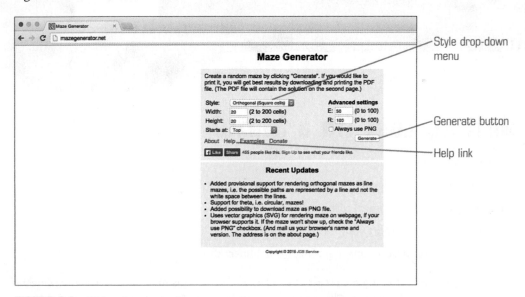

Style drop-down menu

Generate button

Help link

FIGURE 4.1 This simple tool can create some complex mazes.

TIP

Outside exploration

Other maze generators are available, but mazegenerator.net is my favorite. The key is to find one that lets you control both the shape and the complexity of a maze. With mazegenerator.net, you can pick from four different styles (square, hex, triangular, and circular) and tweak the width and length. There are some other advanced settings that I don't cover here, but you can click the Help link to read instructions for every available option.

In Chapter 3, I created a circular maze so that I could place a tower directly in the center. The steps are the same for creating and placing a maze no matter whether you choose a circular maze or the rectangular one that I recommend for your hedge maze in this chapter. To pick the shape, click on the Style box and select your shape. Orthogonal (Square Cells) is the default setting, and it's perfect for creating a rectangular hedge maze.

The Width and Height settings control the dimensions of your maze. (Actually, the Height setting controls the length of the maze. A two-dimensional maze doesn't have a height, but I'll show you how to give it height!) The default settings are 20 for each Width and Height, and you can leave them as is for now. If you click on the Generate button, you'll see a very simple maze appear below the controls, as shown in Figure 4.2.

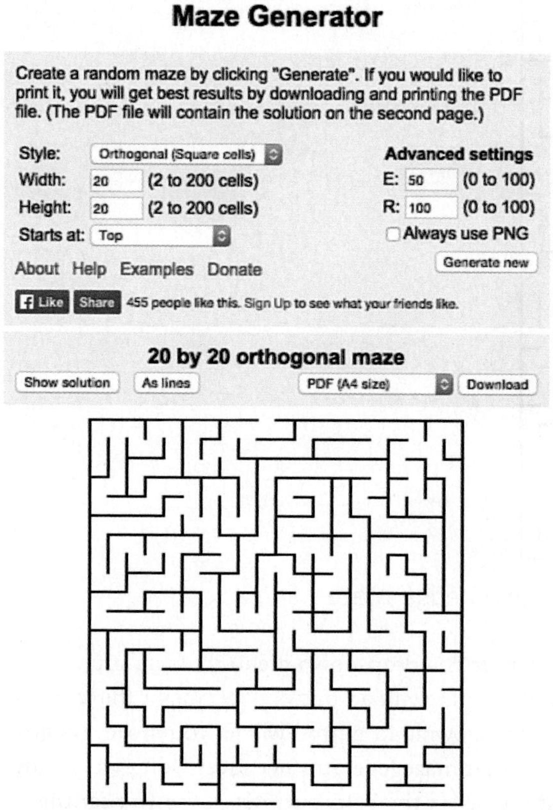

FIGURE 4.2 Click the Generate button to create your maze below the controls.

A square or rectangular maze has an "entrance" and an "exit." But it has no central area like the one found in a circular maze. Feel free to play around with the Width and Height settings to see how changes affect the size of the maze. For your first maze, I recommend a Width setting of 20 and a Height setting of 30 to create a rectangular shaped maze. You could create a larger maze, but later in the chapter, when you start playing with the MCEdit Select tool, you'll appreciate having a smaller maze when it comes to landscaping a flat piece of terrain or placing the maze.

Figure 4.3 shows the simple 20 × 30 maze that will be used as the example in this chapter. Go ahead and create this maze now.

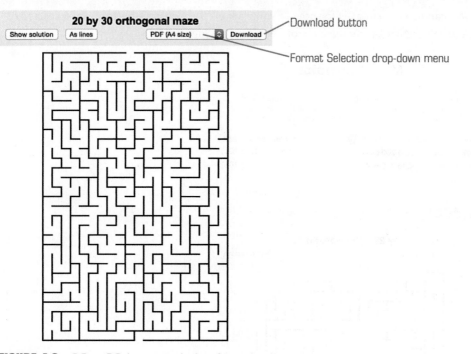

Download button

Format Selection drop-down menu

FIGURE 4.3 20 × 30 is a good size for a hedge maze.

Sitting above and to the right of your new maze is a drop-down menu that lets you select a file type (.pdf, .svg, or .png) as well as a Download button. You might think that selecting the .svg option here and clicking the Download button will let you move straight to Tinkercad, but unfortunately the .svg file that mazegenerator.net saves won't work with Tinkercad. However, there's a quick solution: Select the PNG option (as shown near the bottom of the menu in Figure 4.4) and click the Download button. (Be sure not to choose the PNG (with Solution) option.) The .png file downloads to your computer. Pace it on the desktop or in a folder where you'll be able to easily find it.

FIGURE 4.4 Save your maze as a .png file first.

You're done with the maze generator, so with your web browser still open, point it to online-convert.com, as shown in Figure 4.5.

FIGURE 4.5 You'll be using online-convert.com to change a .png to an .svg.

Converting the Maze with online-convert.com

The online-convert.com website is a very useful website for converting files from one type to another. The site can handle music, video, and other types of files, but in this case you need the Image Converter option. Click on the drop-down menu, as shown in Figure 4.6, and select the Convert to SVG option.

FIGURE 4.6   Select the Convert to SVG option.

When you select Convert to SVG, the site jumps to a page that looks similar to Figure 4.7.

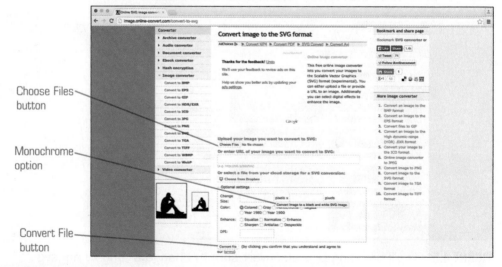

FIGURE 4.7   The Convert Image to the SVG Format page.

Click on the Choose Files button and find the .png file that mazegenerator.net created. Click on the file to select it, as shown in Figure 4.8, and then click the Open button.

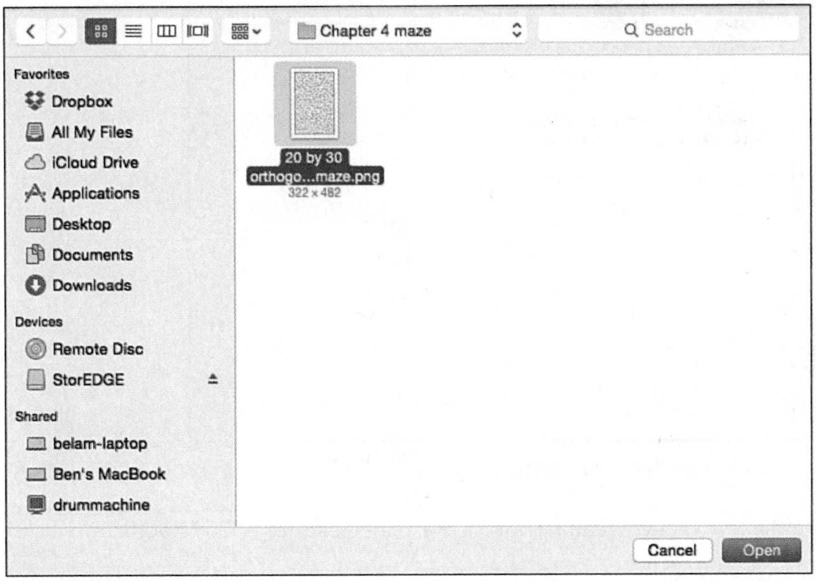

FIGURE 4.8   Find the .png maze file and select it.

Next, click the Monochrome option, as shown in Figure 4.9, and then click the Convert File button.

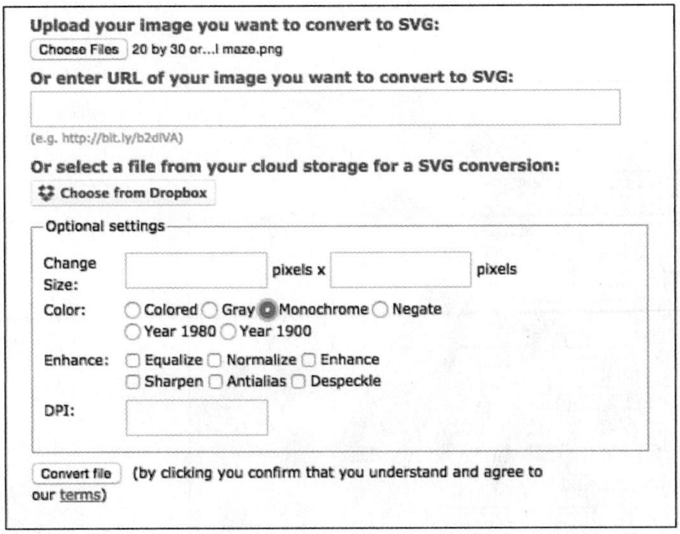

FIGURE 4.9   Select the Monochrome option before clicking Convert File.

The .png file is converted to an .svg file (with the same filename), as shown in Figure 4.10.

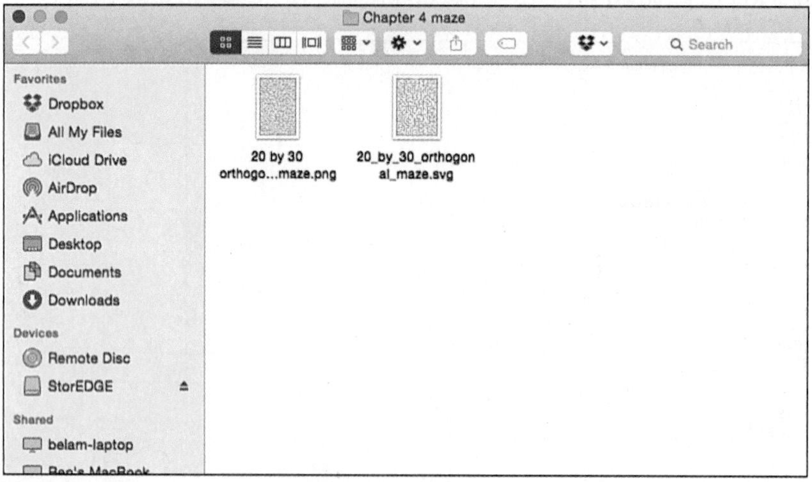

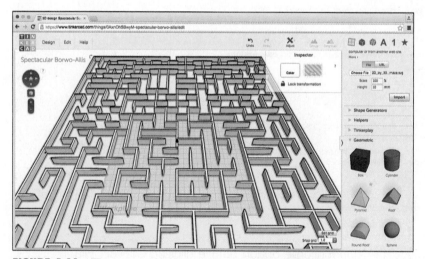

FIGURE 4.10 An .svg maze file is created.

Now that you have the .svg file, you can import it into Tinkercad for a few modifications.

Importing the Maze into Tinkercad

Back in Chapter 2, "Creating Your Own Castle," you saw how to import an .svg file into Tinkercad. I'm not going to cover those steps again here, so refer back to Chapter 2 if you need assistance with that task. As you can see in Figure 4.11, I've imported the maze into Tinkercad, but it's much larger than the workplane. The workplane is just barely visible underneath the maze.

FIGURE 4.11 The maze is imported into Tinkercad.

You need to shrink the maze down a bit, and you also need to remember that 1mm = 1 block in Minecraft. To shrink the maze down, you need to start by zooming out. (Refer to Chapter 2 for instructions on zooming in and out.) Figure 4.12 shows what it looks like after you zoom out, with the entire maze on the screen.

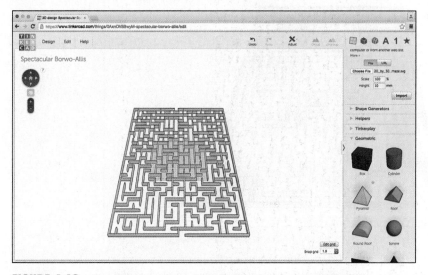

FIGURE 4.12 Zoom out so you can see the entire maze.

Click on the maze once to select it. You know your object is selected when it appears with a blue line around every edge and one of the Resize boxes (small white boxes) in each of the four corners, as shown in Figure 4.13.

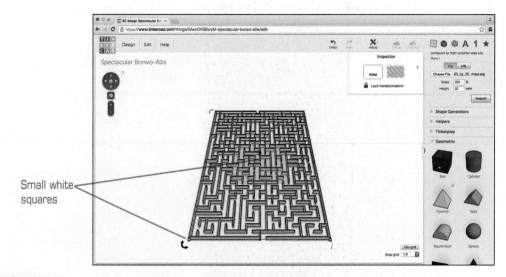

Small white squares

FIGURE 4.13 Select your maze, and four small white squares will appear.

If you hover your mouse pointer over any of the corner white squares, Tinkercad shows you the length and width measurements, as shown in Figure 4.14.

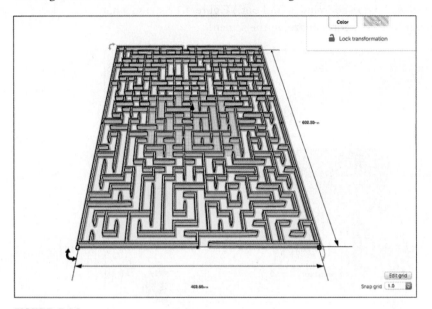
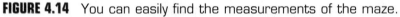

FIGURE 4.14   You can easily find the measurements of the maze.

This maze is 602.50mm long and 402.50mm wide. A maze with dimensions of 602.5 blocks × 402.5 blocks would be huge in Minecraft. It would take days to walk and solve! You definitely need to shrink it down.

If you click and hold on one of the corner white squares and drag, you can reshape the maze. Dragging the lower-right white box to the left will result in a skinny, deformed maze like the one in Figure 4.15.

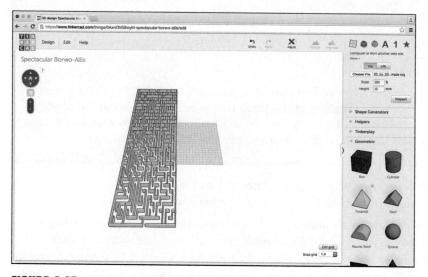

FIGURE 4.15   The maze is much thinner, and it's hard to see a solution.

Likewise, dragging the lower-right white box up (to the top of the screen) results in a crushed maze like the one in Figure 4.16.

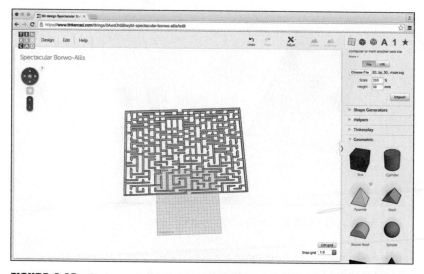

FIGURE 4.16   This crushed maze will also be hard to solve.

TIP

Mistakes are easy to Undo

Any time you make a change in Tinkercad that you don't like, click the Undo button to go back a single step. More clicks of the Undo button will reverse additional changes you've made to your object. If you accidentally crushed your maze by dragging a small white box, just click the Undo button until you get back to the original maze shape.

You want to shrink the maze at a consistent rate—so that the length and width change together and the maze remains looking the same whether it's smaller or larger.

To do this, simply hold down the Shift key on your keyboard while clicking and holding a white corner box. When you drag the white corner box, the length and width will shrink together. Shrink your maze down until it fits on the workplane. Figure 4.17 shows the maze at new dimensions of 75.66 × 113.25; this will be much easier to navigate in a Minecraft world.

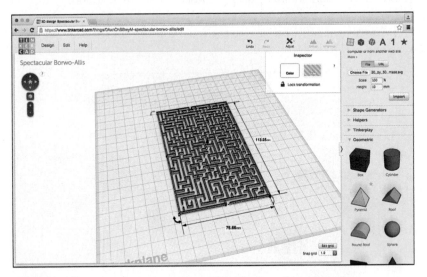

FIGURE 4.17 Shrink the maze until it fits on the workplane.

While the length and width dimensions of the maze are good now, there's still the issue of height. A good hedge maze should be tall enough that you can't see over the edges, which means it should be more than 3 blocks tall. But how tall is the maze right now? To find out, hover your mouse pointer over the single small white square in the center of the maze; the center white box can be a little hard to spot sometimes, so Figure 4.18 shows this box circled.

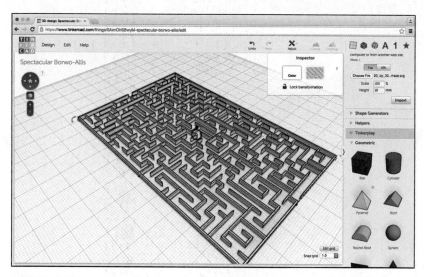

FIGURE 4.18 The center white box can be hard to spot.

When you hover your mouse pointer over the center white box, a small measurement appears, as shown in Figure 4.19.

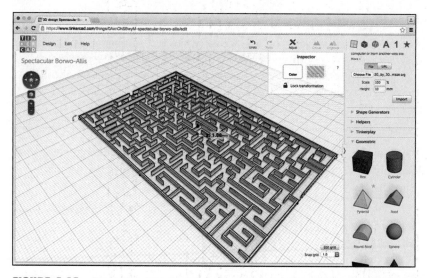

FIGURE 4.19 Find the height of your maze by hovering over the center white box.

The height of this maze is 1.88mm tall, or roughly two blocks. It needs to be taller. You know how to change the length and width of a Tinkercad object, and changing the height is just as easy: Just click and hold on that center white square and drag up to increase the height or drag down to decrease the height. If you drag up to make the maze 4mm high, as shown in Figure 4.20, the maze will end up being 4 blocks tall in Minecraft.

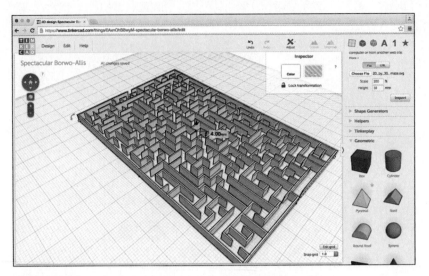

FIGURE 4.20 The hedge maze will be 4 blocks tall.

CAUTION

Be careful with the Shift key and Resize boxes

Do not hold down the Shift key while using the center white box to change an object's height. Doing so will cause the length and width to change as well. If you make any changes to the length and width while holding down the Shift key, the height of the Tinkercad object will automatically change. Always change the height of an object last and ensure that you don't use the Shift key while you make that change.

All that's left now is to export the maze for use with MCEdit. Click on the Design menu and select the Download for Minecraft option, as shown in Figure 4.21. (Leave the default setting of 1mm = 1 block.)

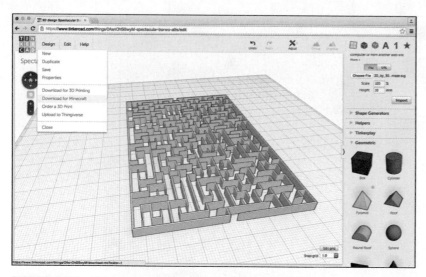

FIGURE 4.21 Export your maze for use with MCEdit.

Move the .schematic file that was created to a place where you'll be able to find it easily. You're almost ready to place your hedge maze, but first you need to create a nice flat space for it in your Minecraft world.

Learning to Use MCEdit's Select Tool

You can use MCEdit to do a lot of amazing things in a Minecraft world, but you need to have a solid understanding of one of its most powerful tools: the Select tool. The Select tool is actually easy to use with only a little practice. In this section, you're going to get that practice by clearing out a flat space for your hedge maze.

Go ahead and open up the MCEdit tool and one of your Minecraft worlds. (Be sure Minecraft is closed before opening MCEdit.) Use the WASD and IJKL keys to navigate around the world (assuming you haven't changed the key mappings—otherwise, use the keys you've assigned to Forward-Left-Right-Back as well as the Pan Up/Down/Left/Right mapped keys) and find a nice big area of land like the one shown in Figure 4.22.

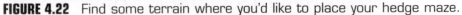

FIGURE 4.22 Find some terrain where you'd like to place your hedge maze.

In Figure 4.22, you can see a section of desert terrain with a couple small hills and some cactus plants. You may have found a different type of terrain, and that's fine: The Select tool will work no matter what type of terrain you have chosen.

Getting down close to the surface at this point will make it easier to understand the Select tool. (If you're high up in the air, the details of the Select tool will be difficult to discern.)

Figure 4.23 shows a good height from the surface, about 5 to 10 blocks above the ground.

FIGURE 4.23   Hover 5 to 10 blocks above the surface.

You can select a tool from the bottom of the MCEdit screen by clicking it. The first tool (from the left) is the Select tool, and in Figure 4.23 it is surrounded by a yellow box to indicate that it is selected. (Go ahead and click a couple other tools to see how the yellow selection box changes, but then reselect the Select tool before continuing.)

With the Select tool selected, move your mouse pointer around on the ground but don't click a mouse button. A small transparent box will follow your mouse pointer around on the screen as you do this, as shown in Figure 4.24.

FIGURE 4.24 The transparent box follows your mouse pointer on the screen.

Move the transparent box toward the left side of your screen and click the left mouse button once. This will "lock" the transparent box onto that location.

NOTE

The Select tool follows the terrain

If you moved the mouse pointer onto a hill, the transparent box will "climb" the hill as the terrain increases in height. While you're practicing, try to click on ground level if possible. If you don't have a large flat area of terrain to practice, use the WASD keys to move around your world to find a large flat area.

This first click will select a piece of terrain or even a block of air. Drag your mouse pointer to the right and down, and you'll see a collection of these transparent blocks begin to appear. This collection of transparent blocks is "selecting" whatever type of block (air, terrain, water, lava, and so on) is found inside the blocks. Figure 4.25 shows an 8 × 8 collection of transparent blocks created.

FIGURE 4.25 Drag your mouse pointer to select a larger area.

You can enlarge or shrink the area by moving the mouse pointer. When you're happy with the selected area, left-click again to lock in the selection size. Figure 4.26 shows a 9 × 11 collection of transparent boxes with a blue box in one corner and a yellow box in the opposite corner. The blue box and the yellow box are used with the Nudge buttons to increase or decrease the size of the selected area.

Blue Nudge button

Yellow Nudge button

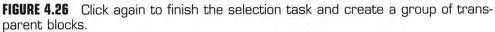

FIGURE 4.26 Click again to finish the selection task and create a group of transparent blocks.

You can increase or decrease the area you've selected by clicking and holding on either the blue Nudge button or the yellow Nudge button and using the WASD keys to expand the selection area. For example, to create the selection area shown in Figure 4.27, I clicked and held on the yellow Nudge button and then press twice on the D key to increase the width from 11 blocks to 13 (from the yellow block's location).

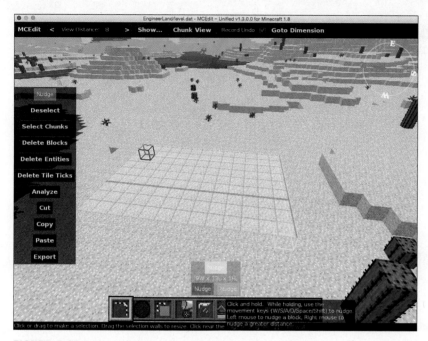

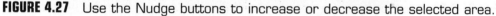

FIGURE 4.27 Use the Nudge buttons to increase or decrease the selected area.

You can also press the A key to reduce the width or the W and S key to add length to the selection area. These keys work the same with the blue Nudge button, but in this case the increase or decrease in size begins at the location of the blue box.

Reading how to do this is one thing. You need to actually try it, so experiment and play around with the WASD keys and the blue and yellow Nudge buttons to see how they actually work. Play around with making that first click and last click to select an area and then use the blue and yellow Nudge buttons with the WASD keys to see what kinds of results you get.

As you're experimenting, take note of one very useful feature with the Select tool. When you have an area selected, the dimensions of this area are displayed above the blue and yellow Nudge buttons. In Figure 4.27, for example, the selected area is 9W × 11L × 1H. That's 9 blocks wide, 11 blocks long, and 1 block in height.

This technique is very useful when you want to select a large section of terrain to fit something in...such as a maze with dimensions of 76 blocks × 114 blocks. By using the Nudge buttons, you can keep pressing the WASD keys (while holding down the blue and yellow Nudge buttons) to select an area equal to the size of a castle, or a maze, or anything else!

But what do you do if some bit of terrain, such as a hill, is taking up part of the area you want to use? In that case, you'll want to select an area as described above but also increase the height of the selection area. To do this, you simply click and hold on top of the selection area and drag up. Figure 4.28 shows that the 9W × 11L × 1H area increased to 9W × 11L × 3H.

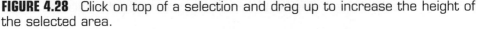

FIGURE 4.28   Click on top of a selection and drag up to increase the height of the selected area.

Using this method, you can select an area of terrain that has lakes, mountains, and even existing buildings on it. By selecting an area in both length, width, and height, you can use another feature of MCEdit to replace any terrain (or other blocks, such as lava or water) with the material of your choosing—or even air. Why would you replace terrain with air? Replacing selected terrain with air is the same as deleting it! By deleting existing terrain blocks and replacing them with air blocks, you can clear out a large piece of land and prepare it for placing a castle or maze.

How do you replace a selection of terrain with air? First, make sure you've selected the terrain you want to clear for your maze. In Figure 4.29, I've zoomed out a bit (by flying higher into the sky) so you can see the entire area that's been selected. Note the dimensions above the blue and yellow Nudge buttons: 77W × 115L × 29H. Selecting this is going to let me carve out a very large area of land, including removing part of that mountain you see on the left side of the screen.

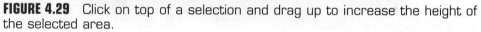

FIGURE 4.29 Click on top of a selection and drag up to increase the height of the selected area.

Once the area is selected, all you need to do is replace whatever terrain is inside the selection area with air blocks. To do this, you need to use the Fill and Replace tool. Press the number 4 key on your keyboard to select the Fill and Replace tool. The screen now looks as shown in Figure 4.30.

FIGURE 4.30 The Fill With screen on the left and the Search screen on the right.

The Search screen has a small field where you can type in the type of terrain you wish to find. If you leave the area blank, the first option in the list below the Search box is Air. Nice.

When you find the terrain you wish to insert into the selected area (which may be the Air option), just double-click it, and it is placed in the Fill With screen on the left, as shown in Figure 4.31.

FIGURE 4.31 Double-click Air, and it appears in the Fill With screen.

All that's left to do now is click the Fill button. A progress bar appears to let you know the Fill process is proceeding. Depending on the size of the area you have selected, this could take a few seconds up to a minute or more. When the process is done, click the Deselect button indicated in Figure 4.32.

Deselect button

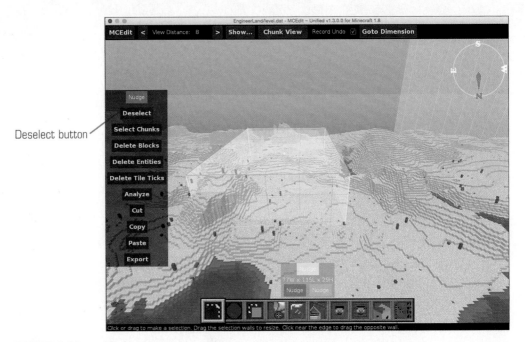

FIGURE 4.32 Click the Deselect button to turn off the selection area.

You should now have a large blank area of terrain, as shown in Figure 4.33. It's a bit strange to see mountains cut in half, but it's a sacrifice you need to make for progress and growth in Minecraft.

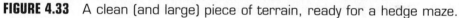

FIGURE 4.33 A clean (and large) piece of terrain, ready for a hedge maze.

With the area empty, you can now import the maze (.schematic) file and place it. (The import process is covered in Chapter 2, so refer back to that chapter for the steps necessary to import a .schematic file if needed.)

Figure 4.34 shows the hedge maze placed in the new empty terrain spot.

FIGURE 4.34 The hedge maze in place and ready to be used.

Right now, the maze consists of simple white stone. You can follow the steps outlined in Chapter 2 if you want to modify the material to something like grass or even lava blocks. (Just don't get too close to lava walls or you can get burned.)

As you can see, using the Select tool allows you to perform modifications to your world quickly and much easier than with block-by-block mining or placement. In later chapters, you'll learn a few more interesting uses for MCEdit, but for now, you can go enjoy your new hedge maze. Be sure to save your work in MCEdit by clicking the MCEdit menu and choosing Save. Then click the MCEdit menu again and choose Quit.

Up Next...

You've seen how easy it is to import .stl files into Tinkercad (from sites such as Thingiverse) or create .svg files using online-convert.com, but not all 3D models you wish to use in your Minecraft world are Tinkercad-compatible. There are many different tools available for creating 3D models, and not all of them save files using the .stl format. Up next in Chapter 5, you'll be introduced to another important 3D model file type and how you can convert it so MCEdit can import it into your Minecraft worlds.

5

Modifying a 3D World

What You'll Be Doing

- Watch Didgee invite Coolcrafter10 to her friends' castle
- Discover the 123D Sculpt+ app
- Select a 3D model with 123D Sculpt+
- Download and install Binvox
- Use Binvox to convert an .obj file to .schematic

Coolcrafter10 could hear laughing coming from around the corner. He ran forward, peeked around the maze wall, and saw Didgee disappear around another corner. "Almost caught you!" he yelled.

The maze was incredible. Didgee had shown Coolcrafter10 how to create the shape of the maze on his computer and then had used Tinkercad to give the maze walls height. Coolcrafter10 had resized the maze in Tinkercad so it would be a certain number of blocks wide in diameter and then plunked it down on some empty land nearby. For the last 10 minutes, the two Minecrafters had been playing a game of hide-and-seek inside the maze.

Coolcrafter10 continued to run after Didgee, who had the map of the maze. He turned corner after corner, following the laughter, until the exit to the inner portion of the maze appeared. Standing in front of the small tower that Coolcrafter10 had chosen to put inside the maze was Didgee, with a big grin on her face.

"Without the map, it would take someone a lot longer to navigate that maze," said Didgee as Coolcrafter10 opened the door to the tower and waved for her to come inside.

"Yeah, I'm glad you couldn't stop laughing, or I might have gotten lost," replied Coolcrafter10 with a smile. "Thanks for showing me how to do that. Tinkercad and MCEdit are some seriously powerful tools."

"They are," said Didgee. "But they're not the only tools available." She looked out the window at the blue sky. "Looks like the storm is long gone. I'm going to have to get on the road."

Coolcrafter10 frowned. "Aw, I hate that you have to leave. Are you sure you can't stay a bit longer?"

Didgee shook her head. "I've got some friends waiting on me at our castle. We've got a big project planned for tomorrow, and I need to get back to my own computer and get my part of the job done."

"I understand," said Coolcrafter10. "But now you've got me very curious about these other tools you mentioned. What do they do?"

Didgee double-checked her backpack for supplies and refilled her water bottle at Coolcrafter10's sink. "Remember how you use Tinkercad to export a .schematic file that can be imported into your world with MCEdit?"

Coolcrafter10 nodded.

"Well, that works great if you've got a 3D object in Tinkercad that you've created yourself or imported from a site like Thingiverse. But sometimes you don't have an .stl file. And other times Tinkercad might not give you exactly the tools you need to create something that's in your mind. Tinkercad is great for creating things with spheres and cubes and pyramids and other shapes that can be joined and morphed, but there are much more complicated 3D objects that you can create only with different software apps."

"Like what?" asked Coolcrafter10.

"Well, take the castle I share with my friends. We've been having some trouble with a local group of bandits. They're not very smart and are very scared of a particular type of monster. We tried to create the monster in Tinkercad, but the final result didn't match what we had in mind. One of my friends found a different software tool that is perfect for creating the monster, but it doesn't save the 3D monster model as an .stl file. It's an .obj file, and Tinkercad can't import .obj files. But that didn't stop us. We found a way to convert an .obj file to a .schematic file, just like Tinkercad does with .stl files. And now we're going to use MCEdit to see if we can get the monster placed to scare off those bandits."

"Sounds like fun—I mean the monster statue, not the bandits," said Coolcrafter10. "I wish I could be there to see it."

Didgee cocked her head and looked at Coolcrafter10. "Why don't you come with me? You'll get to meet my friends, and I can show you some other tools that we've been using to create and modify the land around us."

"I hate to leave my new castle and maze. What if some monsters or griefers start tearing them down?"

Didgee smiled. "I used to worry about that, too. But now I know I can quickly repair or replace anything by using MCEdit and these other tools. I think your castle will be safe, but remember that you can always use MCEdit to erase it completely and put a new one back in its spot—maybe an even bigger castle!"

"You're right," said Coolcrafter10. "I didn't think about that. And I'll bet with my laptop and MCEdit, I can always import a tower or another structure anytime I need it, especially when I'm out exploring and can't get back to my home computer."

"So, are you going to come with me?" asked Didgee.

"Absolutely! I can't wait to see your monster scare away those bandits!"

More Tools Means More Options

Tinkercad is a great tool for importing 3D models you find on sites such as Thingiverse or for importing .svg files. Once you have the file you want in Tinkercad, it's a simple matter of clicking the Design menu and selecting the Download for Minecraft option to download a .schematic file that MCEdit can open and place inside one of your Minecraft worlds.

Later in the book, you'll get some hands-on time actually using the Tinkercad tools to create original 3D models. Tinkercad can import items, but its real strength lies in its toolbars, which allow you to create your own 3D models. Once you create a 3D model and save it as an .stl file, you can modify it—shrink it, enlarge it, rotate it, and even add more features to it over time. Then, when you're done making mods, you use Tinkercad's special ability to create .schematic files for use with Minecraft.

But before you dive into creating your own 3D models with Tinkercad, you should be aware that Tinkercad isn't the only tool around for creating fun models that can be used in Minecraft. There are many other software tools that can create .stl files. If one of them doesn't allow you to download a .schematic file, you can import an .stl file that you create elsewhere into Tinkercad (remember that Tinkercad can import both .stl and .svg files) and then use the Download for Minecraft menu option to create an MCEdit-compatible .schematic file.

Take a look at Figure 5.1, which shows a 3D model of a robot. This robot is one of the standard 3D models you can open and modify using a tablet app called 123D Sculpt+ from Autodesk.

NOTE

The 123D Sculpt+ app

123D Sculpt+ is just one 3D modeling tool that's available for free from Autodesk. It is available from the App Store for iPads running iOS 7.0 and higher and from Google Play for Android tablets running version 4.2 and higher. I'll cover installing and using 123D Sculpt+ in Chapter 6, "Creating Your Own Monster Island." (The 123D Sculpt app shouldn't be confused with 123D+ Sculpt—it's just an older version that is still available for download. Grab the 123D+ Sculpt app for purposes of this chapter.)

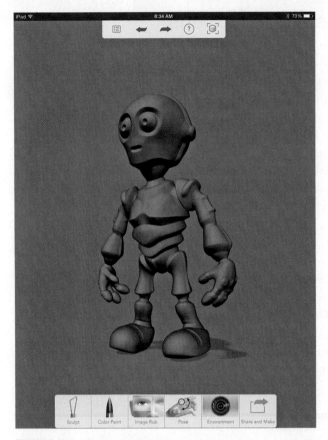

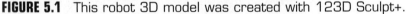

FIGURE 5.1 This robot 3D model was created with 123D Sculpt+.

123D Sculpt+ is fun and easy to use, and you'll see it in action in Chapter 6. For now, there's one important thing you need to know about this 3D modeling app: It doesn't save or export models as .stl or .schematic files. It allows you to download your creations, but when you examine the files, you'll see that they're in the .obj (object) file format. So how can you possibly use a 3D model .obj file from 123D Sculpt+ with Minecraft?

I've mentioned this already in the book, and I'll say it again: Often you'll need to find workarounds when you work with digital tools and software, such as when you need to convert one file type to another. You converted a .jpg to a .svg using the online-convert.com website, and you may be wondering if there's a way to convert an .obj file to an .stl file or even directly to a .schematic file. Yes, there is!

Finding a 3D Model with 123D Sculpt+

In this chapter, I'll show you an example of using a non-Tinkercad application to create a 3D model for use in Minecraft. I'm going to run through the process quickly so you can see what's possible. Then, in Chapter 6, I'll go a bit slower through all the steps and give more details.

It all starts with downloading and loading the 123D Sculpt+ app you see in Figure 5.2.

FIGURE 5.2 The 123D Sculpt+ app lets you view models from other users.

The 123D Sculpt+ app lets you create your own 3D models or view what other app users have designed. If you find something you like, it's easy to save a copy to use as is or modify.

The app also comes with some predesigned models that you can open and play with. Figure 5.3 shows such a model—in this case the robot from before, now rotated around with some color applied. (However, the color really won't make much of a difference, as you'll see when I import this into a Minecraft world with MCEdit.)

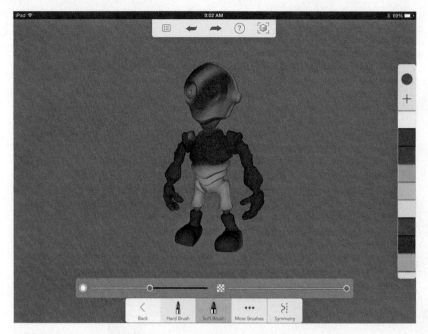

FIGURE 5.3   I've applied some color to my robot.

Once I have a 3D model created, I can save it so I can access it later and make changes if necessary. Figure 5.4 shows the My Sculptures page, with all my models listed—both models I've created and those I've downloaded from other users.

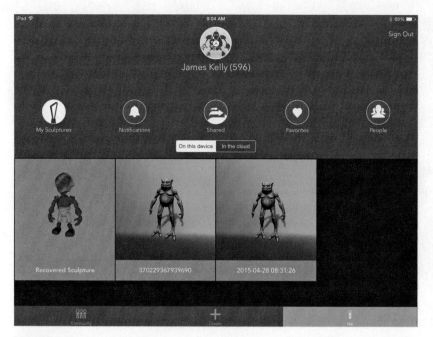

FIGURE 5.4 My 3D models are available on the My Sculptures screen.

NOTE

Share your creations with the world

The app lets you share your models with friends and family. It also lets you follow your favorite 3D model designers and get alerts when they upload new designs. Your own designs could even become popular with other 123D Sculpt+ users, so don't forget to upload them and share them with the world. And should you download someone else's creation, modify it, and then upload the new version, be sure to give proper attribution to the original designer by providing the designer's user name and a link to the original file you copied.

To get this robot into my Minecraft world, I need to download a few files. One file is the .obj file that contains the model's basic shape and design (called the mesh), and a few other files provide additional details, such as the colors and textures (called skins). The 123D Sculpt+ app makes it very easy to get these files to my computer via email, as shown in Figure 5.5.

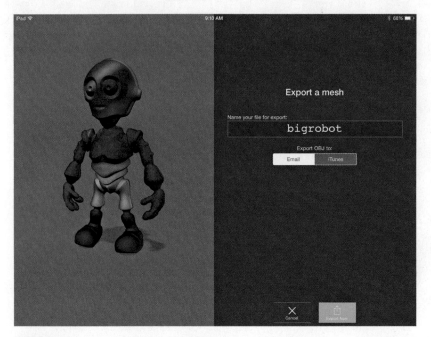

FIGURE 5.5 I can email 123D Sculpt+ model files to my computer.

When I choose to export the model this way, the app emails me a zipped file that I can save to my computer (see Figure 5.6).

FIGURE 5.6 The .obj file is compressed inside the zip file emailed by 123D Sculpt+.

When I open up the zip file, I see the three files shown in Figure 5.7. The only file I'm interested in is the one that ends with .obj; in this case, it's called bigrobot.obj.

Name ^	Type	Compressed size	Password p...	Size	Ratio	Date modified
bigrobot	PNG image	2,879 KB	No	2,880 KB	1%	4/28/2015 9:11 AM
bigrobot.mtl	MTL File	1 KB	No	1 KB	27%	4/28/2015 9:11 AM
bigrobot.obj	OBJ File	6,344 KB	No	25,428 KB	76%	4/28/2015 9:10 AM

FIGURE 5.7 The .obj file is the one I need for my Minecraft world.

After I save the bigrobot.obj file to a folder where I'll be able to easily find it later, I need to convert that .obj file to a .schematic file. I've got a great tool for making this conversion, but as you're about to see, it's not as "pretty" as other tools I've been introducing to you. But just as you should never judge a book by its cover, you should also never judge a piece of software until you've used it and decided whether it's useful to you.

NOTE

Mac and Windows options for .obj files

You may have noticed from the screenshots in Figures 5.6 and 5.7 that I'm using a Windows computer. Don't worry, Mac users. I'll be providing some additional details in Chapter 6 on how Mac users can convert .obj files to .schematic files.

Converting Files with Binvox

During my search for tools to convert .obj files to .schematic files, I found quite a few solutions, but most of them required owning a piece of expensive software. Not everyone can afford to spend hundreds or even thousands of dollars on powerful design software, so I kept looking. And I finally found a solution that both works and is free. It's called Binvox, and once you figure out its basic controls, it's quite easy to use.

I'll go into the details of using Binvox (including downloading and installing it) in Chapter 6, so for now you can just sit back and let me give you a brief overview of the process for converting .obj files to .schematic files in Binvox.

These days, software is almost always graphical in nature, with drop-down menus and pop-up alerts and all sorts of visual aids. But years ago, a lot of software was text based: You just typed a command or two on the keyboard and pressed the Enter key. Binvox is such a command-line tool. This means you won't be double-clicking an icon on the desktop or tapping the name of an app on a tablet. Instead, Binvox's work is all done from what's called a command prompt. You can see the Windows command prompt in Figure 5.8.

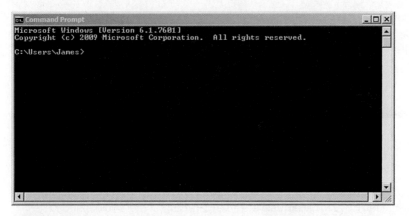

FIGURE 5.8 Binvox does its work at a command prompt.

NOTE

A command prompt can be useful

I won't be going into a lot of detail about using a command prompt here, but for now just know that command prompts are really useful: You can access every folder you have on your computer from a command prompt if you know the right commands. You'll learn more in Chapter 6.

I've copied the bigrobot.obj file into a folder called vox_package that was created when I installed Binvox. Figure 5.9 shows the contents of the vox_package folder. Look closely, and you should see the bigrobot.obj file, toward the top of the list.

binrobot.obj file

FIGURE 5.9 Looking inside the Binvox folder of files.

There's also another file called binvox.exe, which is the executable file for the actual Binvox app (or program) that you will run. You run a command prompt program by simply typing in the name of the .exe file and pressing Enter. In this case, if I type **binvox** and press the Enter key, I get a long list of explanations about how to use the binvox.exe program, as shown in Figure 5.10.

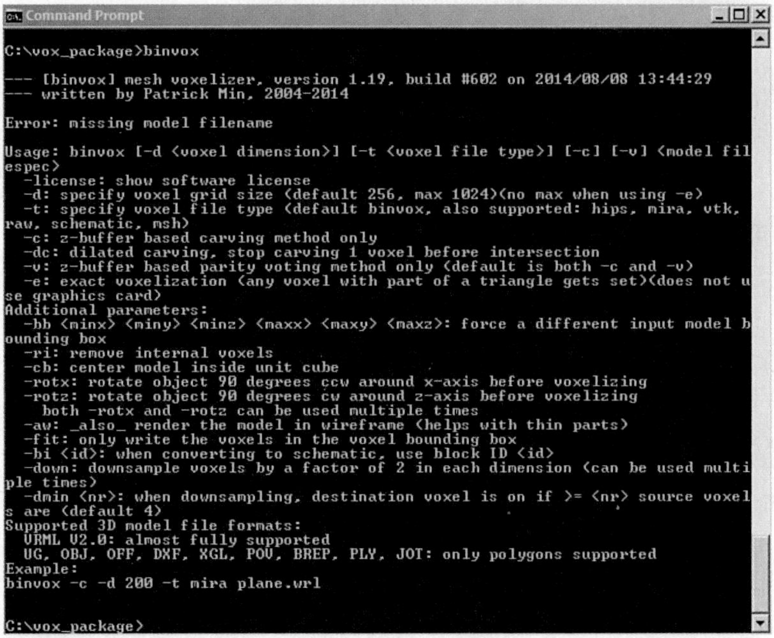

FIGURE 5.10 Some strange stuff appears on the screen when I run Binvox.

All I need to do to get binvox.exe working properly and converting my .obj file to a .schematic file is to type the following at the command prompt (and be aware of the lowercase usage and enter the command exactly as shown):

```
binvox -t schematic bigrobot.obj
```

When I type that bit of text and press Enter, a strange thing happens. Another window appears on the screen, with lots of crazy-looking rows of numbers (see Figure 5.11).

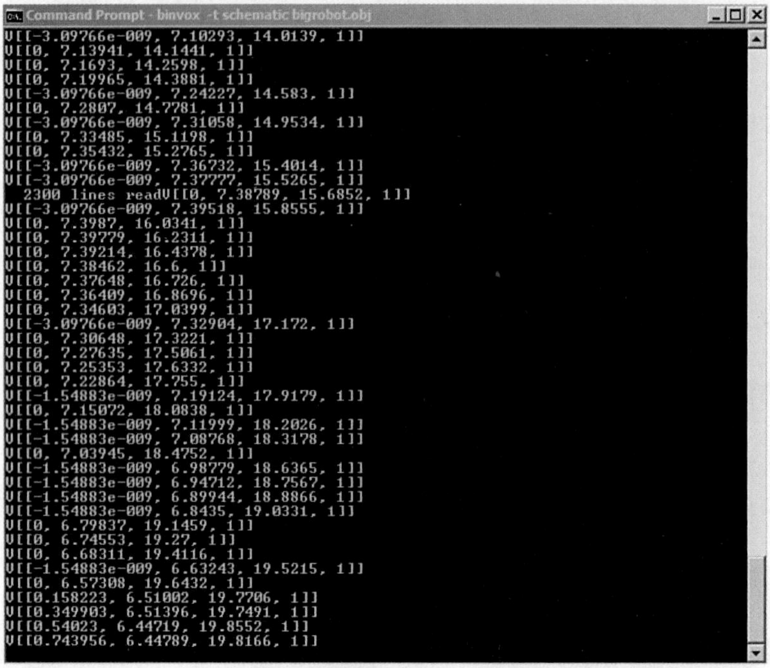

FIGURE 5.11   The Binvox program starts the conversion.

The numbers and other characters scroll up from the bottom of the screen and off the top, and they move much faster than I can read. You shouldn't even try to read that stuff. Just wait about 8 to 10 minutes for Binvox to finish its work; it's taking the data stored in the .obj file that defines the shape and structure of the 3D model its changing that into the .schematic file format that MCEdit can read.

At some point, yet another window appears, containing a colorful shape of the 3D model, as shown in Figure 5.12. As part of the conversion process, this shape changes from a top view to a side view and on to other angles. The conversion process takes a little time, so be patient.

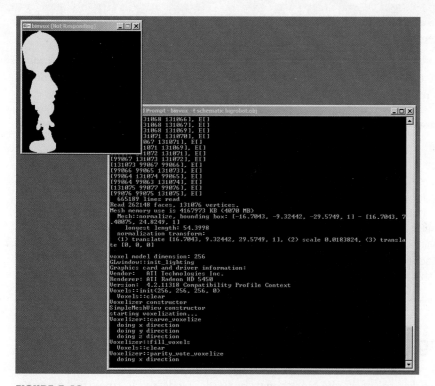

FIGURE 5.12   The model goes through a number of conversion steps.

When the conversion process is done, I take another look in the vox_package folder and see that there's a new file called bigrobot.schematic, as shown in Figure 5.13. Woo hoo!

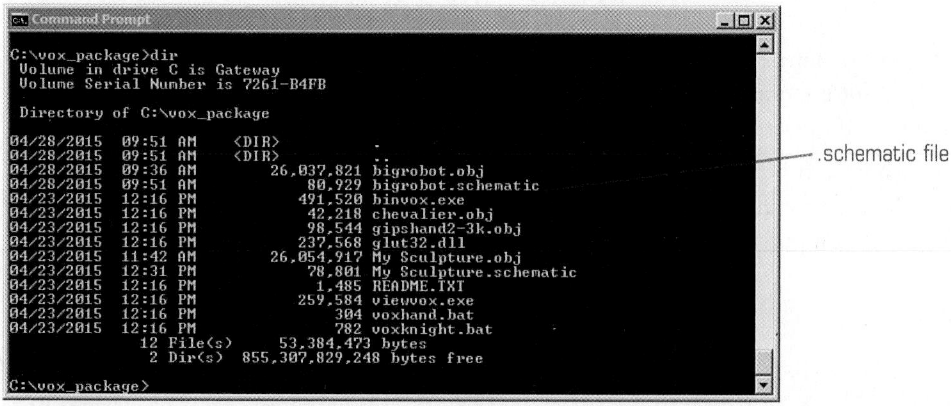

FIGURE 5.13   I've now got a bigrobot.schematic file!

Now that I have a .schematic file, I can use MCEdit to import the robot into one of my Minecraft worlds.

I've got Minecraft and MCEdit installed on both my Mac laptop and my Windows desktop computer. Since I used my Windows computer to do the Binvox conversion, I'll stick around and import the robot model with MCEdit.

NOTE

I've got Minecraft and MCEdit installed on both my Mac laptop and my Windows desktop computer (and the worlds I create and edit on each computer are compatible). Since I used my Windows computer to do the Binvox conversion and the .schematic file is on my computer, I'll use MCEdit to import the robot into one of my other Minecraft worlds. I could just as easily copy the bigrobot.schematic file over to my Mac laptop and import it there, but I want to show you that most of the processes in this book can be done with both Windows and Mac machines.

Importing and Sizing the Robot

Remember that when you use Tinkercad for creating .schematic files, at one point in the process you are asked to specify the block size to be used. The default is 1mm (millimeter) is equal to 1 block, so a 50mm-tall object in Tinkercad will be 50 blocks tall in Minecraft. Knowing this is helpful for sizing 3D models and helping you find suitable locations for them in your Minecraft worlds.

There's a slight problem with the .obj file created in 123D Sculpt+. You can't specify the dimensions (height, length, and width) of a 3D model in the app. You may have noticed that during the Binvox conversion process, I was never asked to specify a size for the robot 3D model. But I'm not worried because I know that MCEdit will allow me to modify the size of an imported object before I place it permanently.

Let's take a look at how to modify the size of my imported robot using an MCEdit control. Figure 5.14 shows that I'm inside MCEdit, and I've opened up one of my worlds (found on my Windows computer), called TheGreatWild.

FIGURE 5.14 This island needs a guardian.

Just as Easter Island has those huge monoliths staring out at the ocean, I'd like to place my big robot facing out at the ocean, warning away any unfriendly visitors.

NOTE

Easter Island monoliths

There are a lot of theories about the large stone faces that line the shore of Easter Island. One of them is that the stones were meant to look like giants that lived on the island. The idea is that the "giants" would scare away anyone approaching the island. You can read more information on Easter Island, including theories on how the island's inhabitants made and transported these giant stones, by visiting http://en.wikipedia.org/wiki/Easter_Island.

I've found a suitable place for the robot and clicked the Import button to start the process. As you can see in Figure 5.15, however, the green box that indicates the size of my robot is very large—too large. It almost completely covers both islands!

Scale Factor
value

FIGURE 5.15   My imported robot is just too large for my purposes.

Thankfully, MCEdit allows me to resize the robot before placing it. To do this, I need to click on the Scale Factor value box (the default is 1.0) and change it to 0.5 (half size) or even 0.25 (one-quarter size). But even after I try out 0.25, I can see that the robot is still too large (see Figure 5.16). (You might also notice the shape of the robot: He's lying down rather than standing on his feet! Don't worry. I'll fix that shortly.)

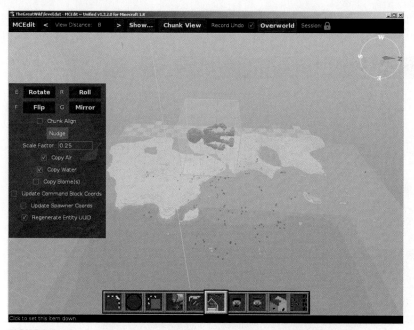

FIGURE 5.16 The 0.25 scale factor is still a bit too large.

I try changing the Scale Factor value to 0.15 and think that I have found the perfect size for my robot, as shown in Figure 5.17.

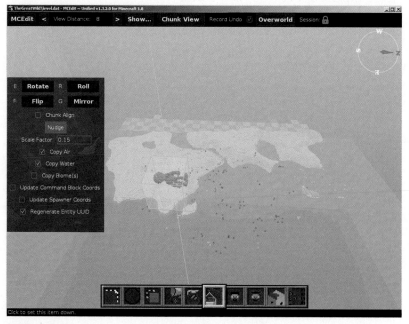

FIGURE 5.17 My robot is ready to be placed.

I click the spot where I want to place my robot, but notice in Figure 5.18 that he's still lying down, so I need to correct his orientation.

FIGURE 5.18 My robot is placed, but he's lying down.

I'll use a combination of clicks on the Rotate and Roll buttons to get the robot standing up. After a few test clicks, I've got the robot standing up, but now I see that I'd like him to be more centered on the shore of the left island.

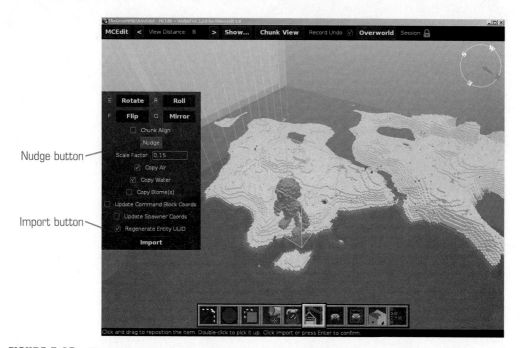

FIGURE 5.19 The robot is facing the ocean, but I'd like to move him a bit.

By clicking and holding down the Nudge button, I can use the WASD keys to move him forward, backward, left, and right. Figure 5.20 shows that I've got the robot right where I want him.

FIGURE 5.20   My robot is right on the shoreline, guarding my island.

All that's left to do is to click the Import button to finalize the import action. When the import is finished, I click on the MCEdit menu (in the upper-left corner of the screen) and select the Save option.

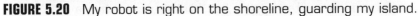

NOTE

Binvox doesn't care about colors

The robot's colors don't carry through during the conversion process. I can go in and use blocks of different colors if I want to give him some color, but I like the pure gray stone color because it reminds me of the Easter Island faces.

After closing down MCEdit, I open up my TheGreatWild world in Minecraft and take a walk to visit my new island guardian (see Figure 5.21).

FIGURE 5.21 Now that's an island guardian!

I could have some fun and import 10 or 20 more copies of the bigrobot.schematic file and place them all around my island to create my own version of Easter Island...but with giant robots.

Binvox Opens Up Many Possibilities

None of what I've done in this chapter would be possible without the ability to convert .obj files to .schematic files that Binvox provides. Being able to make this file type conversion opens up many more opportunities for my Minecraft worlds. Just as Thingiverse.com allows me to browse and find interesting .stl files to import into Tinkercad (and then into Minecraft via MCEdit), there are also online libraries of free .obj files (such as the one offered by TurboSquid at http://www.turbosquid.com/Search/3D-Models/free/obj) that you can browse to find fun and interesting 3D models.

One final thing: The 123D Sculpt+ app isn't the only app out there that can create 3D models using the .obj file format, but it is one of the most fun apps to use. I'll go into a few of the basics of using it in Chapter 6, but it's not hard to figure out on your own, so feel free to download it and try it out now.

Up Next...

Before this chapter, you already knew that Tinkercad allows you to convert .stl files (and .svg files) into .schematic files that MCEdit can import into your Minecraft worlds. Now you also know about Binvox, a command-line program that can convert .obj files into .schematic files. All that you need to do now is get some more instructions on installing and using the 123D Sculpt+ app and the Binvox program. Up next in Chapter 6, I'll provide a more detailed explanation about using 123D Sculpt+ and Binvox so you'll have another couple tools for your Minecraft digital tool belt.

6

Creating Your Own Monster Island

What You'll Be Doing

- Create your own monster with 123D Sculpt+
- Download, install, and use Binvox
- Use MCEdit to import your monster
- Resize and rotate your monster

As you saw in Chapter 5, "Modifying a 3D World," not every 3D object that you download or create is saved as an .stl or .schematic file. There are dozens and dozens of file formats that exist for 3D models, and not all of them are compatible with MCEdit, which means you can't directly import them into a Minecraft world.

Fortunately, one of the most popular 3D model file formats, .obj, is 100% compatible with MCEdit...if you know how to properly convert it for use with MCEdit. And that's exactly what you're going to learn in this chapter, along with how to use a special tool for creating 3D models.

The steps in this chapter might seem a little overwhelming at first, but if you read carefully and actually perform the steps, you'll find that they're not all that difficult. As with baking a recipe or assembling a piece of furniture, they key is to follow the steps in the right order. Do that, and you're going to discover a fast and easy way to add some amazing creations to your Minecraft worlds. And it all starts with a fun app for iPad and Android tablets called 123D Sculpt+.

TIP

123D Sculpt+—for tablets only

If you don't have access to a tablet, feel free to skip this chapter. Unfortunately, Autodesk hasn't yet released a version of 123D Sculpt+ for Windows and Mac computers. It only works on iPads and Android tablets. However, it might at some point be released for Windows and Mac computers, so be sure to keep an eye out at www.123dapp.com for updates to the 123D Sculpt+ application.

Monster Making for Beginners

Creating a monster is super-easy if you've got 123D Sculpt+ installed on your iPad or Android tablet. Links to the App Store or Google Play can be found at http://www.123dapp.com/sculptplus (scroll all the way to the bottom of the page) to download the free app to your tablet. Once it's installed, you should see an app icon like the one shown in Figure 6.1.

FIGURE 6.1   Download and install the 123D Sculpt+ app on your tablet.

NOTE

123D Sculpt+ on iOS and Android

Screenshots of 123D Sculpt+ in this chapter are taken from the iOS version running on an iPad. The app looks and works the same on Android tablets, minus a few subtle visual differences due to the way the two tablets display information (such as fonts and buttons). The design tool, however, works the same, so Android users shouldn't have any trouble finding and using the same tools and buttons shown here in the iPad version.

If you've ever used clay to mold and shape something with your hands, then you won't have any problem understanding the main use of 123D Sculpt+. This app lets you create 3D models by dropping a "lump" of clay on the screen and then offering you various tools to shape the "clay" and add details. Of course, you do all this on the touchscreen, using your fingers.

After opening the Sculpt+ app, you see a series of buttons (as shown in Figure 6.2) near the top that offer you the ability to view 3D models created by other Sculpt+ users. You can tap the Popular button to see what Sculpt+ users believe to be some of the best creations or use the Featured and Recent buttons to find current designs. The Search allows you to use keywords to find 3D models that fit your interests. If you find something you like, you can save a copy to your tablet and make changes to it (such as changing colors) if you like.

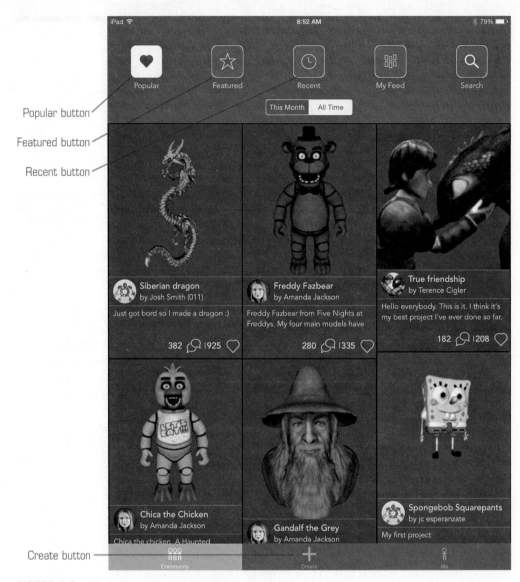

FIGURE 6.2 The menu in the Sculpt+ app.

But the real power of Sculpt+ is that it allows you to make your own models, and to do that, you need to tap the Create button at the bottom of the screen. After you tap the Create button, you're given three choices, as shown in Figure 6.3.

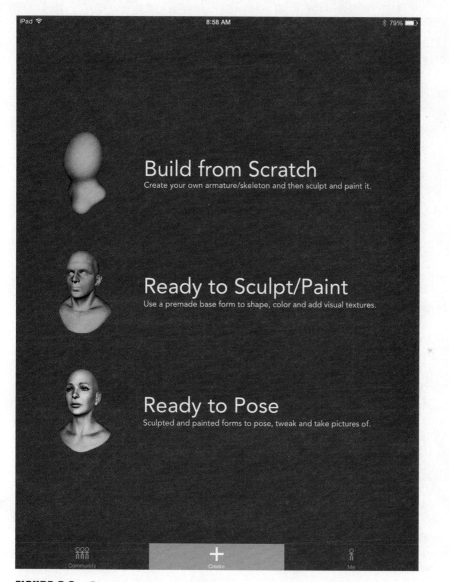

FIGURE 6.3 Create a custom object or a predesigned one.

The Build from Scratch option is the most basic starting point, offering up clay models in various shapes such as body, head (bust), and a few others. These clay shapes are pretty generic, as you can see in Figure 6.4. The "clay" has no details other than just the basic shape of an object.

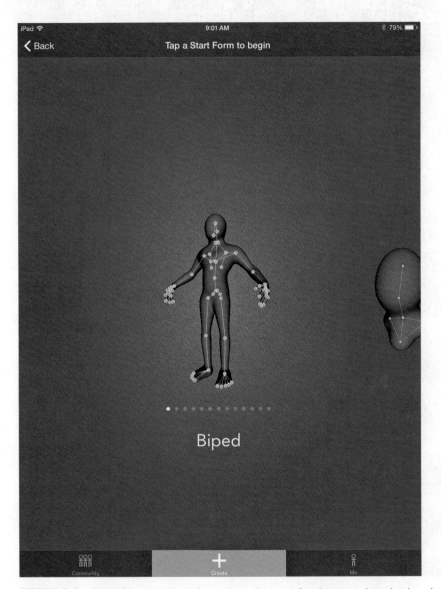

FIGURE 6.4   The Biped object has the shape of a human but lacks detail.

The other two options, Ready to Sculpt/Paint and Ready to Pose offer up detailed 3D models that have already been sculpted in digital clay. These two options are actually great starting places as all the detail work has already been done, and you can just modify the colors and poses. Figure 6.5, for example, shows a cartoonish male figure that you can select after tapping the Comic Man option displayed on the screen. The figure starts out colorless and standing in a rather boring pose.

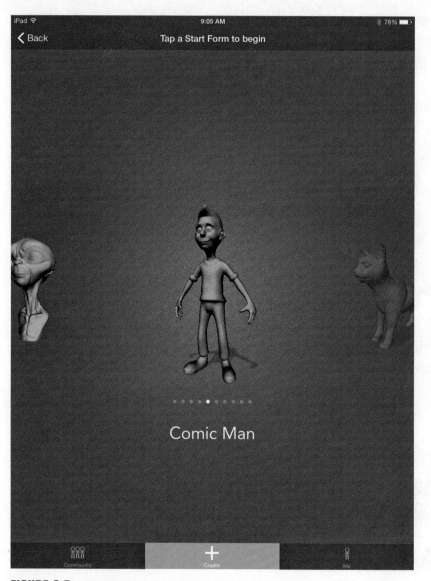

FIGURE 6.5 A detailed model that lacks color and action.

While you can certainly choose one of the predesigned options, I highly encourage you to test the Build from Scratch option and start with a clean model that lacks details. If you select the Biped object, you get all the tools shown in Figure 6.6 for modifying it.

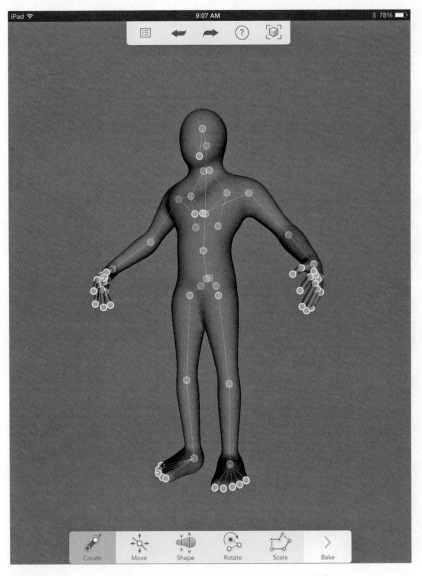

FIGURE 6.6 The Biped clay model is ready for modification.

All those blue dots are joints you can tap in order to move part of the model. Figure 6.7 shows that I've selected the Rotate button and tapped on the shoulders to move the arms (like a zombie lurching toward you).

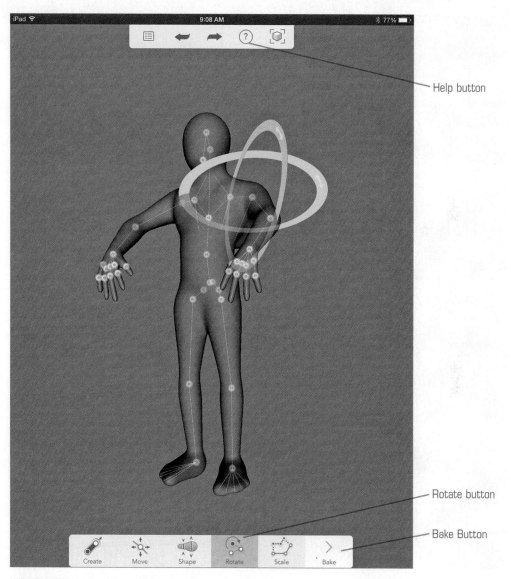

Help button

Rotate button

Bake Button

FIGURE 6.7   Modifying the Biped model with the Rotate button.

If you tap on a button and then tap the Help button, you get a more detailed description of how to use a particular tool, as shown in Figure 6.8.

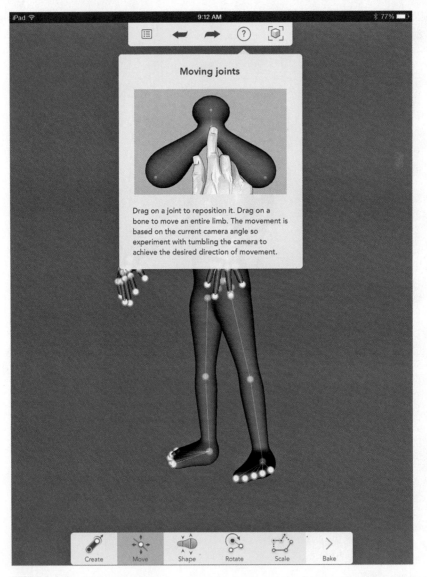

FIGURE 6.8 Tap a tool button on the bottom and then the Help button at the top.

You can shrink, enlarge, rotate, and "mold" the clay with the buttons along the bottom, and you can also add new appendages or features with the Create button. It will probably take you some time to figure out every tool and how it can best be used to add details to your model, so be sure to spend some time with each button and play with your model to see what you can create. When you're done, you tap the Bake button to make a permanent 3D model like the one in Figure 6.9. Once you have this baked model, you can further sculpt it and paint it.

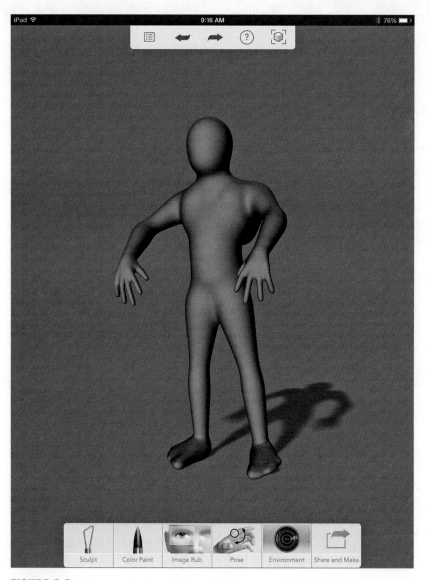

FIGURE 6.9 You can add color to your creature by using the Color Paint button.

NOTE

123D Sculpt+ colors don't matter to MCEdit

Remember that any colors you apply to your 3D model in 123D Sculpt+ will not carry over into Minecraft. MCEdit will import your design, but you'll have to use its Select tool and Fill With tool to apply colors to various Minecraft blocks.

The Sculpt button allows you to add fine features such as noses or warts or claws, but once again, keep in mind that most fine details do not carry over into a Minecraft world since your design will be made of hundreds—or maybe even thousands—of blocks. A wart may look funny on your monster's face, but it might not be large enough to be made out of a block or two that visitors to your world will be able to distinguish.

One tool that can make a huge impact is the Pose button. Tap this button and then tap on various locations of your model, and you'll be able to drag your finger and move a leg or arm or other appendage anywhere you like. Figure 6.10 shows that I've moved the creature's left arm up in a threatening manner.

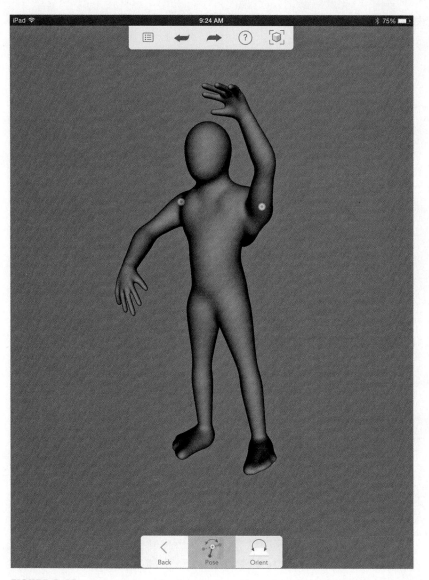

FIGURE 6.10 Pose your design by tapping on areas of the body and dragging.

When you're done posing, sculpting, and coloring your model, you tap the Share and Make button (in the bottom-right corner). This button offers four options, as you can see in Figure 6.11.

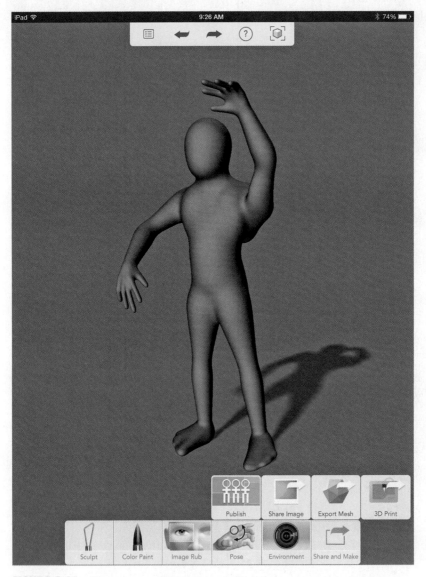

FIGURE 6.11 There are different ways to export your model.

In this case, you want to press the Export Mesh button.

NOTE

Printing and sharing options with 123D Sculpt+

By tapping the Publish button you can share your design with other Sculpt+ users. The Share Image button allows you to post a photo of your design to Facebook or Twitter or email it to a friend. The 3D Print option allows you to order a plastic model of your design from a company called Sculpteo (www.sculpteo.com). This costs money, but it's a fun way to get a physical 3D version of your very own creature to set on your desk.

Tap the Export Mesh button, and you'll see a screen like the one in Figure 6.12.

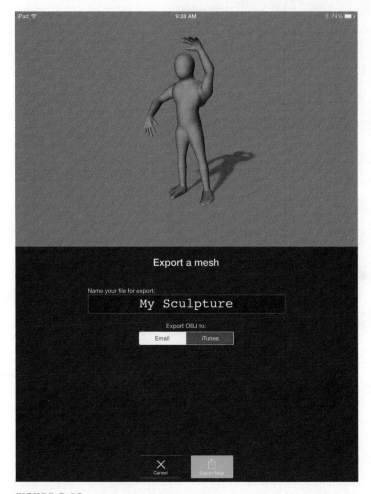

FIGURE 6.12 Use the Export Mesh button to download your model's file.

Notice that the Email option is selected; you'll need to provide an email address the app can use to send the model's file as an attachment. You can modify the name of your object by tapping in the My Sculpture box and typing a new name, such as MyMonster, as shown in Figure 6.13.

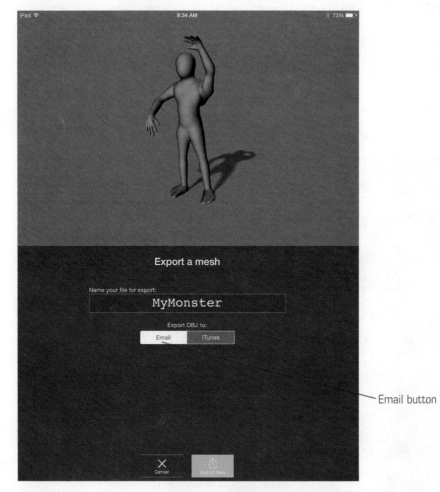

Email button

FIGURE 6.13 Give your design a new name and select the Email option.

Tap the Export Now button, and your tablet's email app will open and allow you to select a recipient for your file, as shown in Figure 6.14. Tap Send button, and your model is sent! Keep in mind that the file being sent is not an .stl or .schematic file; it's an .obj file.

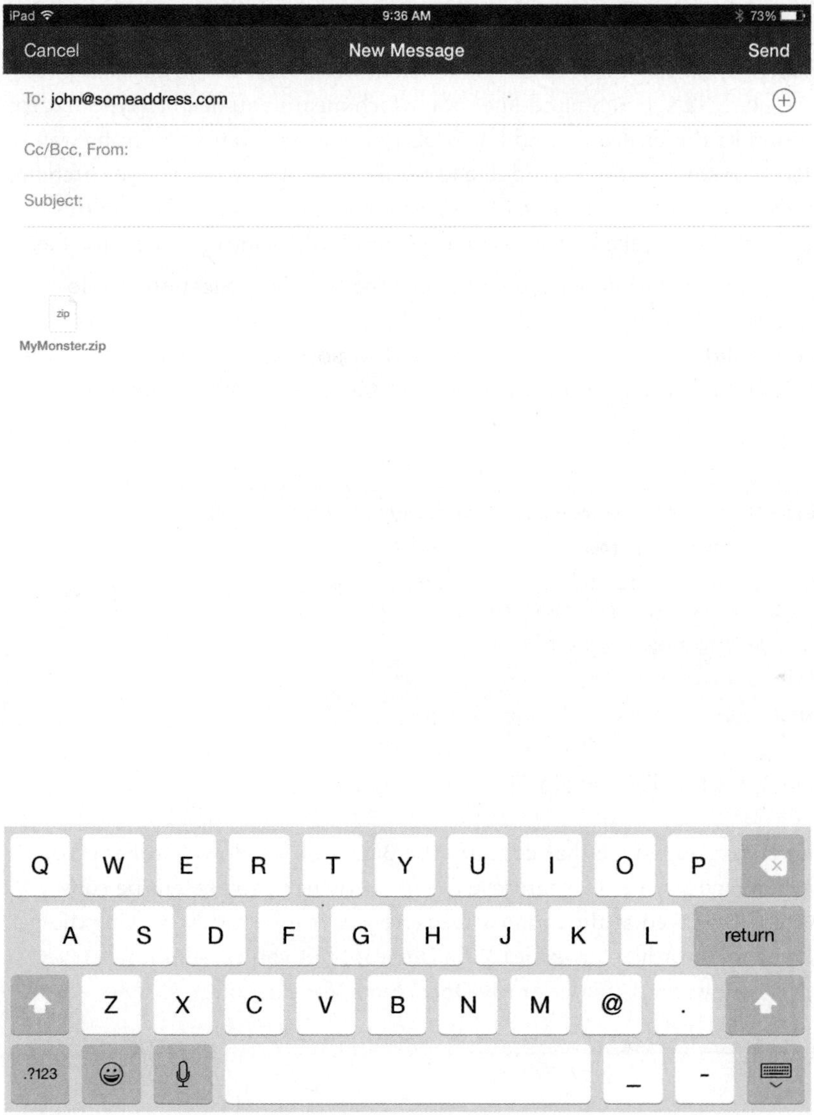

FIGURE 6.14 Type in an email address and tap Send.

Next, you need to download the model's .obj file to a computer where you'll be performing the next part of the process—using the Binvox tool to convert your model to a .schematic file that will work with MCEdit.

Using Binvox

As you read in Chapter 5, Binvox might be a little different from most of the applications you probably use regularly. It's a command-line tool, which means you need to type text to tell the tool to perform its duties. Command-line tools typically have very little in the way of graphics or buttons or sounds. Command-line tools like Binvox may not be eye-catching, but they're sometimes the only option you have to perform certain tasks on files. In this case, Binvox will convert the .obj file that was emailed from Sculpt+ into a .schematic file.

Before you can use it, you need to download and install the Binvox application. To do this, point a web browser to http://minecraft.gamepedia.com/Programs_and_editors/ Binvox#Download, scroll down a bit until you find the Download section, and click on the vox_package.zip link for Windows or the binvox link for Mac, as shown in Figure 6.15.

Download [edit]

Windows: vox_package.zip ⟐ This distribution gives you everything you need in one download, including

The individual programs can be updated by direct download: binvox ⟐, viewvox ⟐.

Another alternative is Auto-Binvox.zip ⟐, a CMD batch that simplifies the process of voxelising any file, an model in a directory and then runs binvox and viewvox in turn. The downside is that you can't easily conti

The GLUT ⟐ library must be downloaded separately in order to run viewvox.

Mac (Snow Leopard, OS X 10.6.8): binvox ⟐, viewvox ⟐.

Linux (Fedora 13, 64-bit): binvox 64-bit ⟐ 32-bit ⟐, viewvox 64-bit ⟐ or 32-bit ⟐.

FIGURE 6.15   Download the Binvox zip file to your computer.

When you click this link, a zipped file that contains the Binvox files is downloaded to your computer, as shown in Figure 6.16. You can save the file anywhere you like but be sure to make note of where it is saved at the moment because you're going to be moving the contents of the zipped file shortly. (I saved it to the Desktop, but you can put it wherever you like, such as in the Downloads folder or My Documents, for example.)

FIGURE 6.16   The Binvox tool is downloaded as a zipped file.

Once the Binvox zipped file is saved, click on the Start button and then choose Computer, as shown in Figure 6.17.

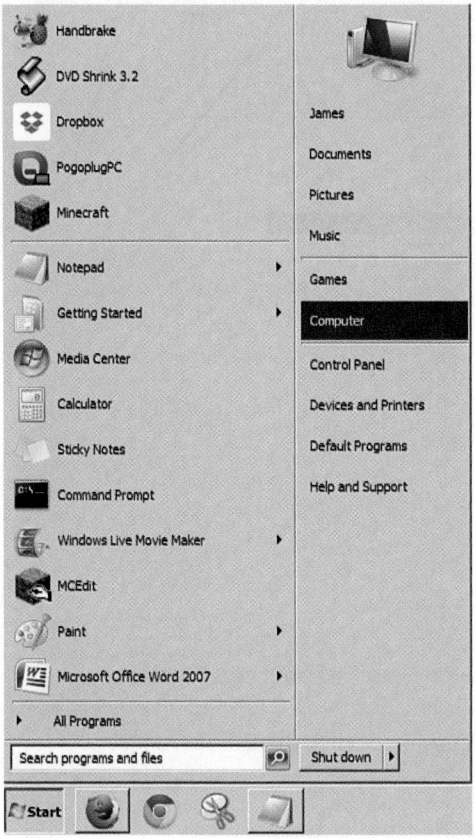

FIGURE 6.17 Open the Computer window.

Double-click on the hard drive (the C: drive) for your computer and create a folder called vox_package, as shown in Figure 6.18.

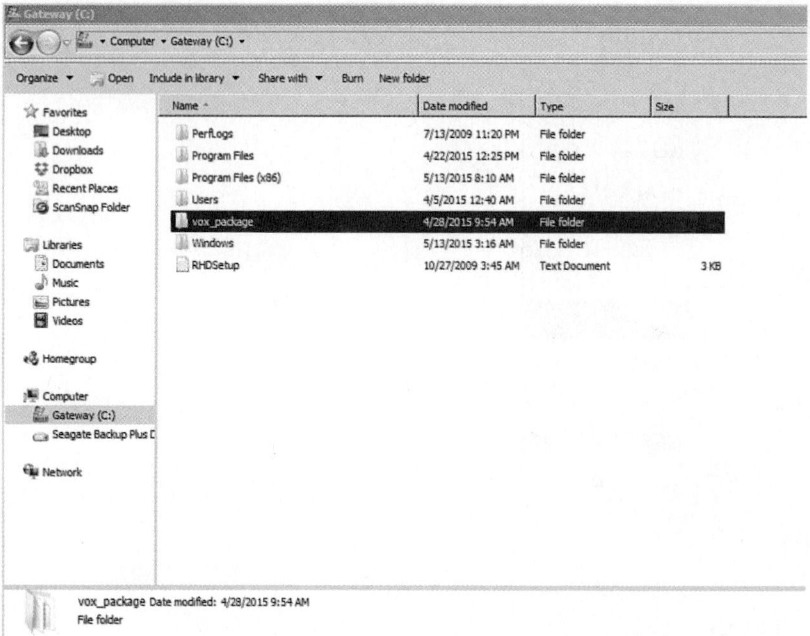

FIGURE 6.18   Create the vox_package folder on your computer's C: drive.

Next, double-click the vox_package.zip to open it up. Then click the Extract All Files button, as shown in Figure 6.19.

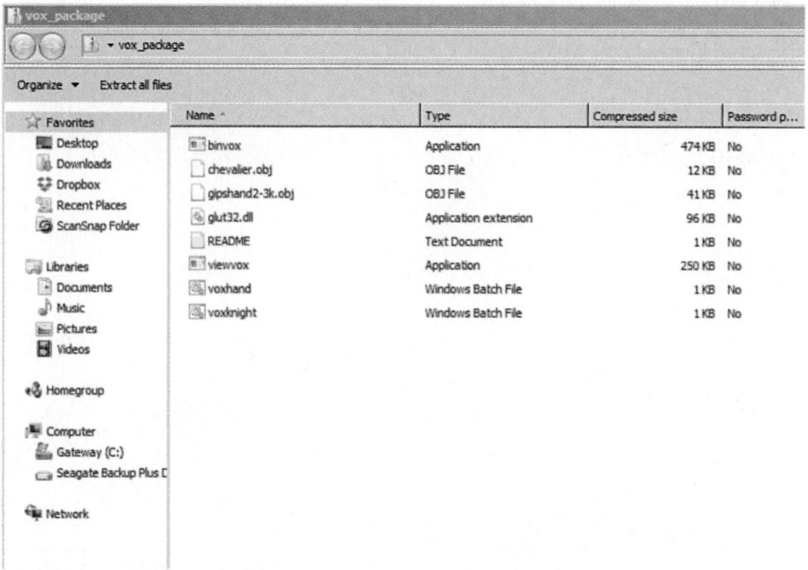

FIGURE 6.19   Extract the zipped files to the folder you created on the C: drive.

When the Extract Compressed (Zipped) Folders dialog appears (see Figure 6.20), click the Browse button and find the vox_package folder you created on the C: drive and click Extract.

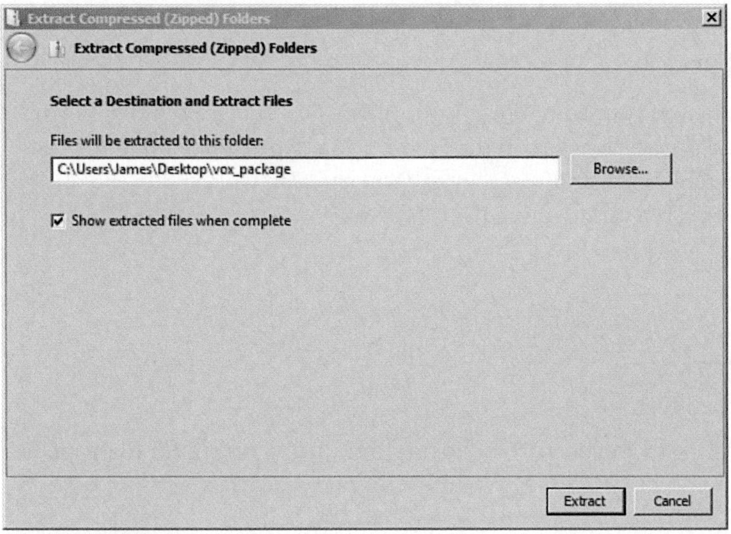

FIGURE 6.20 Save the Binvox files to the vox_package folder.

Double-click the zipped file that contains the 3D model you created in 123D Sculpt+. Click the Extract button, as shown in Figure 6.21, and extract these files to the same vox_package folder you created on the C: drive.

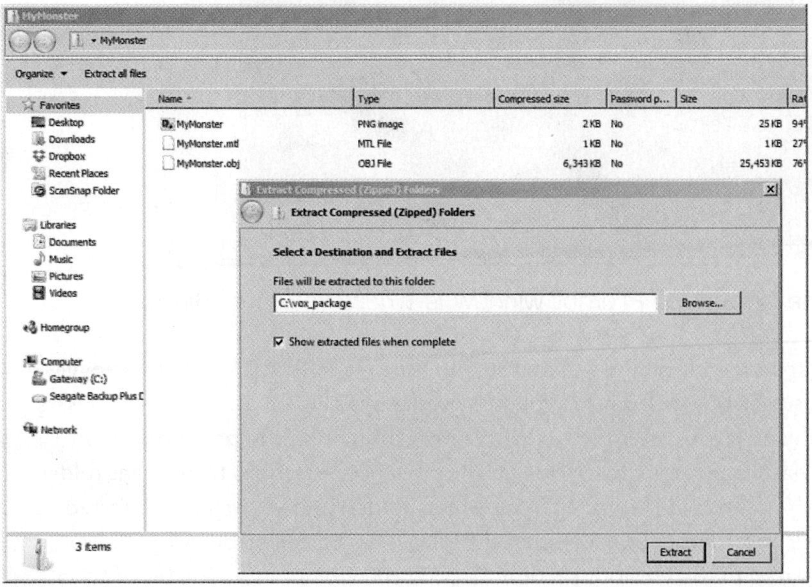

FIGURE 6.21 Save your 3D model files to the C:\vox_package folder.

At this point, you have a vox_package folder stored on your Windows computer's C: drive. It contains the Binvox files and your 3D model files from Sculpt+. Now it's time to use Binvox to convert the .obj file to a .schematic file.

Converting with Binvox

With the vox_package folder on your computer's C: drive, it's now time to run the Binvox command-line tool. To do this, click again on the Start button, type **command** in the text box at the bottom (see Figure 6.22), and press Enter. (You can also type **cmd** in the text box if command doesn't open up the windows seen in Figure 6.23.)

FIGURE 6.22   Type **command** in the text box to launch the Command Prompt window.

The Command Prompt window appears, as shown in Figure 6.23.

FIGURE 6.23   The Command Prompt window is where you'll run Binvox.

Your screen may appear a bit different than the one shown here because you'll be logged in as a different user (with a different username). Notice that Figure 6.23 shows C:\Users\ James> with a blinking cursor after the >. (Where my Command Prompt window says James, yours will have your username.) This bit of text simply describes the current folder. In this case, I'm not interested in looking in my James folder, and you're not interested in looking in the folder that has your username, either. We both need to be using the vox_ package folder created in the previous section. Getting there requires a little bit of typing.

First, you need to change to the root of the C: drive—the highest point of everything stored on the hard drive of the computer. To get there you simply type the following:

cd \

Then you press the Enter key. The \Users*username* part disappears, and you're left with simply C:>, as shown in Figure 6.24.

FIGURE 6.24 Get to the root of the C: drive.

Remember that you created a vox_package folder on the C: drive, and getting there requires a little more typing:

cd vox_package

Then press Enter. The Command Prompt screen now shows your location as the vox_package folder (see Figure 6.25).

FIGURE 6.25 The vox_package folder is the destination on the C: drive.

Now that you're here, all that's left to do is run the Binvox tool. Back in Chapter 5, I showed you that simply typing **binvox** at the command prompt displays a list of helpful instructions. Feel free pull up those instructions if you like.

To convert your .obj model, you need to know the filename of the 3D model. If you can't remember it, type **dir** at the command prompt, and you get a list of all the files in the vox_package folder, including your 3D model file, as shown in Figure 6.26. (In my case, it's called MyMonster.obj.)

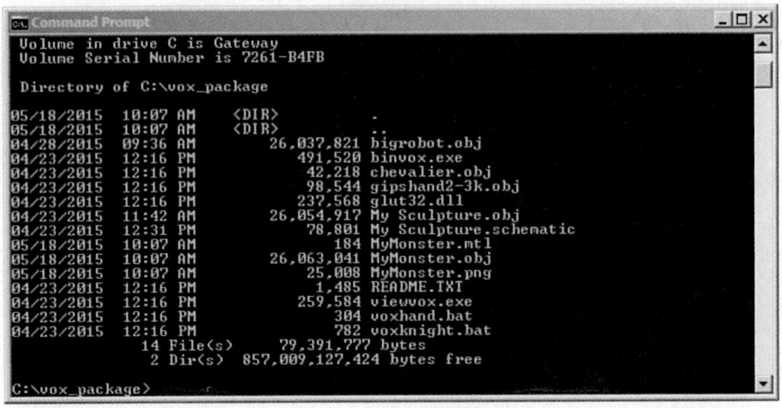

FIGURE 6.26 Find your 3D object's filename.

Once you have the filename, type the following at the prompt:

```
binvox -t schematic filename.obj
```

Instead of *filename*, though, you type the name of your own 3D model file. Keep in mind that it is case-sensitive, so you need to type uppercase and lowercase letters exactly as they appear in the filename. In my case, I typed the following, as shown in Figure 6.27:

```
binvox -t schematic MyMonster.obj
```

FIGURE 6.27 Enter the binvox command along with your model's filename.

Press the Enter key after you've typed in this command, and then you can sit back as the conversion process starts. This process can take anywhere from 8 to 10 minutes, depending on the complexity of your model. You'll see a stream of numbers scrolling up on the Command Prompt window, as shown in Figure 6.28. This means Binvox is doing its job.

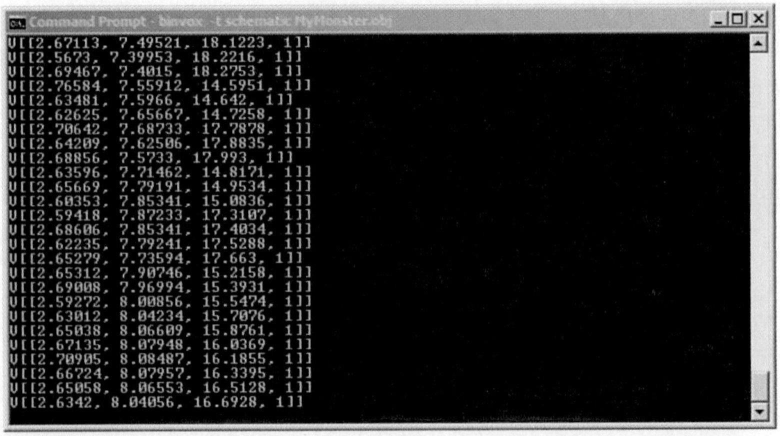

FIGURE 6.28 A stream of numbers scrolls up during the conversion.

At some point in the conversion, a small screen appears near the Command Prompt window, as shown in Figure 6.29. Don't touch the keyboard or click on anything. Just let it keep going.

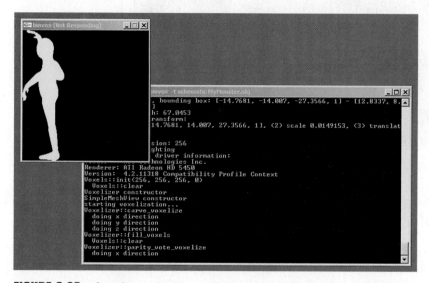

FIGURE 6.29 Another window containing some simple graphics appears.

When the conversion process is done, the Command Prompt window shows the word "done" all by itself on the last line, as shown in Figure 6.30.

FIGURE 6.30 The conversion process is complete.

If you type **dir** at the command prompt now, you see a new file in the listing that has the .schematic file type, as shown in Figure 6.31. If you see that file, you're ready to import it with MCEdit.

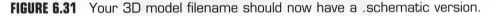

```
Command Prompt                                              _ □ X
 Volume Serial Number is 7261-B4FB

 Directory of C:\vox_package

05/18/2015  10:35 AM    <DIR>          .
05/18/2015  10:35 AM    <DIR>          ..
04/28/2015  09:36 AM        26,037,821 bigrobot.obj
05/18/2015  10:25 AM           491,520 binvox.exe
05/18/2015  10:25 AM            42,218 chevalier.obj
05/18/2015  10:25 AM            98,544 gipshand2-3k.obj
05/18/2015  10:25 AM           237,568 glut32.dll
04/23/2015  11:42 AM        26,054,917 My Sculpture.obj
04/23/2015  12:31 PM            78,801 My Sculpture.schematic
05/18/2015  10:07 AM               184 MyMonster.mtl
05/18/2015  10:07 AM        26,063,041 MyMonster.obj
05/18/2015  10:07 AM            25,008 MyMonster.png
05/18/2015  10:35 AM            56,709 MyMonster.schematic
05/18/2015  10:25 AM             1,485 README.TXT
05/18/2015  10:25 AM           259,584 viewvox.exe
05/18/2015  10:25 AM               304 voxhand.bat
05/18/2015  10:25 AM               782 voxknight.bat
              15 File(s)     79,448,486 bytes
               2 Dir(s)  856,985,432,064 bytes free

C:\vox_package>
```
.schematic file

FIGURE 6.31 Your 3D model filename should now have a .schematic version.

You can keep that file where it is or copy it elsewhere, but you need to be sure it's located on the computer where you have Minecraft and MCEdit installed. Once you are sure that the file is in a safe and appropriate spot, you can open up MCEdit and get ready to import your design into a Minecraft world.

Placing a Monster with MCEdit

By this point, you should be very comfortable using MCEdit to import .schematic files into your Minecraft worlds. I'm not going to go over all those steps again here, so please refer to Chapters 2, "Creating Your Own Castle," and 4, "Getting Lost (in a Maze)," if you need help with the Import option.

You have learned how to use Tinkercad to define the size of an imported object. You do this by specifying how many millimeters are equal to 1 block in the Minecraft game. The default is 1mm = 1 block, and if you leave this default, a 50mm-tall object created in Tinkercad will be 50 blocks tall in your world.

With 123D Sculpt+, you didn't have an opportunity to define the height of your object, did you? Some applications allow you to define the height, length, and width of objects you create, but not all of them do. This often doesn't become apparent until you import an object into Minecraft with MCEdit and discover that the imported object is so large you can't fit it anywhere! Figure 6.32 shows an imported creature (surrounded by the green box) that is way too big for the island.

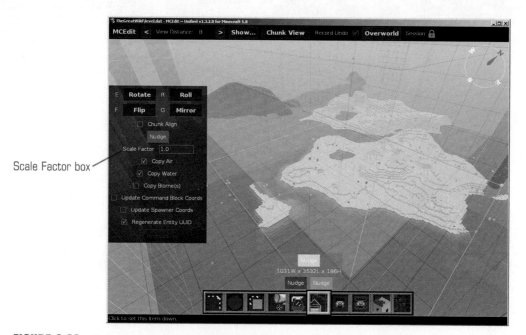

Scale Factor box

FIGURE 6.32 Sometimes an imported object is too big for the screen.

In such a case, you need a tool to reduce the size of the imported object. One way to do it is to use the Scale Factor box (visible in Figure 6.32). A value of 1.0 means actual size, so if you type in a value of 0.5, the imported object will be cut in half (because 0.5 = 50%, 0.25 = 25%, and 0.10 = 10%), as shown in Figure 6.33. This is better, but the model is still too large.

FIGURE 6.33 Decrease the size of an imported object using the Scale Factor box.

Figure 6.34 shows the Scale Factor set to 0.3. But as you can see, there's still a slight problem.

FIGURE 6.34 This size is good, but is the creature asleep?

With Tinkercad, your imported object is always right-side up, but depending on what you created with the Sculpt+ app, your imported object may not necessarily be standing on two legs (or four...we are talking about a monster, right?). Take a look at Figure 6.34, and you'll notice that the creature is not exactly standing on solid ground.

Fortunately, MCEdit has a fix. You click on the screen to place your model as close as possible to its final resting place. (Don't worry: If you miss, it's easy to fix, as you'll see shortly.)

Once the object is placed in your world, click the Rotate, Roll, and Mirror buttons until you get the model properly oriented. This may require some experimenting with different clicks. Rotate moves the object so that it moves through various north, west, east, or south facings with each click. Mirror simply changes whether the object faces forward or backward, and Roll rotates the object around like the hands on a clock, to 12, 3, 6, and 9 positions (or 0-, 90-, 180-, and 270-degree positions).

Figure 6.35 shows a creature standing on his own two legs. The problem now is that he's standing in water.

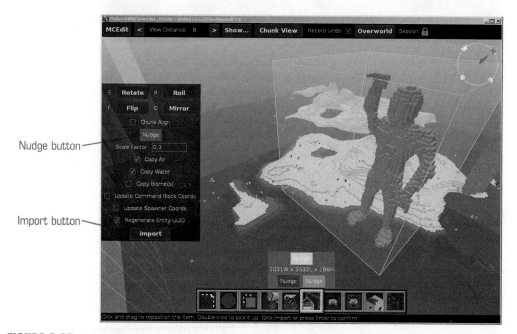

FIGURE 6.35 The object is standing, but his ankles are in the water.

You need to nudge the creature back a little bit to get him on dry land. Easy!

To move your object around, click and hold down the Nudge button (just below the Rotate, Roll, Flip, and Mirror buttons) and then use the WASD keys to move the object. Each tap on one of the WASD keys will move the object forward, left, right, or back. Click on the Import button when you're done to lock in the object and then click the MCEdit menu to save your changes.

Figure 6.36 shows the monster nudged right into place on the shore of the island, ready to scare off invaders.

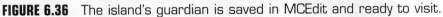

FIGURE 6.36   The island's guardian is saved in MCEdit and ready to visit.

Now all that's left to do is close down MCEdit and open up that world in Minecraft to see the new addition. As you can see in Figure 6.37, the stone guardian is doing his job perfectly, greeting friendlies and hopefully scaring off bad guys.

FIGURE 6.37   Island Guardian, offering protection since 2015.

Up Next...

So far, the projects in this book have involved viewing a structure or animal or other imported object on your computer screen. The objects you see on the screen are also flat... two dimensional. How would you like to be able to see your Minecraft worlds as if you were actually standing in the game, looking at your surroundings with your own two eyes? That distant mountain range would actually look far away, and those nearby trees would look close enough to reach out and touch.

In the next chapter, you're going to discover a simple and inexpensive method that will let you share your favorite scenes from your favorite Minecraft worlds in wonderful 3D!

7

Seeing Your World in 3D

What You'll Be Doing

- Coolcrafter10 meets PackRat and Prism
- Having fun outside the Minecraft game
- Examining the Oculus Rift
- Obtaining your own 3D Viewer
- Taking screenshots of your Minecraft worlds
- Creating 3D Image Cards for viewing

As the forest cleared, Didgee waved back at Coolcrafter10. "Come on. We're almost there! My friends and our castle are just over this small hill."

Coolcrafter10 walked a bit faster, catching up with his new friend as they reached the top of the hill. Standing next to Didgee, Coolcrafter10 looked down at the valley below and gasped. A castle unlike any Coolcrafter10 had ever seen reached high into the clouds. "That's where you live?" asked Coolcrafter10.

"With my friends," replied Didgee. "We've shared it for a year now, and we just keep making changes to it."

Coolcrafter10 shook his head. "It's incredible. I wish I'd brought my camera to take a photo. I'd love to show it to my family."

"I'm sure we have a camera somewhere you can borrow. Come on. I'll introduce you to my friends."

Coolcrafter10 stepped carefully as he followed Didgee down the steep path cut into the hill's side. In the distance he could see some sheep grazing outside the castle's main entrance, and a few horses were being chased by two figures in armor.

At the bottom of the hill, Didgee waved at the two figures: "Prism! PackRat!"

The two figures waved back and began walking toward Didgee and Coolcrafter10. Coolcrafter10 could see one was a boy and one was a girl. They looked like twins. As the two groups met, Didgee hugged them both and turned to smile at Coolcrafter10.

"Prism and PackRat, this is my new friend, Coolcrafter10. Cool, meet Prism and PackRat," said Didgee.

The girl smiled and waved. "Hey, I'm Prism. Where did you get that backpack? Did you make it or buy it? It looks like it's made of dragon scale. Is it heavy?"

The young boy shook his head and stuck out his hand. "I'm PackRat. Forgive my sister. She'll ask a million questions if you let her."

Coolcrafter10 shook PackRat's hand and nodded at the castle. "It's okay. I have that many questions about your castle there."

Prism beamed. "Well, we can take turns then. Why don't both of you come inside and rest, and we can visit. I really want to hear all about Didgee's latest adventures away."

Coolcrafter10 followed Didgee and her two friends as they began walking toward the castle. He whistled as he got closer. "I don't think any of my friends have ever built anything this impressive."

"That reminds me," said Didgee. "Don't we have a camera somewhere, PackRat? Cool wanted to take a photo of the castle." She followed Prism through the doorway and into the entry hall of the castle where she dropped her bag and sat down on a nearby chair. "Have a seat, Cool. I'll bet you're as tired as I am."

Coolcrafter10 nodded and sat down next to Didgee. "I'd love to email my friends a photo of that castle. It's not as good as standing here in person looking at it, but it'll do...if you can find a camera."

Prism jumped a bit. "Oooh, oooh! PackRat, maybe we can test out our new project and give Coolcrafter10 something better to share with his friends!"

Didgee's left eyebrow went up, and she smiled. "New project? Have you guys been working on something without me?"

PackRat grinned and began digging through a nearby cabinet. "Well, you were gone for a few weeks, Didgee. Plenty of time for Prism and me to find something new and fun to do. And yes, Prism, I think the castle would make a great test of our new idea. We can show them before we tackle building the guardian monster on the hilltop."

"Tell me," said Didgee. "Don't hold back if you've got some new tool to make Minecrafting easier and more fun."

"Oh, you're going to love it," said Prism. "It's so much fun to do."

Coolcrafter10 looked at Prism, then PackRat, then Didgee. "Didgee has been showing me some of the amazing tools that your group uses for Minecrafting, and now you're telling me you have yet another special tool?"

PackRat nodded and pulled out a camera. "It's not a tool for crafting, but I think you'll both like it. How would you like your friends to be able to see a picture of our castle in 3D, just as if they were standing outside looking at it?"

Didgee and Coolcrafter10 both smiled. "Show us."

Having Fun Outside Minecraft

Most of this book's lessons involve creating something and then taking it into a Minecraft world. So far, you've used Tinkercad and Thingiverse and 123D Sculpt+ to find or create objects that are converted to .schematic files. You've also used MCEdit to import the .schematic files into a Minecraft world of your choosing. Basically, for all the projects you've seen so far in this book, you've done something outside Minecraft and then used MCEdit to move it inside Minecraft.

But in this chapter and Chapter 8, "Viewing Your Worlds—Full 360!" I'm going to show you a couple interesting projects that start inside a Minecraft world first and then have you leave the game for some fun.

To better understand what we'll be doing, I want you to take a look at your surroundings right now. You live and breathe in a three-dimensional world. Objects have length, width, and height, and objects can be described as being near or far away. Most humans have two functional eyes that allow them to see the world around them and determine when something is close or distant; we call this depth perception, and it's an ability that helps us navigate the world around us. With both eyes open, you can easily figure out whether something is within reach of your hands. A driver in a vehicle can determine a safe distance to put between the front bumper of her own car and the car in front of her to avoid a collision. Baseball players can decide how much energy to put into throwing a ball to get it from third base to first.

Once again, look around you and mentally decide what is close and what is far away. Once you've done this, close one eye. Now examine the same surroundings and determine how near or far away objects are. Did you notice that something changed when you closed one eye? That happened because seeing out of only one eye causes you to lose your depth perception. You can still see things around you, but it's much more difficult to determine what is near or far because your 3D world is now more of a 2D world.

Two-dimensional objects are flat—they have length and width, but they lack height (or depth). When you play Minecraft and view your world on a computer screen, you're actually looking at a flat screen. The world is three-dimensional because you can move around in it, but it's still a 2D representation because the game's imagery is displayed on a two-dimensional screen. You know the trees in Figure 7.1 are in the distance but only because they are smaller, and your brain knows that smaller objects displayed in Minecraft are small because they're far away.

FIGURE 7.1   Those trees are far away, but they're still two-dimensional objects.

As you move around in Minecraft, the software performs calculations that determine what is displayed on your screen. Turn left, and whatever is to the left of your avatar is displayed. Look straight ahead, and objects that are close and far are both displayed together on the 2D screen. Both of your eyeballs are seeing exactly the same image. Because of this, your brain sees the Minecraft world exactly as you'd see it if you had one eye closed. Try it! Look at the screen with both eyes open and then close one. Nothing changes. You're getting closer to the secret of how our eyes work.

It's your brain's ability to combine a left image and a right image (from your left and right eyeballs) into a single image that provides you with three-dimensional vision and depth perception.

And now you're probably beginning to realize that the image of your Minecraft world on a computer screen presents exactly the same image to both your left eye and your right eye. You may be playing in a 3D world, but you're not seeing it in three dimensions. Your surroundings don't jump out at you like they do in a 3D movie How might you be able to see your Minecraft worlds in such a way that mountains truly appear in the distance and Creepers are actually getting closer and closer to you? Believe it or not, there are ways to experience Minecraft in this manner.

For now, just know that it is possible. There are several ways you can view your Minecraft world in 3D. In this chapter, we'll look at two of them: One is very expensive, and the other is not. Let's look at both and then see how you can use the inexpensive option to see your Minecraft worlds as they really should be seen—in amazing 3D!

Viewing with the Oculus Rift

There are more than a few solutions to viewing computer screen images in 3D, but I'm going to focus on just two in this chapter. One way is to use a specialized device that can easily cost more than the computer that runs Minecraft but provides constant 3D imagery as you play your game. The other is a small $3 device that is easy to obtain but lets you view only a single 3D image that you select from your game (similar to viewing photographs of an event rather than a video).

The expensive device is called an Oculus Rift, and you can see it in Figure 7.2.

FIGURE 7.2   The Oculus Rift.

The Oculus Rift attaches to your computer, and for many applications (including games like Minecraft), it provides your left eye and your right eye with two different images. You wear it over your eyes as shown in Figure 7.3 and use a joystick or mouse and keyboard while viewing what is displayed on the two screens in front of your eyes. While you're wearing a Rift, your brain combines these two images, and you end up being able to view the game (or other application) in 3D. Mountains in the distance actually appear far away in Minecraft. A nearby sheep appears close enough to touch.

FIGURE 7.3 You wear the Oculus Rift like a pair of goggles.

It's an amazing technology that is sure to change the way we play games, but right now it has two limitations. First, it's not out yet. As I'm writing this book, the group that is building and testing the Oculus Rift is stating that it will be released in early 2016. It remains to be seen if the company will make that deadline as the Oculus Rift has had a number of setbacks. It will eventually be released, but there's always a risk that another company could come out with something much sooner—and possibly with even better capabilities.

The second limitation is one I've already mentioned—price. The Oculus Rift is likely to be priced around $350. This price doesn't include the computer that will also be needed, and it's quite possible that the computing power needed for Oculus Rift to operate properly could require you to purchase a computer that is significantly higher in price that the Oculus Rift.

NOTE

Two 3D viewing technology options

You can read all about the Oculus Rift at the official website, as well as receive updates about its release. Point a web browser to https://www.oculus.com to learn more. And while you've got a web browser open, you'll definitely want to read and see details about Microsoft's take on 3D technology called HoloLens. Visit https://www.microsoft.com/microsoft-hololens/en-us and be sure to watch a video (https://youtu.be/xgakdcEzVwg) on one possible future for Minecraft that uses holographic technology to view your worlds.

Ultimately, however, price and release date don't matter. Game players around the world will be flocking to buy the Oculus Rift so they can see their favorite games in full 3D. And maybe you'll be one of those Oculus Rift users who will get to experience Minecraft in full 3D! For now, however, you'll just have to wait like most everyone else until the Oculus Rift is released. But that doesn't mean you can't get a little preview of what Minecraft will look like in true 3D....

Imagine for a moment being able to share your favorite castle or mountain or other locale in Minecraft with your friends and family in 3D. Imagine letting people see these sites as if they were actually standing in your world. Would you like to know how to do that? I thought so.

Using a 3D Viewer

This chapter's project has two parts to it—the first involves obtaining a special 3D viewer and the second involves taking screenshots of various Minecraft scenes in your world and editing them for use with the 3D viewer. You might be familiar with a very popular 3D viewer called the View Master. This has been a popular toy for kids for decades, using small paper discs with small images (printed on plastic film) to provide 3D images for viewing. You don't have to make your own paper discs, however—with the 3D viewer described below and the steps later in this chapter for taking screenshots, you'll have all you need to make your own homemade 3D images.

First, the easier task—obtaining a 3D viewer. There are a number of places on the Internet that sell them, and you can search online for "3D viewer" and sift through the various shapes and sizes. The one I recommend is made by a company called Loreo. You can visit http://www.loreo.com and scroll down the page to look at the various 3D viewer models they sell. Most of them are made from heavy cardstock with special small lenses mounted inside. My favorite is the Loreo Lite 3D Viewer, which folds flat and can be stored easily or even sent through the postal service in a regular envelope. Best of all, the Loreo Lite 3D Viewer is less than $5 (including shipping). Figure 7.4 shows the Loreo Lite 3D Viewer.

FIGURE 7.4 The Loreo Lite 3D Viewer.

> **TIP**
>
> 3D viewers come in many shapes and sizes and materials. If you buy one, just make certain that it is the two-lens variety that can be used for stereoscopic photography. (*Stereoscopic* means that two images are viewed with the viewer—an image on the left and an image on the right.) You'll see examples of these types of photos later in the chapter.

Ordering a 3D viewer is easy, but you'll have to wait a few days or weeks for it to arrive. Thankfully, you can start creating the 3D images that you'll use with the 3D viewer right away, and you'll have plenty of them ready to go when the viewer arrives.

There are two ways you can create your 3D images:

- You can use JPEG files that you view on your computer screen.

- You can have 4×6 photographs printed.

I'll show you how to do both methods, although my preferred method is the second one. There's just something really fun about a stack of 3D photos that you can take to share with family and friends (along with your 3D viewer).

Both methods start in a Minecraft world. I'm going to open up one of my favorite Minecraft world and get ready to create some 3D images.

Taking Minecraft Screenshots

Take a look at Figure 7.5, and you'll see that my game avatar is standing on flat ground, looking at one of the recent additions to my world, the monster guardian from Chapter 6, "Creating Your Own Monster Island." In the distance, you can see another large statue.

FIGURE 7.5 A two-dimensional monolith placed in my world.

As I stare at this screen, I close my right eye and look at what's shown in Figure 7.5. Next, I open my right eye and close my left eye. And I see exactly the same image shown in Figure 7.5. That's because this is a 2D image.

What I need to do is take two screen captures (also called screenshots or screen grabs). One screenshot should show what my in-game avatar would see if he closed just his right eye. The other screenshot should show what my in-game avatar would see if he closed only his left eye. These two images will simulate how a real person's eyes see two slightly different versions of the same view. But how do I do this?

First, notice in Figure 7.5 that you can see my tools, my health and food bars, and my hand. I'd like for those to go away so I can see more of the surrounding landscape. Fortunately, Minecraft makes this really easy. Press the F1 key in Windows or press Fn key on a Mac keyboard and then press the F1 key. (This is the default setting—if you've made changes to your key assignments, you may need to check to see the key combination you used as a replacement.) Doing this causes your avatar's hand and the other visuals to disappear, leaving behind an unobstructed view, as shown in Figure 7.6.

FIGURE 7.6 Hide your avatar's hand and the health, food, and tools icons.

Next, move your mouse around until you're happy with the full screen view. It's best to have whatever you wish to be the main focus of the image centered on the screen. In Figure 7.6, you can see that I've got the large stone figure centered.

Once you have a mountain or castle or other object centered, it's time to take your first screenshot. Carefully move your hand away from the mouse or touchpad. You do not want to change the current view on the screen by looking around or accidentally moving the mouse/touchpad.

To take a screenshot, in Windows, press F2. On a Mac, hold down the Fn key and press F2. (Again, these are the default settings—change them back or check the Options settings for key assignments if you've made changes.) This first screenshot will represent what is seen by your avatar's right eye. (I'll tell you in a moment where to find the screenshots that are stored on your computer.) Figure 7.7 shows the screenshot I got when I did this.

FIGURE 7.7 My avatar's right-eye view of the stone monument.

After taking the first screenshot, use the A key to move to your left. Press the A key long enough to say "One Mississippi" and release it. Be careful not to move the view onscreen with the mouse or touchpad; the only movement that should occur is that your avatar moves slightly to the left. Take another screenshot with the F2 key (or Fn+F2 on a Mac), and you're done taking screenshots for now. You can repeat this procedure as many times as you like in as many locations and worlds in Minecraft as you desire. It's these matched pair of images that you'll be using with your 3D viewer to see your various Minecraft scenes as if you were standing right there in the digital world.

Figure 7.8 shows the screenshot I took after moving my avatar slightly to the left. Compare it to Figure 7.7. Although Figures 7.7 and 7.8 look pretty much identical, you'll notice some subtle differences between the two if you look carefully. (For example, look at the small cloud to the right of the monument's hand. In Figure 7.7 there's a larger gap of blue sky between the cloud and the wrist than there is in Figure 7.8.)

FIGURE 7.8 My avatar's left-eye view of the stone monument.

Next, I'm going to use this pair of screenshot to create a 3D image card that can be used with a 3D viewer.

NOTE

Collecting your worlds' sites as 3D image cards

Using the method described here, you can easily create a nice collection of 3D image cards, showing various interesting sites in your world. You can go so far as to create a small scrapbook for each of your worlds that holds the famous sites and creations you've added. You'll learn how to create 3D image cards later in the chapter.

Locating Your Screenshots

Before you can use your 3D viewer, you need to locate the screenshots you took, rename them, and then resize them on your computer screen so they can be properly viewed.

The folder holding your Minecraft screenshots will vary depending on whether you are using a Windows or Mac computer.

Finding Minecraft Screenshots on a Windows Computer

If you're a Windows user, click on the Start button and in the Search box at the bottom, type in **%appdata%**, as shown in Figure 7.9, and press the Enter key.

FIGURE 7.9   Start the hunt for your Minecraft screenshots.

Windows will display a list of folders, including one called .minecraft. If you double-click the .minecraft folder, you'll see a list of folders like the one in Figure 7.10.

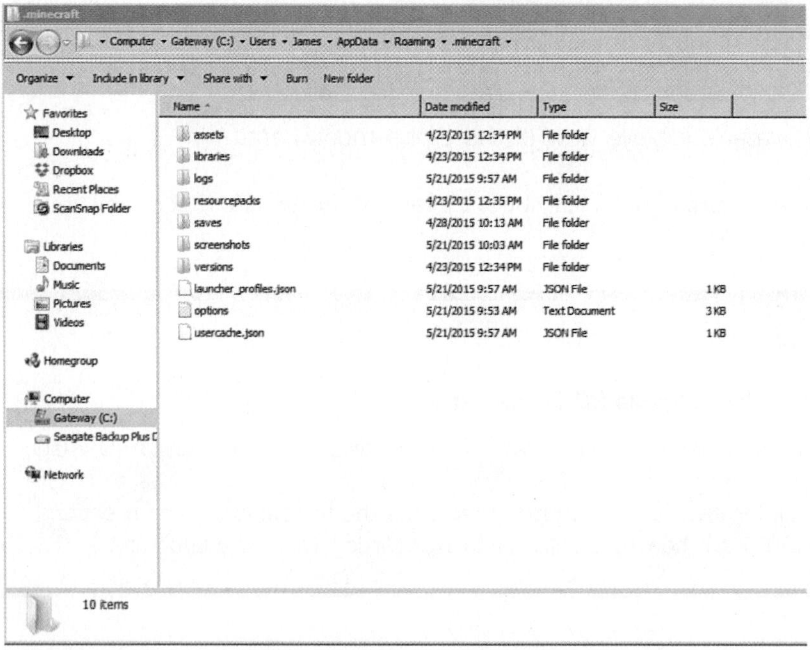

FIGURE 7.10   Your screenshots are stored here somewhere...but where?

In case you didn't spot it already, double-click on the screenshots folder (which in Figure 7.10 is the sixth folder down the list). Any screenshots you've taken will appear here. Figure 7.11 shows the two screenshots I took.

FIGURE 7.11 My Minecraft screenshots are stored here.

Copy these images to a folder that you'll be able to more easily find; I copied them to a "Minecraft Screenshots" folder I created on my desktop. I also like to copy them to a thumb drive so I can take them to have them printed.

Unless you're curious about how to do this on a Mac, you can jump to the "Preparing Your Screenshots" section, where I'll show the next steps.

Finding Minecraft Screenshots on a Mac

To find your screenshots on a Mac, open the Finder window (shown in Figure 7.12), click on the Go menu, and select Go To Folder.

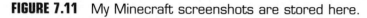

FIGURE 7.12 Start your screenshot hunt with Finder.

A small box like the one in Figure 7.13 opens. In the box, type in **˜/Library/Application Support/minecraft/screenshots** and press the Enter key.

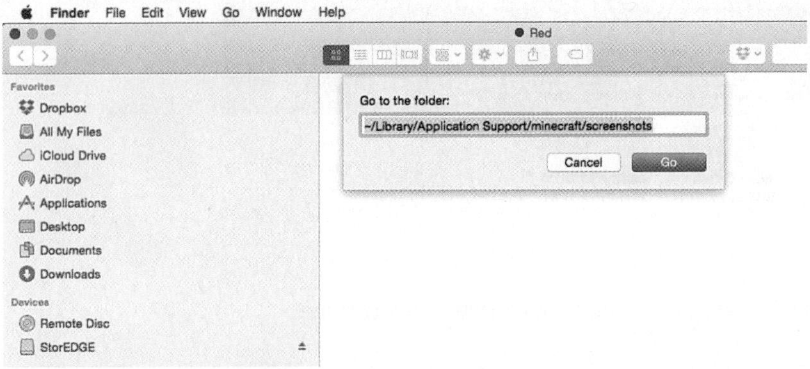

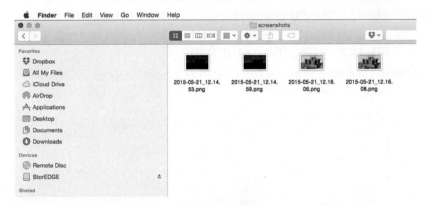

FIGURE 7.13 Use the Go to the Folder box to jump straight to the screenshots.

The screen changes to show the contents of the screenshot folder, as shown in Figure 7.14.

FIGURE 7.14 Minecraft screenshots stored on a Mac.

Copy these images to a folder that you'll be able to more easily find; I've copied them to a "Minecraft Screenshots" folder I created on my desktop. I also like to copy them to a thumb drive so I can take them to have them printed.

Once you've got the screenshots where you can easily access them, it's time to prepare them for viewing.

Preparing Your Screenshots

To properly use your 3D viewer, you have to place the image pairs side-by-side. It's important that the screenshot taken for the right-eye view is placed on the right and the other screenshot (the one for which you moved your avatar slightly to the left) is placed to the left. Figure 7.15 shows that I've placed these two images side-by-side on my Windows desktop.

FIGURE 7.15 Place the screenshots side-by-side.

When I double-click them, they open using the Windows Photo Viewer, which lets me resize them by clicking and dragging on the lower-right corner of the window.

TIP

Distinguishing between left and right images

If you can't remember which screenshot goes on the right, look at the filenames. A computer names screenshots based on the date and time the image was taken. For example, I have two screenshots with filenames 2015-05-21_10.01.11 and 2015-05-21_10.01.14. The numbers before the underscore show the date (May 5, 2015), and the numbers after the underscore (separated by periods) show the time. You can see that I took the one with the timestamp 10.01.11 (10:01 and 11 seconds) before the one stamped 10.01.14 (10:01 and 14 seconds), so that makes the first file my right-eye view and the other my left-eye view. You can rename these files "left view" and "right view" if it helps.

It's important to shrink the photos down a bit. The Loreo Lite 3D Viewer works best when both the left and right images are no more than 3 inches wide, making for a 6-inch-wide pair of images. It's hard to tell in Figure 7.15, but these images on the screen are about 3 inches wide and 1.5 inches tall.

To view the 3D image, you simply hold up the 3D viewer so that your left eye is looking through the left lens while your right eye is looking through the right lens. Try to center it by getting your nose lined up with the dividing line that runs vertically between the two images. Look through the viewer, and your Minecraft world should suddenly jump to life as you view it in 3D!

If you're a Mac user, you perform the same steps with your screenshots, but the images will open in the Preview app. Once again, place them side-by-side and shrink them a bit so both images are no more than 3 inches or so wide. Figure 7.16 shows that I've placed two screenshots on my Mac screen together. You can look at the filenames in the right and left images to see that the 2015-5-21_12.16.06 file is on the right and the 2015-5-21_12.16.08 file is on the left. It only took two seconds for me to shift my avatar to the left and take the left-eye image.

FIGURE 7.16 Screenshots paired on a Mac screen.

Using this method, you can store a bunch of screenshot pairs that you can share with friends and family members on your computer screen. (Rename them things such as Monument_Left and Monument_Right so you can more easily find them and open them together.)

Even though this is an easy way to view Minecraft worlds in 3D, I much prefer to have printed copies because I can make something I called 3D image cards.

Creating 3D Image Cards

3D image cards are easy to make and fun to share with your friends. To make them, you need to have your screenshots printed. There are many options out there, from online ordering with companies such as www.snapfish.com to using a self-serve kiosk like you find at stores like Walgreens or Target.

You'll want to have them printed as 4×6 photos, and if the option exists for matte (versus glossy), choose it. Online ordering is usually slower since the photos must be mailed to you, but they typically have a lower cost per photo to print. Self-serve kiosks often print them out immediately (or within an hour), but they're usually a few pennies or more extra per photo. (There's an in-between option, too: You can send your photos to a store like Walgreens and pick them up in the store a short time later.)

Figure 7.17 shows six photos I had printed at a self-serve kiosk. You can't tell from the figure, but the photos are very bright and vivid, and the detail is amazing.

FIGURE 7.17   Six images that will be turned into three 3D image cards.

Feel free to put them side-by-side as 4×6 photos and take a look. You'll probably find that, without a 3D viewer, you don't get a 3D effect at all.

Remember that most small portable 3D viewers work best with images that are about 3 inches wide. So the next step is to trim down the photos. In my case, I simply trimmed 1 inch from the left and 1 inch from the right of each photo, leaving the main point of interest, as shown in Figure 7.18.

FIGURE 7.18 Trim down the photos in width.

Once the photos are trimmed down, use a bit of clear tape to secure the photos together, as shown in Figure 7.19. Before taping, remember to check that the right-eye view and left-eye view are in their proper places and flip over both pictures together to keep their left/right orientation.

FIGURE 7.19 Tape the two images together (on the back) to create a single card.

Another option is to place the two photos over a piece of cardboard or cardstock and trace around the edges. Then you can cut out the tracing and glue down the photos to create a more sturdy 3D image card.

And that's it. Repeat as often as you like and build up a nice collection of 3D image cards that you can take with you (along with a 3D viewer) to share the amazing designs and creations from your various Minecraft worlds. I've yet to meet anyone who isn't amazed the first time they get a glimpse of 3D scenes from Minecraft, and I'm sure you'll get the same response.

Up Next...

We're not done with 3D projects yet. Up next in Chapter 8, I'm going to show you another way to make scenes from your Minecraft worlds come to life as a 3D video. Best of all, the software required is 100% free, so you can get started right away while you wait on your 3D viewer to be delivered.

Viewing Your Worlds—Full 360!

What You'll Be Doing

- Take screenshots of your favorite Minecraft sites
- Learn to use 123D Catch
- Create a 360-degree viewable model of a Minecraft site

Until we can all get our hands on a tool such as the Oculus Rift that can give us a real-time 3D view of our Minecraft worlds, we'll have to do with substitutes. You learned about one option in Chapter 7, "Seeing Your World in 3D," using an inexpensive 3D viewer and pairs of screenshots taken from inside a world.

If you've created a few 3D image cards, you've likely discovered just how fun it is to view your worlds in 3D...and how easy it is to create the cards. But there's one drawback to the cards that really stands out when you compare it to this chapter's project, and that is that the 3D image cards you create using screenshots give you only a single 3D view of a favorite Minecraft creation or site. Depending on whether you took the screenshots from the front or from the left or from above, that's the 3D view you'll get with your 3D viewer. If you wish to see a site or creation in 3D from a different angle, you've got to take more screenshots (and create more 3D image cards if you wish to have a portable version to share with friends).

If you have a castle that you'd like to see in 3D from the front, left, and right sides, and also from the back and from above, you'll have to create five (or more) sets of 3D image cards. It's not a big problem, but there's another method you can use to view your Minecraft creations in 3D that does away with creating multiple cards. You can view a snippet of your Minecraft world from all angles with just a slight movement of your mouse. It's like walking around a real object in front of you and seeing it from all sides,...but instead of a real object, you'll be viewing a Minecraft object or location on your computer screen from any angle you like. And even better, you can save your 3D-viewable objects on your computer so they can be shared, or you can create a small movie of your 360-degree exploration.

This process has two steps, and it's not difficult. In the following sections you should follow along in your own Minecraft world so you can duplicate what you see me doing in one of my own Minecraft worlds.

> **NOTE**
>
> **Special 360-view software runs on Windows**
>
> The software used to create these 360-degree viewable objects is free, but it's only available for iOS and Android tablets/phones and for Windows PCs. To write this chapter, I used my Mac laptop to take the Minecraft screenshots and my Windows desktop PC to run the special software. If you don't have access to a Windows computer, you might be able to convince a friend or family member to install the software so you can see the final results for yourself.

Creating a 3D Model with Photos

Imagine that you have a favorite (small) toy sitting on top of a flat desk. You can walk around the table and view the toy from different angles, including from directly above and from down low, where it sits on the table. Now imagine that you have a camera in your hands and are told to take as many photos as possible so that someone in a different room can look at the photos and be able to see every side of that toy (except for the bottom).

> **NOTE**
>
> **Pretend you won't look at the bottom (but you know you will)**
>
> The only side not visible would be the underside, where the toy rests on the table. You could set the toy on a clear glass table and take photos from underneath, but for now let's just assume that seeing the underside isn't as important as seeing all the other sides.

With all those photos, someone who has never seen your toy would at least be able to get a much better idea of what it looks like from any angle because they could look at all your photos—from the left, from the right, from above and behind, and even from above. If you took enough photos, other people would be able to determine from them the shape and colors and textures of your toy. As a matter of fact, if you took enough, you'd probably have quite a few photos that overlap a little in what they show.

Now, imagine that there is a piece of special software that can "stitch" together a 3D model of your toy, based on all those photos you took. If the photos were good quality and you didn't miss any sides or angles, the software should be able to re-create your toy as a 3D model on the screen. They you would be able to use your mouse to move "around" and "above" the toy as if it were an actual object.

Well, that software exists. As a matter of fact, there are a lot of different applications available that can do this sort of thing. The one I'll be using in this book is a free application called 123D Catch (http://www.123dapp.com/catch). It's from Autodesk, the same company that owns Tinkercad and 123D Sculpt+ you saw back in Chapter 5, "Modifying a 3D World." With 123D Catch, you can take up to 70 photos that the software then stitches together to create a 3D model. It's available for iOS devices (iPhone and iPad) as well as Android devices. It's also available as an application for a Windows computer. (Unfortunately, there isn't an OS X version for Mac users yet but you can try the browser version of the app at http://apps.123dapp.com/catch/.)

To use the app on a phone or tablet, you open the app and use the device's built-in camera to take a series of photos. As you can see in Figure 8.1, the software provides a small wheel that changes as you move around an object (such as my milk shake).

FIGURE 8.1 The 123D Catch app running on an iPhone.

When you take a photo, one of the small circular slices turns blue, giving you a visual indicator of where you've already been so you don't miss a side of the object. You need to take a minimum of 18 going around an object and 6 going around the object at a slightly higher view. While 24 photos sounds like enough, the software actually performs best when you take many many more—up to 70 photos.

As you work your way around an object, snapping photos, the app saves the photos until you're done. Then you upload the photos to Autodesk, which goes to work on your photos, stitching them together to create what will (hopefully) be a good 3D representation of your object.

If you'd like to see just how powerful this software is, point a web browser to the gallery of user-submitted 3D models found at http://autode.sk/1J5Ha1p and look around. If you have a phone or tablet with the 123D Catch app installed (covered in the next section), you can view objects from the gallery onscreen and rotate around as shown in Figure 8.2.

FIGURE 8.2 A 3D model of a dollhouse from two different angles.

Using 123D Catch, you can create 3D models of just about anything that can be photographed, including people. (Taking a bunch of photos of a person, however, can be tricky: They must remain very still until you are finished. If they move, the final 3D model will be blurry.)

Most people use 123D Catch to create 3D models of real objects like cars or artwork or famous buildings, and this is exactly what the app was designed to do. But after I discovered 123D Catch and played around with it, I began to wonder whether it would work with Minecraft. The only way to find out was to try, so I did. And guess what? It works! Let me show you how.

Starting with Screenshots—Lots of Them

The 123D Catch app running on a phone or tablet has a drawback: It can only be used to take photos with the device's camera. The app (running on a phone or tablet) doesn't allow you to upload preexisting photos to the Autodesk stitching service. But the Windows PC version of the software doesn't have this limitation. As a matter of fact, it works best if you take photos ahead of time (with any digital camera) and then upload those photo files to your computer so that the 123D Catch application can import them.

Why am I telling you this? Because it's not like you can jump inside a Minecraft world with a real camera and start taking photos. The only tool available to you to take "photos" of your Minecraft worlds is a screen capture tool. Fortunately, Minecraft has a built-in screen capture tool that works great.

If you can find a way to move around a Minecraft creation (like a castle or giant statue) and take a bunch of screenshots, you can use the 123D Catch app to stitch those screenshots together to create a 3D model of the subject of your screenshots.

TIP

Take screenshots in Creative mode worlds

Using Creative mode in Minecraft is about the only way you can take the necessary screenshots because you'll need to be flying around your object, high up in the air— flying is disabled in Survival mode. If you set the Allow Cheats option to ON (done when creating a world and clicking the More World Options button), you can enable flying as well as the ability to toggle back and forth between Survival and Creative.

How many screenshots should you take? Obviously, the more the better. I've found that using between 60 and 70 screenshots produces the best results, but you can experiment to see if fewer screenshots can get you the results you want.

Capturing Screenshots

It all starts by finding a snippet of your Minecraft world that you wish to view in a full 360-degree manner. Take a look at Figure 8.3, and you'll see what I've selected as the subject for my screenshots. Download the monolith (see TIP below) used in the example below and place it in one of your own worlds and follow along with my instructions.

FIGURE 8.3   Find a site in your world that you'd like to see with a full 360 view.

TIP

Grab an Easter Island monolith for your own world

You can download this object, called Maoi (and created by user alienOOO), by visiting http://www.thingiverse.com/thing:144668.

Place the stone guardian where you like, fly up in the air a bit (double-tap the space bar and hold it down on the second tap to fly up, and hold the Left Shift key to fly down) and then begin by taking a bunch of screenshots as you move around the stone figure.

Recall from Chapter 7 that you can hide the toolbar, health bar and other items by pressing F1 in Windows or pressing Fn+F1 on a Mac. This will also make your arm or any tool you're holding disappear, giving you a nice clean screenshot (press F2 on Windows to take a screenshot or Fn+F2 on Mac), as shown in Figure 8.4.

FIGURE 8.4 Hide the toolbar view and prepare to take a lot of screenshots.

To take the screenshots, use the A key (to move left, or clockwise) to move around your object. Avoid touching your touchpad (or a mouse) so that your view of the object and the screenshots that will be taken are all from the same elevation from the ground.

Take your first set of screenshots as you move completely around the object. This means picking a good starting point you can remember. (In this case, try looking at the statue's nose, as shown in Figure 8.5.)

FIGURE 8.5 Start in a specific spot and try to end there.

Since there are 360 degrees in a complete circle, try to take 30 screenshots at this elevation. This means taking a photo every 12 degrees (360/30 = 12). Another way to think about this is to visualize a clock face where your object sits in the center of the clock (the point where the hands spin). You'll want to try to take a picture at the even minutes—2 minutes, 4 minutes, all the way up to 58 minutes—and eventually you should find yourself back at your starting position.

To do this, use a combination of pressing the A key and moving your mouse (or touchpad) to rotate the view so you're always looking at the object and keeping it in the center of the screen. It's important not to move too far away from or get too close to the object; the goal is to stay at roughly the same distance from the object as you move and take screenshots from all the various angles. After you've completed a small move, press the F2 key on Windows or Fn+F2 key on a Mac. Then move to the next spot and take another. And another.

Notice in Figure 8.6 that I've moved about one-quarter of the way around the object. At this point, I've taken about 8 screenshots.

FIGURE 8.6   About 8 screenshots down and 22 to go.

Figure 8.7 shows what it looks like after I've taken 17 screenshots: I'm now facing the back of the statue. (It doesn't have to be exact, but try to get about 30 photos by the time you finish your first time circling your object.)

FIGURE 8.7 Halfway through the screenshot trip.

Finally, come back around, and you should be looking at the object from almost the front. At this point you should have somewhere around 26 to 30 photos.

FIGURE 8.8 Finishing up the first circle around the statue.

You're not done yet, however, when you finish that first circle. To really give a 3D model the best chance to look great, you need to increase your elevation a bit (past the halfway point on the height of the subject) and take another round of screenshots. The good news is that you can take fewer photos here, but you don't want to take fewer than 12. As you can see in Figure 8.9, I've raised myself a bit higher (by holding down the Spacebar to fly up a bit) and am looking down at my statue from a bit above it.

FIGURE 8.9 Move up a bit higher and take another round of screenshots.

Finally, move closer to your object so that you're almost looking down on it from above. Figure 8.10 shows you how close I get—basically close enough so that I can see the top of the object and the edges of where it meets the ground, all in one screen. Take about eight screenshots as you circle the object from this elevation.

FIGURE 8.10 Get close and take a few screenshots from slightly above the object.

You want to end up with close to 60 images or more. Remember that the 123D Catch software has a limit of 70 uploaded images, so you should delete a few that look too similar.

If you're not sure how to locate your screenshots, refer to Chapter 7. As described there, the location will be different depending on whether you took the screenshots on a Windows computer or a Mac.

TIP

Taking screenshots with Minecraft Pocket Edition

Can you take screenshots on a tablet with Minecraft Pocket Edition? Absolutely! However, you'll need to transfer the screenshot images to a Windows computer, so use a service like Dropbox or sync your tablet to download those images. Also, you may need to do some digging to find out the proper way to take screenshots on your device. With an iPad, you press and hold the Power button (on top) and the Home button (just beneath the screen) at the same time. For other tablets, the method varies.

Find and collect these screenshots into a single folder, as shown in Figure 8.11.

FIGURE 8.11 You should have a nice large collection of screenshots.

Converting Image Files

Once you have your 60 or so screenshots, you're almost ready to move on to using the 123D Catch app, but there's still one last step that may be necessary. The 123D Catch app only accepts certain file types, the main ones being JPEG/JPG and TIFF. But Minecraft takes screenshots using the PNG file type. This means you'll need to convert your PNG files to JPG images.

For Mac users, this is an easy task: Select all the screenshots (go to Finder, select Edit, and click on Select All), right-click on any of the selected images, and choose Open With, Preview. Once in Preview, you'll see all your screenshots scrolling down the left side in thumbnail view, as shown in Figure 8.12.

FIGURE 8.12 Open the screenshot collection in Preview on a Mac.

Once again, select all the thumbnails by clicking the Edit menu and choosing Select All. All the screenshots will be selected. Click on the File menu and choose Export Selected Images, as shown in Figure 8.13.

FIGURE 8.13 Choose the Export Selected Images option.

A window like the one in Figure 8.14 appears. Select the folder where you wish to save your files and choose the JPEG option in the Format drop-down menu. (You can also click the New Folder button to create a new folder to keep things organized.) Click Choose to complete the conversion, and then wait about 30 seconds for it to complete.

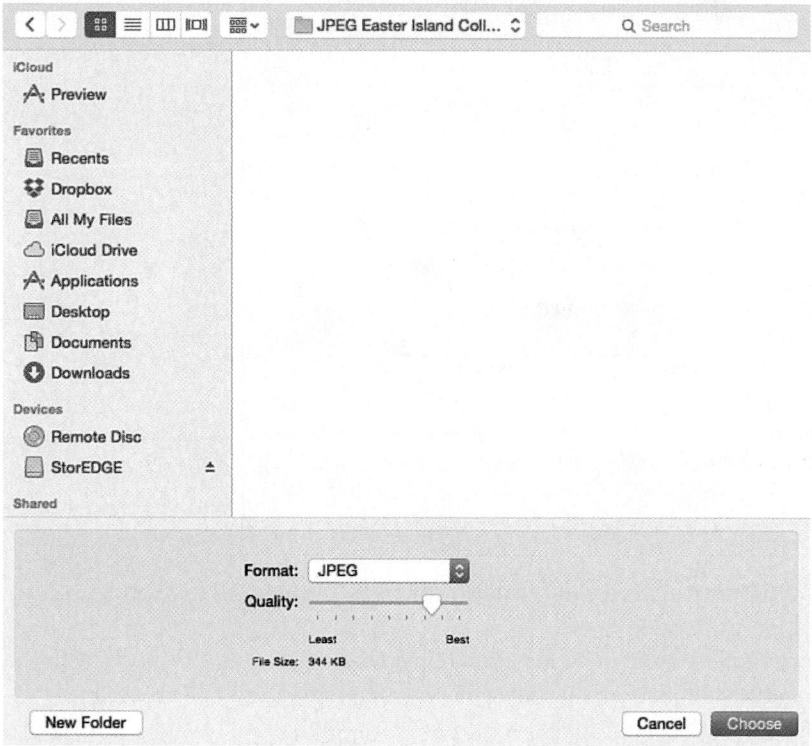

FIGURE 8.14 Change the file type to JPEG and start the conversion.

You'll need to get this collection of JPEG images to a Windows computer, so use a USB flash drive or cloud storage (such as Dropbox) to copy them over.

If you're a Windows user, you might remember that you've already used online-convert.com in previous chapters. You can use it to convert a PNG to JPG, but it's slow going because it requires you to convert one image at a time. More useful would be a conversion tool that can do all the conversions at once—a batch conversion tool. There are a number of free ones available online. Do an online search for "batch image convert tool," and you'll find them.

One free and simple one is ImageBatch, found at imagebatch.org and shown in Figure 8.15. Download and run it: Select the folder containing the PNG files and specify a folder where you wish to save the JPEG conversions. Check the JPEG box only, click on the Start button, and you're done.

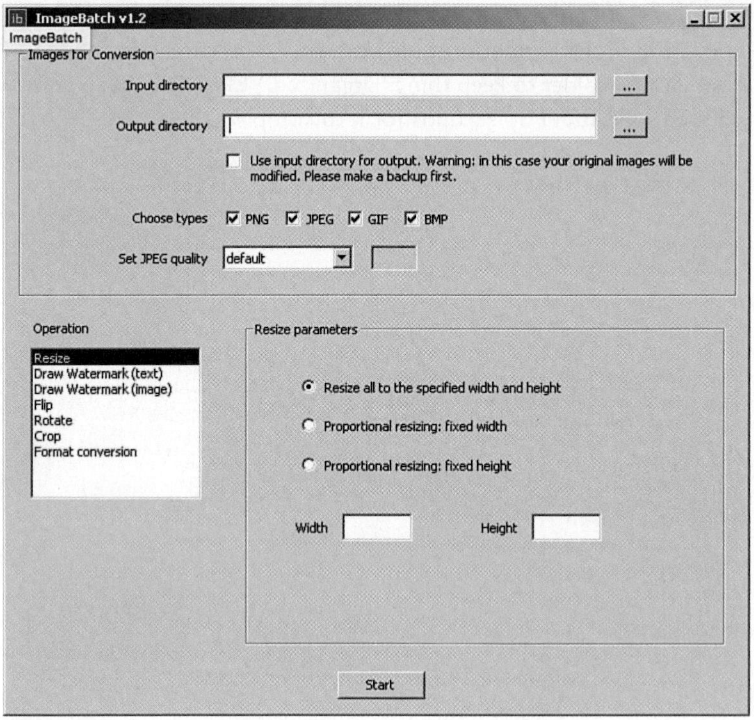

FIGURE 8.15 Windows users can use ImageBatch to convert PNG files to JPEG.

Once you've got your collection of JPEG files, you're ready to create your 3D model with the 123D Catch app. In the next section, I'll show you where to find it and how to use it.

Using 123D Catch to Create 3D Models

123D Catch is a free app from Autodesk that you can get for your Windows computer. Just visit http://www.123dapp.com/catch, scroll down the page about halfway, click on the PC Download button, and follow the instructions to install it.

After you've installed the application on your Windows computer, double-click it, and you'll see a screen like the one in Figure 8.16.

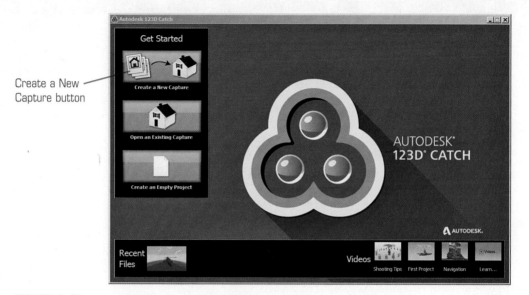

Create a New Capture button

FIGURE 8.16   The 123D Catch application running on Windows.

I'm not going to go into super-detail on all the special tools available with the 123D Catch application, but just know that after you've created your 3D model with the app, you can also use its editing tools to erase or delete areas of the 3D visual that you don't like or want floating around. You'll want to spend some time experimenting to discover the best ways to present your 3D models, but before you can do that, you've got to have a 3D model to view! Let's take care of that now.

Uploading Your Image Files

Click the Create a New Capture button to open a browsing window where you'll need to browse to your new JPEG images and select them all. To do this, hold down the Shift key and click on the first image in the list and then scroll down (while still holding Shift) and click on the last image. You've now selected all the images, as shown in Figure 8.17. (If you count carefully, you'll see that I took a total of 59 images.)

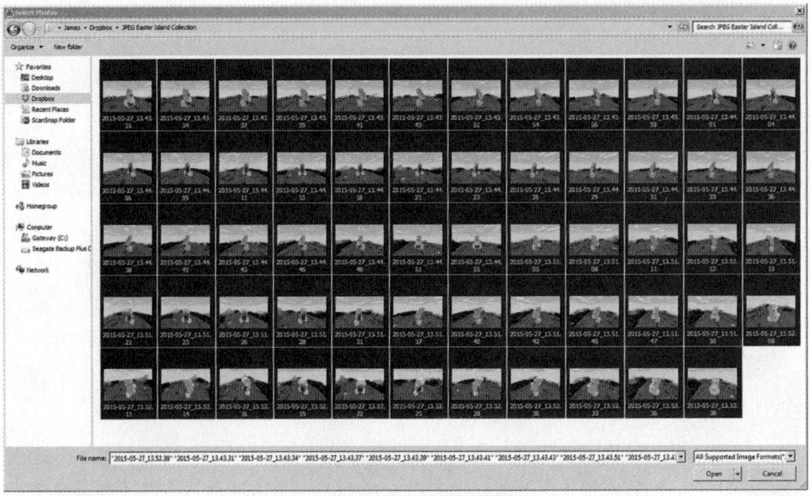

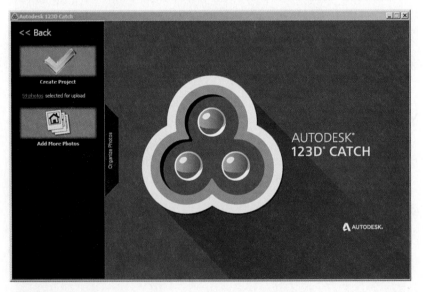

FIGURE 8.17 Select your JPEG screenshots.

With the screenshots selected, click on the Open button. The 123D Catch screen displays a large green check mark button, as shown in Figure 8.18.

FIGURE 8.18 Screenshots uploaded and ready to be stitched together.

Click on that check mark, and a new window appears, as shown in Figure 8.19. You'll need to provide some information, including the email address you want the application to use to send you a message when the 3D model is completed.

FIGURE 8.19 Provide some information about your model.

Tags are required, but a description isn't. Click the Create button when you're done providing the information, and accept the Terms of Service (that appears in a pop-up window) by clicking the OK button. A new window appears, as shown in Figure 8.20, to let you know the process has, and the app is uploading the images to Autodesk.

FIGURE 8.20 Images begin to upload.

Running the Create Capture Process

The uploading of the images doesn't take long (maybe a minute or so). The next step is the Create Capture process, and it can take a while. I've had one model created in about 10 minutes, but another one took a few hours. The time it takes depends partly on how many users are submitting images, so be patient! Figure 8.21 shows what it looks like when the Create Capture process has started.

FIGURE 8.21 The Create Capture process can take a while to complete.

When the Create Capture process is completed, your 3D model will be downloaded to the 123D Catch software installed on Windows and opened so you can view the results. Figure 8.22 shows my monument open in the 123D Catch application on Windows.

FIGURE 8.22   A 3D model created with 123D Catch.

Notice that small white camera outlines appear all around the monument. These are the locations I took the screenshots, as calculated by the 123D Catch application. Don't worry—these will go away.

Along the top of the screen are various tools you can use to move around the screen and edit your model. If you have a scroll wheel mouse, you can use the wheel to zoom in and out on your model. Figure 8.23 shows what it looks like after I've zoomed out a little.

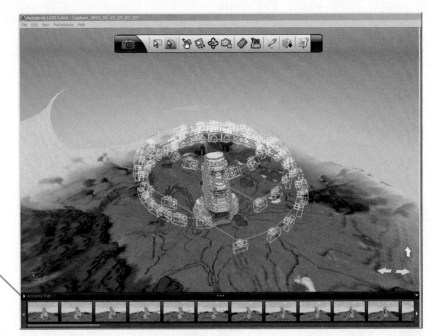

Animation Path
button

FIGURE 8.23 Zoom out to see your entire model.

Why does the surrounding Minecraft scenery look blurred? Blur is caused by having too few images of an area for the 123D Catch app to display in better detail. In this case, I was focused on the monument, not the surrounding forest and plains. Therefore, I didn't get enough photos showing the trees and grass to make them clear; the application does its best to display those areas based on what screenshots it did have with those areas in the image. This is why the image is sharper closer to the monument and more blurry further away from the monument.

There's just not enough room in this chapter for me to go over every tool in detail, but if you click the Help menu, you'll find an option labeled Online Content. Click that to gain access to online tutorials and help with all the various toolbars available. There is one tool, however, that I want to show you because it's really fun to use.

In the lower-left corner of the screen, click the Animation Path button to open up the toolbar shown in Figure 8.24.

Create Default
Animation Path
button

FIGURE 8.24 Open up the Animation Path toolbar.

Next, click the Create Default Animation Path button. A blue spiral surrounds your central object, as shown in Figure 8.25. (You can create a custom path, but it's tricky. The default animation path works fine.)

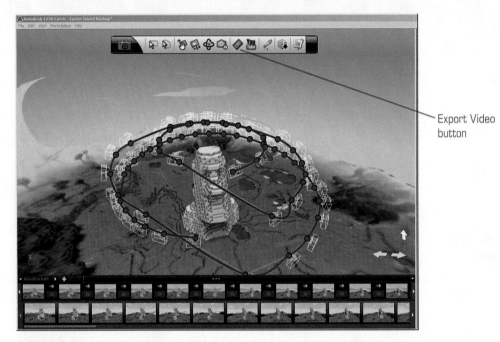

Export Video
button

FIGURE 8.25   Allow the application to create a default path to follow.

Click on the Export Video button (it's to the left of the YouTube button on the toolbar), and the window shown in Figure 8.26 appears.

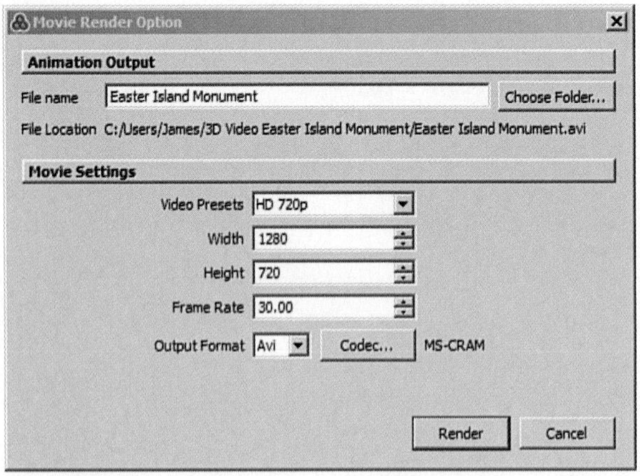

FIGURE 8.26   A video configuration screen.

If you know a lot about video configuration, feel free to tweak the settings. Otherwise, give the video a title and click the Choose Folder button to specify a location for the video that will be created. Accept the rest of the default settings (which will work 99% of the time) and click on the Render button. The video creation process takes a few minutes to complete. When it's done, you end up with a small animation video you can share with friends and family members that show your Minecraft feature in 3D as the camera zooms around and up and down. Figure 8.27 shows my video playing on my computer.

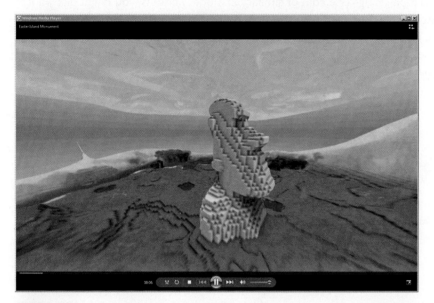

FIGURE 8.27 A video provides a tour of your newly created 3D model.

NOTE

View the Easter Island monolith video

If you like, you can view my upload in the 123D Catch gallery by visiting http://www.123dapp.com/catch/Easter-Island-Minecraft-Tour/4006221.

Be sure to click on the File menu and save your project. This way you can visit it later if you want to do some editing (such as deleting some of the surrounding countryside).

All in all, you've just learned a pretty slick way to share some of your best Minecraft designs as 3D models that can be viewed in real-time 3D vision on a computer screen. It's a great way to get a little glimpse into how playing Minecraft with a device such as the Oculus Rift (see Chapter 7) will feel and look.

Up Next...

You've been using Tinkercad to create .schematic files to use with MCEdit, but did you know that Tinkercad is also a perfect tool for creating your own 3D models? If you can't find what you need on Thingiverse.com or similar 3D model websites, you might just want to make it yourself! Tinkercad's got plenty of features that allow you to add and merge shapes to create your own unique 3D models. In the next chapter, you'll learn about some of the basic Tinkercad features and see how they are used to create an original object (a futuristic city) that can be imported into a Minecraft world.

Custom Creations, Part 1

What You'll Be Doing

- Watch Coolcrafter10 go to the ocean for a surprise
- Create objects that you can't find on Thingiverse
- Work with shapes and groups of shapes

Coolcrafter10 and Didgee sat on a couch, taking turns looking through the 3D viewer at the various 3D image cards they had created using PackRat's instructions. On the other side of the room, Prism sat at her laptop and smiled at a video of their castle as it rotated around, giving her a 360-degree view of their home.

"This is amazing," said Didgee. "Now we can take along these 3D image cards when we visit our friends and show them our designs. They'll be able to see our creations as if they were actually standing right in front of them."

PackRat nodded and smiled, "It was a nice surprise to see it worked. I honestly didn't know if the 3D effect would be good or bad."

"Oh, it's good," said Coolcrafter10, holding up a card and staring at it with the 3D viewer. "This tree looks much closer than the castle behind it. And the clouds disappear into the distance."

Prism laughed out loud, and everyone looked over at her. "I can zoom in and out and fly up above this 3D model of the waterfall behind the castle. You really outdid yourself with this project, PackRat."

Coolcrafter10 and Didgee nodded in agreement.

"Thank you," said PackRat. "But Didgee, you haven't seen Prism's project yet."

Didgee looked from PackRat to Prism. "Okay, so what have you been working on while I was gone, Prism?"

Prism stood up from the laptop and held up her hands. "I'm still learning my way around the software, but I've been teaching myself how to use more of the Tinkercad tools. You wouldn't believe some of the things you can do inside Tinkercad."

"Can you show us?" asked Coolcrafter10.

"Sure, but I don't think it's as impressive as PackRat's 3D images," said Prism.

"She's too humble," said PackRat. "Her project is just as cool. Come on, let's go outside, and you can see for yourself. Show them, Prism."

Prism motioned for the others to follow her. She picked up her laptop, closed it, and the four Minecrafters left the castle. Prism led the way, up a different hill than the one Coolcrafter10 and Didgee had walked down a few hours earlier. As the group reached the top of the hill, a vast ocean became visible. The reflection of the sun was bright on the water, and Prism and PackRat shielded their eyes from the light. But Didgee and Coolcrafter10 just stood, mouths open, forgetting the glare and focusing instead on the sight before them.

Didgee pointed out into the water. "You designed that?" she asked.

Prism nodded. "It only took an hour or so. I used a combination of predesigned buildings from Thingiverse plus my own designs with the Tinkercad tools."

Coolcrafter10 couldn't believe his eyes. A futuristic city floated over the ocean, with dozens of buildings in various shapes and sizes and colors. Twisting through the city and up and down and all around the buildings was what appeared to be a rollercoaster. "Who lives there?" asked Coolcrafter10.

PackRat laughed, "No one right now. Prism and I have been hollowing out some of the buildings, but honestly we haven't gotten much work done. The rollercoaster is just too much fun to ride."

"You've got to show us how you did this," said Didgee. "I knew Tinkercad was a powerful tool, but this is way beyond what I thought was possible."

Prism smiled. "I'll show both of you, but you'll be surprised at how easy it is. Tinkercad isn't all that difficult once you figure out a few basics. Let's head back to the castle, and I'll show you."

"Oh, come on, Prism. That can wait. We can't show them this and expect them not to want to go out and take a ride." PackRat began walking down the hill toward a pier that stretched from the shoreline to the beginnings of the city's streets. "I'm going for another ride."

Coolcrafter10 looked at Prism and then at Didgee. "Uh, yeah, I'm going for a ride," he replied with a grin. "I want to learn, Prism, but later, okay?" He took off running after PackRat.

Prism shrugged at Didgee. "Go on. I've got a few tweaks I plan on making tonight, so take a ride while the city is still open to visitors. In a few hours, I'll have to close it down for a while."

Didgee laughed. "Thanks, Prism. You build a nice city, by the way," she yelled back as she ran to catch up to PackRat and Coolcrafter10.

Prism looked down at her laptop and then back to her friends. She placed the laptop carefully on the ground and ran down the hill. "Wait for me!"

Creating Your Own Designs with Tinkercad

In the previous chapters, you've learned how to use a variety of tools to create some amazing things in your Minecraft worlds. With most of those tools, however, you have found and imported designs created by others. Thingiverse.com is a library where people can upload their 3D models for others to use, and you learned how to search and find interesting items and then import them into Tinkercad. Once in Tinkercad, you used the Download for Minecraft option to create a .schematic file that MCEdit could use to place your object inside a world. (You also learned how to find .obj 3D model files that couldn't be imported into Minecraft but could be converted to .schematic files using Binvox.)

Using the methods you've already learned, you can add an unlimited number of objects to your world in a very short amount of time (compared to building them block-by-block). Want an Eiffel Tower in your world? Thingiverse has plenty of Eiffel Tower .stl files to download. Looking to add a tyrannosaurus rex to scare off intruders? The 123D Sculpt+ app has a fearsome looking one that you can grab (as an .obj file to convert with Binvox) and place wherever you like.

Thingiverse.com and other websites like it have thousands and thousands of models available for free download, and chances are that something you have in mind for your worlds already exists as a 3D model that someone has graciously created and uploaded for the world to use.

But what if you've got something in mind that can't be found on Thingiverse.com? Maybe you'd like some combination of a castle with a dragon's head as the entrance? Or maybe you'd like to place a 3D model of your own house in a Minecraft world? There are lots of things you can probably imagine adding to your world that do not exist on Thingiverse or similar 3D model repositories.

Obviously, you can build those things block-by-block, the old-fashioned way. But if you've spent any time building anything in Minecraft, you know that building can be time-consuming. Sometimes you have no choice but to build things a little at a time, especially if you're testing out different looks or features. At other times, you may be working with a group of people (maybe on a shared Minecraft server) to create something unique and can't use MCEdit to open and edit the world. But most Minecraft players, if given the chance, would prefer to spend less time building their creations and more time enjoying them and playing in and around them, right?

There may be times when you know what you want to build but you can't find it on Thingiverse or another repository, and you absolutely want it as fast as possible. That's when it's time to go outside Minecraft and try your hand at creating what you want with a tool that lets you design things quickly rather than block-by-block. Tinkercad is one such tool. However, although you've been using it throughout the book, you've only used about 5% of its features. Now it's time to get a crash course in how to use its other features. It's one of my favorite computer-aided design (CAD) apps, and it can help you build amazing creations.

NOTE

Tinkercad is free and well supported

There are other free CAD applications out there, but Tinkercad shines for many reasons. It's free, it doesn't require software to be installed on your computer (just a web browser), and it's well supported by the folks at Autodesk, the company that owns Tinkercad.

In the remainder of this chapter and in Chapter 10, "Custom Creations, Part 2," you're going to learn to use many of the basic tools that are built into Tinkercad. The best way to learn how to use them...is to use them! That's why I'm going to suggest right now that you open up a web browser, log in to Tinkercad, and follow along in the building of the futuristic city that will be this chapter's project. When you see me use a tool, click on that tool and perform the same step I describe. Your final result doesn't have to look exactly like mine, though. As long as you understand how the various tools work, you'll be in good shape and ready to design your own custom creations in Tinkercad.

Starting a New Project

You've read it previously in this book, but I'll say it again: Tinkercad is a CAD application. CAD—computer-aided design—is a type of software that lets users create three-dimensional models on a computer. These objects can be rotated, shrunk, enlarged, twisted, and much more. Some CAD applications are easy to learn, and some are difficult to grasp. Whether you choose to use Tinkercad as your CAD application is up to you, but keep in mind that some CAD applications can cost hundreds or thousands of dollars, and often that price includes features and tools that you may never use. For this reason, I always encourage any-one learning CAD to start easy. And cheap. Tinkercad is free, and using it is a great way to take a test drive of CAD and determine whether you like it.

NOTE

A more detailed source on Tinkercad

I wrote a book that covers about 90% of Tinkercad's features: *3D Modeling and Printing with Tinkercad: Create and Print Your Own 3D Models.* (Autodesk's software developers are always adding more, so there may be a few things it doesn't cover.) There's no way I can cram in everything found in that book into a few chapters in this book. So if you find that you like Tinkercad and want to learn how to use some of its powerful design features, that's the book you'll want to grab and read.

I covered how to create a Tinkercad account back in Chapter 1, "Taking Over a Castle," so go back to that chapter if you need help getting started. Once you're signed in, you'll be able to view your user screen and all the various models you've created (or imported) and modified. If you're logging in for the first time, you won't have any projects to view.

Once you're logged in, click the Create New Design button to open up a blank Tinkercad project like the one shown in Figure 9.1.

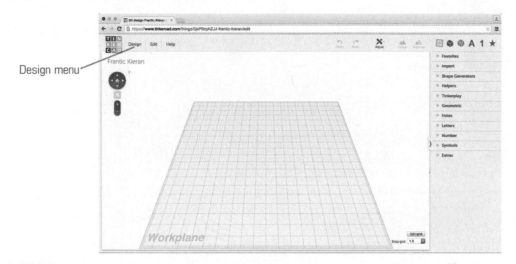

Design menu

FIGURE 9.1 A new Tinkercad project starts with an empty workspace.

When Tinkercad opens a new project, it gives it a strange name. If you're following along, your project probably isn't named Frantic Kieran, like the one shown in Figure 9.1.

To get rid of Tinkercad's meaningless-to-you name, you need to rename a project and save it. So right now, click on the Design menu and select the Properties option, as shown in Figure 9.2.

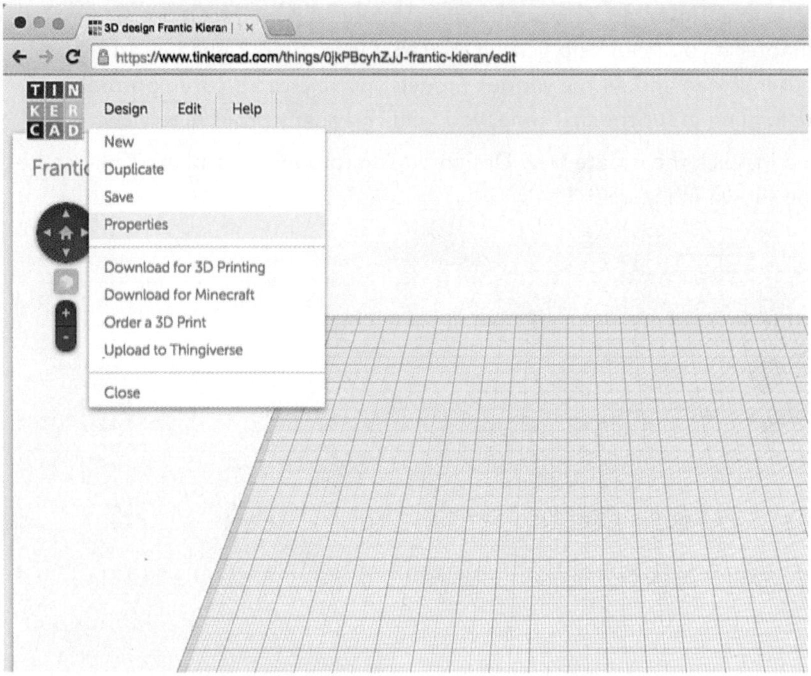

FIGURE 9.2   Use the Design menu to rename a project.

You can change the name of your project by typing in a new one in the Name box, as shown in Figure 9.3. You don't have to worry about the other settings in this window right now, but just know that if you change the Visibility option from Private to Public, other Tinkercad users will be able to view your design and download it. Click the Save Changes button to commit your name change.

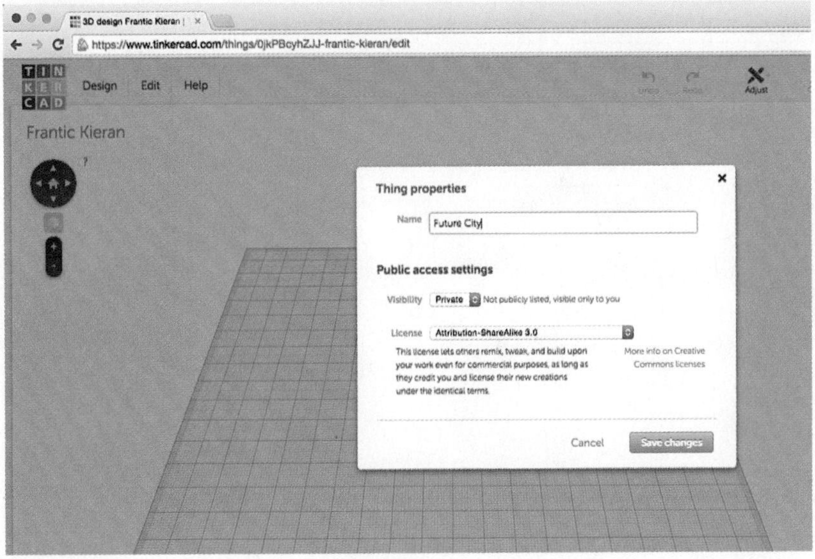

FIGURE 9.3 Change the name of your project.

After you've changed your project name, you can return to the Design menu and choose the Save option as often as you like. (Keep in mind that Tinkercad automatically saves your changes every few minutes.)

Running down the right side of the screen are collections of shapes and other items that you can drag and drop onto the workplane. These objects are organized into categories such as Geometric, Letters, and Symbols. A few of the categories offer tools instead of objects, and you've already seen the Import category used in previous chapters, when pulling in an .stl file into Tinkercad.

Figure 9.4 shows the Geometric category opened up. (The triangle that points to a category name points down when clicked on and expands to show that category's contents.) As you can see, this category has a bunch of shapes, such as Box, Pyramid, and Sphere.

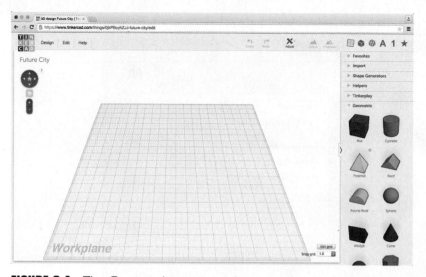

FIGURE 9.4 The Geometric category is opened and displaying its contents.

Running from left to right along the top of the screen are some menus (Design, Edit, and Help) and some other useful tools, including the Undo and Redo buttons. You'll learn about some of these in this chapter and Chapter 10. (The Help menu offers some video tutorials, so definitely check them out when you have some time.)

I could spend this chapter's remaining pages going over each button and tool in detail, but that wouldn't be much fun. You know what's fun? Learning by doing. So let's get right to it and start creating something fun that will also be useful in a Minecraft world. Take a look at Figure 9.5, which shows a futuristic city. By the time you're done with this chapter, you'll have your very own version of this city, and it will be ready to be imported into one of your Minecraft worlds with MCEdit.

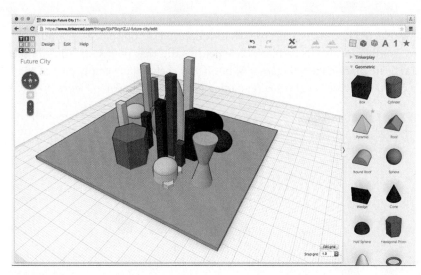

FIGURE 9.5   My futuristic city was built with nothing but the basic Tinkercad tools.

Don't believe me? I know it looks a bit complicated, but I'm going to show you how to create it easily and quickly. It all starts by dragging a Box object onto the workplane.

Breaking Ground on the Future City

Move your mouse pointer over the Box object (in the Geometric category) and click and hold as you drag a copy of the box onto the workplane. Try to center it on the workplane and release the mouse button to drop it in place, as shown in Figure 9.6.

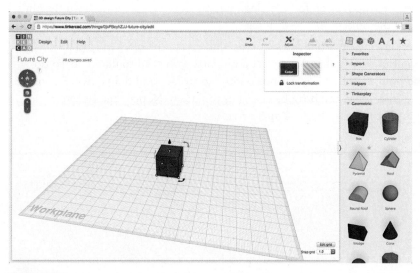

FIGURE 9.6   The city starts with a simple Box object.

When you drop an object on the workplane, that object is automatically selected. You can tell that an object is selected because it has little white squares in various places around its edges and on its top surface. It also has a black cone near its top that points up. You can see these white boxes and the black cone in Figure 9.6, but if you click on any empty part of the workplane, the object will be deselected while remaining in place, as shown in Figure 9.7.

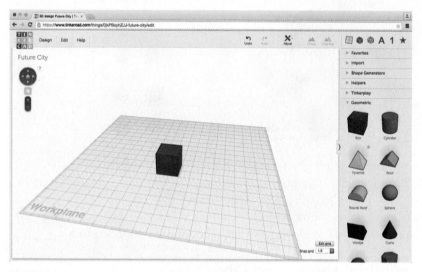

FIGURE 9.7 The Box object is not selected.

Click an item to select it again. If you have two or more objects you want to select at the same time, you can click-and-hold the mouse button as you drag a selection window around the objects. Another option for selecting multiple objects is to hold down the Shift key while clicking on the objects you wish to select.

Before you start adding my city's buildings, you need to create the piece of land it will sit on. To do this, you can modify that Box object a bit. First, you need to flatten it. To do this, you click and hold on the little white box on its top surface and drag down. Figure 9.8 shows that as you drag down, the Box object begins to flatten. Notice that Tinkercad displays the thickness—in this case, 4mm (4 millimeters).

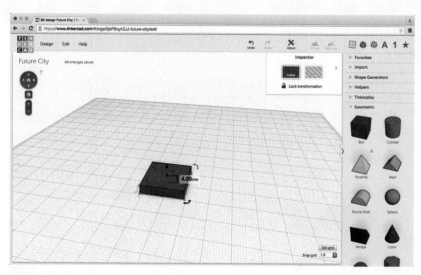

FIGURE 9.8 Flatten that box!

Flatten the box down so that it's only 2mm thick. Then it's time to stretch its length and width. To do this, you can click on any of the four white squares that are visible in the corners. If you click and hold while dragging away from the flat Box object, it widens or lengthens (depending on the direction of the drag). Notice in Figure 9.9 that the width and length are different values (55mm and 59mm, respectively), but the height remains at 2mm.

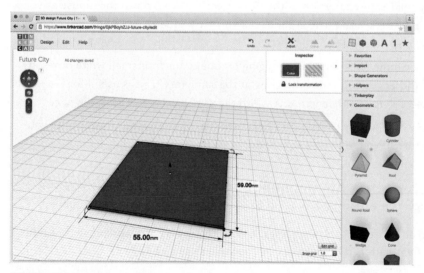

FIGURE 9.9 Stretch that box!

Use a combination of the little white boxes in the four corners to drag and stretch the flattened box until you're happy with it. Figure 9.10 shows the box expanded to fill about one-third of the workplane.

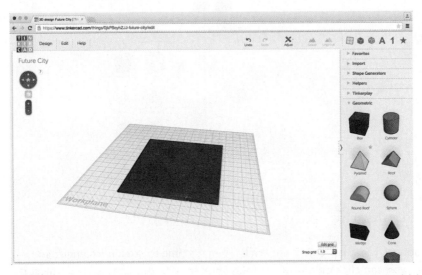

FIGURE 9.10 Now that the city streets are made, it's time to add buildings.

Before you start adding buildings, here are a few things to test with your flattened Box object:

- Click on any solid-colored portion of the Box object and hold down the mouse as you drag it. The Box object will move around. Use this technique to move and place objects exactly where you want them.

- If you hold down the Shift key while dragging on one of the four small white boxes in the corners, the length and width will grow at the same rate. This is useful for keeping a square's perfect shape (with length and width the same value) as it grows in size.

- Rotating the workplane by clicking and holding down on both mouse buttons as you move the mouse. If you're using a touchpad, press down with two fingers and pivot to get the same effect.

- Roll the scroll wheel on top of your mouse to zoom in and out on the workplane. Or, with two fingers on a touchpad, drag up to zoom out and drag down to zoom in.

Now it's time to add a skyscraper. Drag another Box object onto the workplane (but not touching the current flattened Box object), as shown in Figure 9.11.

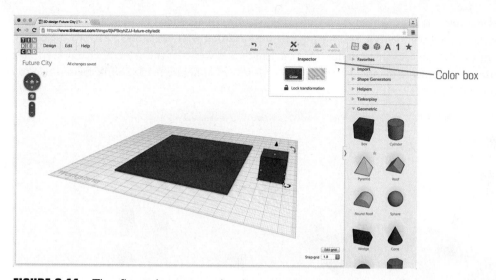

Color box

FIGURE 9.11   The first skyscraper begins to take shape.

The new Box object has the same color as the flattened one. This is fine, but changing the color will make it easier to see all the different city objects you'll be adding. To do this, click on the new box to select it (if it isn't already selected) and then click on the Color box to see a selection of colors, as shown in Figure 9.12. Click on a color—maybe a blue—to select it for the object.

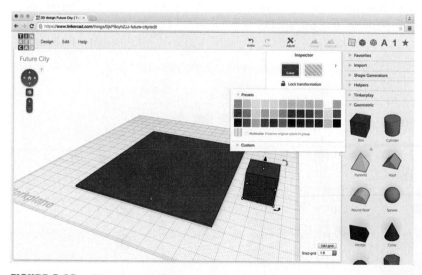

FIGURE 9.12   Change the color of an object.

A skyscraper should be tall but not too wide or long. To get the size and shape you want, hold down the Shift key while dragging one of the corner white squares in toward the center of the Box object. This will decrease the length and width of the skyscraper but keep those measurements identical to each other, as shown in Figure 9.13. Shrink them down to around 4mm.

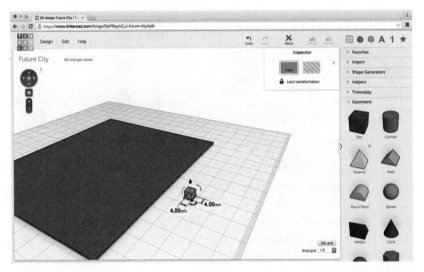

FIGURE 9.13 Shrink down the box but keep its length and width the same value.

Now it's time to send that skyscraper into the sky. Click and hold on the white square on the top of the Box object and drag up, as shown in Figure 9.14. Send it up to about a height of 50mm.

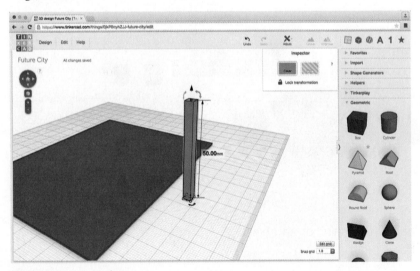

FIGURE 9.14 Raise the box up above the workplane's surface.

Now all that's left to do is place the skyscraper. Select it and then click and hold on any colored spot (but not on the little white squares or the black cone), drag it, and drop it where you want it. Figure 9.15 shows the skyscraper placed near the center of the flattened Box object.

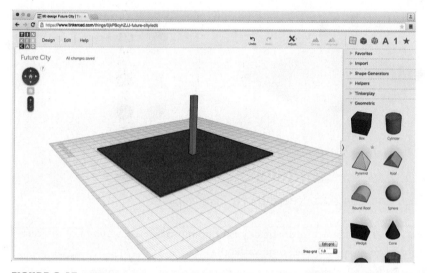

FIGURE 9.15   Place your new skyscraper on the flattened Box object.

That's one building down. Now you just need to create 50 more. Just kidding! While you can easily create 50 new skyscrapers by dragging out 50 Box objects and changing their length, width, and height, there's a much faster way to do this.

First, select a skyscraper. (If you have only one, it's an easy choice.) Then press Ctrl+C in Windows or Command+C on a Mac to copy. Then press Ctrl+V in Windows or Command+V on a Mac to paste the copy on the workplane. The copy will slightly overlap the original, so click and hold on the copy and drag it where you want it and release the mouse button to drop it in place.

Press Command+V or Ctrl+V as many times as you like. Each time you do, Tinkercad places another copy of the skyscraper. Figure 9.16 shows six copies pasted on the workplane and dragged to various parts of the city. You'll notice that they're not all the same size, though. That's because I've also clicked on the little white square on the top of each skyscraper and changed the height so the buildings don't all look the same.

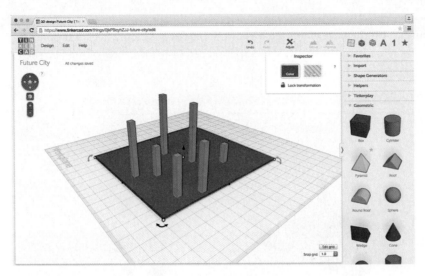

FIGURE 9.16 Copy and paste to create more skyscrapers.

It's starting to look like a city, but a futuristic city isn't going to be just a bunch of tall rectangular boxes, right? There needs to be some variety!

Fortunately, Tinkercad has a lot more shapes than the Box object. Let's try some!

Drag out a Sphere object and change its color as shown in Figure 9.17.

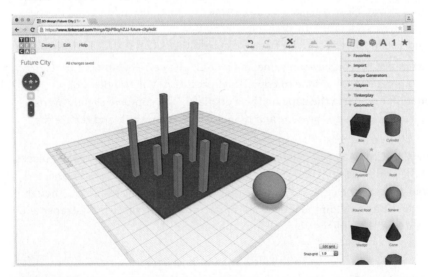

FIGURE 9.17 Every futuristic city should have a sphere. Or a dozen.

You can shrink or enlarge the Sphere (while keeping its perfect spherical shape) by holding down the Shift key as you drag one of the four corner squares. If you don't hold down the

Shift key, you can twist the Sphere object into unusual shapes such as the watermelon-shaped object in Figure 9.18 by dragging any of the four corner squares or even the one on top.

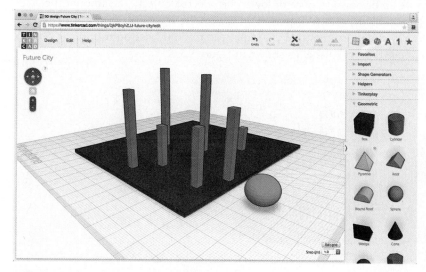

FIGURE 9.18   A flattened sphere.

After you've created a spherical building that you're happy with, try to drag it onto the city streets and see what happens. As you can see in Figure 9.19, part of the building is "buried" in the city streets. How do you make sure the entire sphere is visible?

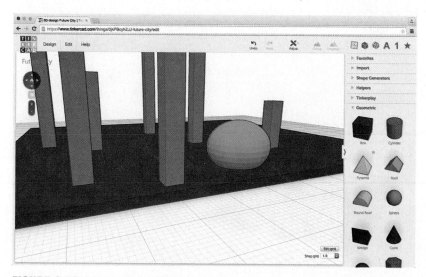

FIGURE 9.19   Part of the sphere is hidden by the city streets.

This is an easy fix. Once again, click on the object to select it. Remember the black cone that appears near the top of an object? When you click and hold down on that cone, you can move the mouse up or down to raise or lower the selected object. The amount the object is moved (up or down) will be displayed on the screen. If the flattened Box object you placed for the city streets is 2mm thick, all you need to do is raise up the Sphere object so that it's 2mm above the workplane, as shown in Figure 9.20.

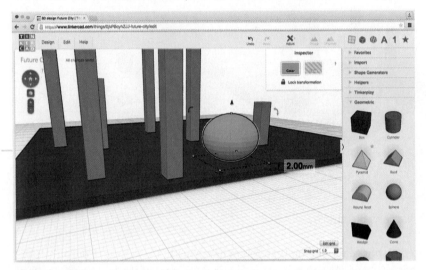

FIGURE 9.20 Raise (or lower) an object by using the black cone.

When the spherical building is the right height above the city streets, you can copy and paste to make more. Figure 9.21 shows a couple more spherical-shaped buildings added to the futuristic city and reshaped for variety.

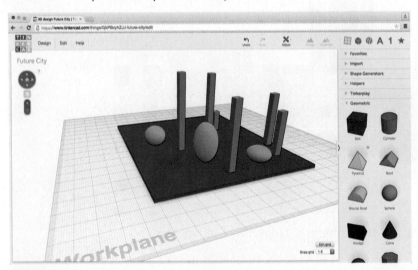

FIGURE 9.21 Toss a few extra sphere-shaped buildings on the map.

You can experiment with some of the other unique shapes in the Geometric category list. Figure 9.22 shows a few Hexagonal Prism objects, a Paraboloid object, and a couple Torus objects added to the city. In this figure, you can see that I've pulled in the buildings to tighten up the spaces between them, and I've changed the sizes and shapes and colors of many of the buildings. There's nothing added to this city that you can't do yourself with the skills you've already picked up.

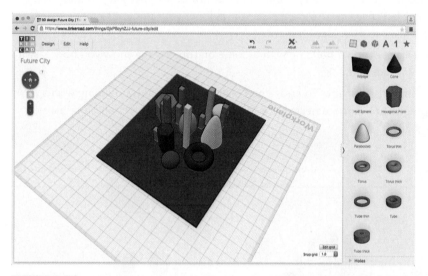

FIGURE 9.22 More fun shapes added to the workplane as buildings.

TIP

Use unique colors for objects to be imported with MCEdit

While you're in Tinkercad, change up the colors of the buildings as much as possible. When you import an object with MCEdit, the MCEdit tool will try to match up a block material with the color you've selected in Tinkercad. If all the buildings in the city are the same color, they'll all be made of the same material in a Minecraft world. (You can change each one with MCEdit by selecting each building and changing the block type, but that is a time-consuming process.) If you give different parts of your models unique colors in Tinkercad, they'll stand out better after they're imported into Minecraft.

The futuristic city is starting to look like a city, with plenty of buildings in different shapes and sizes. But so far, you've only used the basic shapes in the Geometric category. It might be nice to have some buildings that are combinations of basic shapes. Imagine a round building with a dome on top, or how about a Pyramid-shaped building that rests on a round base? There aren't any limits to what you can design if you know how to use the tools properly, so before we finish up this chapter, let's look at a few more Tinkercad tools that let you do some really interesting things in your futuristic city model.

Designing Custom-Shaped Buildings

In this section, you'll continue to use the Geometric category, but feel free to explore some of the other categories, such as Letters, Numbers, or Symbols. It's your city, so add what you like. Stack three buildings next to each other to spell out your initials. Create a giant building with your favorite punctuation mark.

I mentioned in the last section a building with a dome on top. Let me show you how easy it is to make something like that.

You can overlap Tinkercad's shapes to create new shapes. So to make a building with a dome, start by dragging two new objects onto the workplane—a Cylinder and a Sphere—as shown in Figure 9.23.

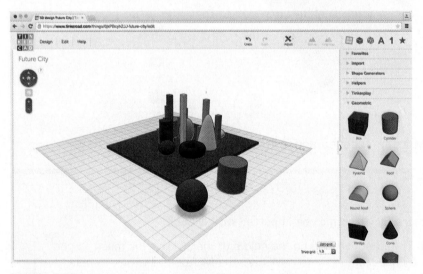

FIGURE 9.23 Part of the sphere is hidden by the city streets.

Both the Cylinder and the Sphere objects have a length and width of 20mm in this case, which is perfect if you want half of the sphere to be placed on top of the cylinder to give it a rounded, dome-shaped roof.

To get the sphere on top of the cylinder, you need to raise the sphere by using the black cone. As shown in Figure 9.24, a shadow underneath the sphere indicates that it's floating above the workplane.

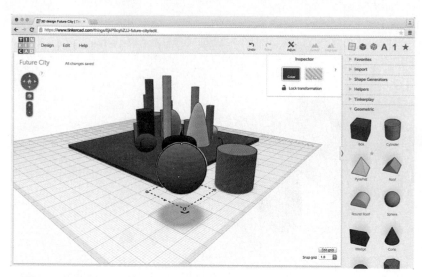

FIGURE 9.24 Raise up the Sphere object.

Next, drag the sphere so that it begins to merge into the cylinder, as shown in Figure 9.25.

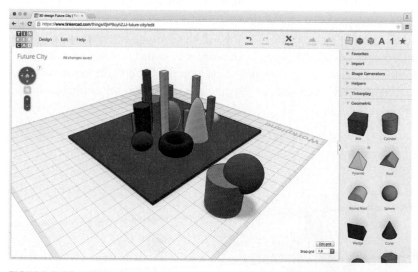

FIGURE 9.25 Blend the Cylinder and Sphere objects.

With a little more dragging, carefully move the sphere into place so that it blends perfectly with the sides of the cylinder, as shown in Figure 9.26. You may have to raise or lower the sphere a little until you get a smooth transition from cylinder to sphere.

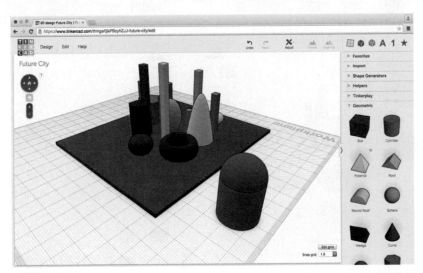

FIGURE 9.26 A cylinder and sphere together make a nice-looking building.

You can move the cylinder and sphere together by selecting both (using the Shift key or dragging a selection box around them) and placing them in the city where you want them.

Notice that the sphere and cylinder are different colors. If you leave the building like this, when you import the city using MCEdit, the building will have orange-colored blocks on the bottom and blue blocks on top. But what if you want the domed building to be all the same color? To do that, you select both objects and click on the Group button to combine both objects into a single object. Then you can pick a color to apply to the entire building, as shown in Figure 9.27.

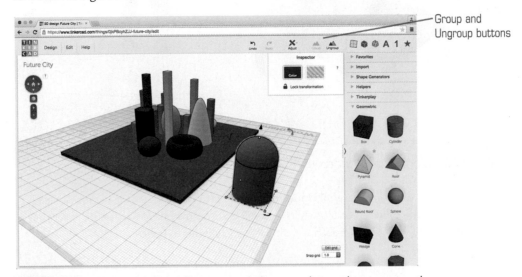

FIGURE 9.27 Group objects if you need them to have the same color.

You can continue to add additional shapes (by overlapping them) to the domed building and then click on the Group button to turn them into a single object. Grouped items can also be separated again by using the Ungroup button; grouped objects can always be ungrouped, even after saving a model. Weeks or months later, should you decide you wish to break up a collection of grouped objects, Tinkercad will always remember how to break up a single object into its various smaller parts.

Figure 9.28 shows a few other shapes added to the domed building and grouped together. (You can easily get this effect by dragging some Hexagonal Prism objects onto the workplane, shrinking them down a little, and then dragging them so they go inside the cylinder just a small amount.)

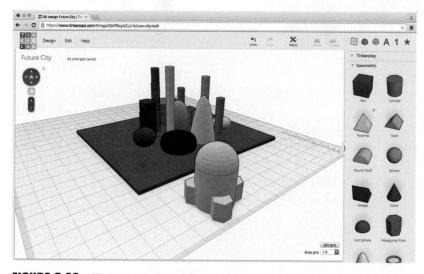

FIGURE 9.28   The domed building now has some extra components.

Once you're happy with the building, you can shrink or enlarge it by using the little squares. Figure 9.29 shows the domed building shrunk a bit and also flattened.

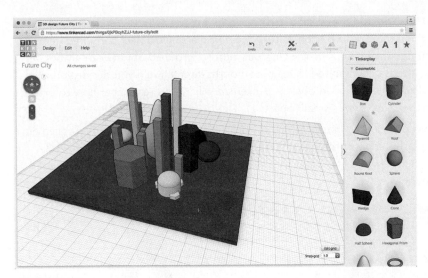

FIGURE 9.29 The flattened domed building is dragged and put in place.

Let's build one more building—this one hourglass shaped—before wrapping up this chapter. This one might sound a little complex, but once you know the actual "trick" to doing it, you'll be using that trick a lot.

Start by dragging out two Cone objects, as shown in Figure 9.30.

Adjust tool

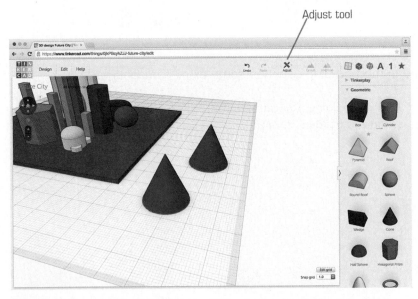

FIGURE 9.30 Two Cone objects will make an hourglass building.

To make an hourglass, you need to flip one of the cones. There are a couple ways to do this, and I'm going to show you the easiest method now. (The other method involves rotating pieces, and you'll learn how to do that in Chapter 10.)

First, select one of the cones click the Adjust tool, and select the Mirror option, as shown in Figure 9.31.

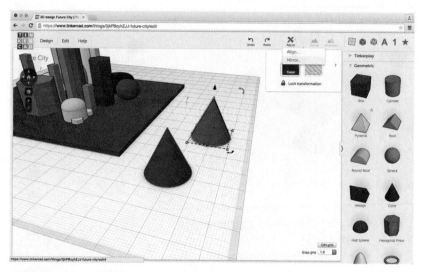

FIGURE 9.31 Choose the Mirror option.

After you click the Mirror option, three double-arrows appear near the selected cone, as shown in Figure 9.32.

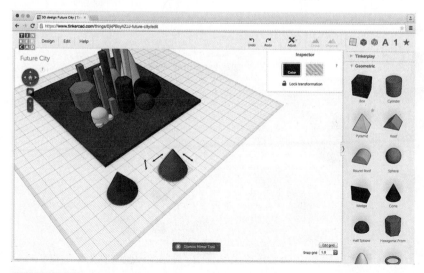

FIGURE 9.32 Control arrows let you quickly make changes to an object.

Each of these double-arrows causes the selected object to flip in the directions the arrows are pointing. To flip it vertically (upside down), click on the double-arrow that points up and down. (The other two double-arrows allow you to flip the object front to back or left to right.) Figure 9.33 shows what happens to the selected cone.

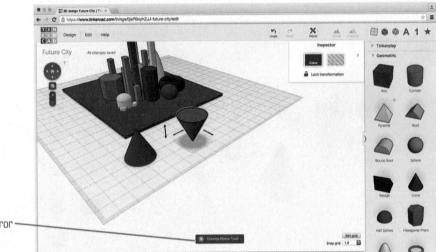

Dismiss Mirror Tool button

FIGURE 9.33 The cone is flipped upside down.

Click the Dismiss Mirror Tool button to turn off the Mirror option and then use the black cone to raise the upside-down cone a little. Finally, drag the upside-down cone until it blends with the other cone, group the two cones, and resize the combined object a little bit...until you end up with an hourglass-shaped building like the one shown in Figure 9.34.

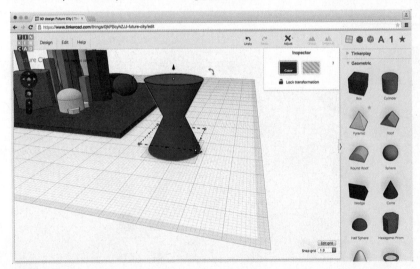

FIGURE 9.34 One unique hourglass-shaped building made easy.

After dragging the hourglass building into place, make some color changes to the city's buildings (including changing the street color to gray) and do a few more copy, paste, and resize operations to create a futuristic city like the one shown in Figure 9.35.

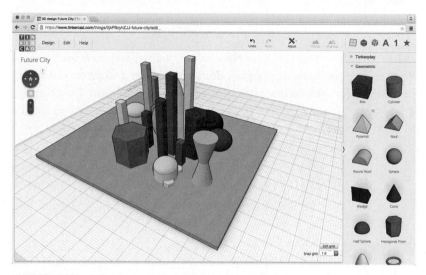

FIGURE 9.35   The futuristic city is complete!

Now all that's left to do is click on the Design menu, select Download for Minecraft, and use MCEdit to import the city into one of your worlds. Figure 9.36 shows the futuristic city sitting proudly out in the ocean.

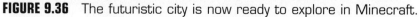

FIGURE 9.36   The futuristic city is now ready to explore in Minecraft.

You can do a lot more with the city. You can use a few more Tinkercad tools to create even crazier buildings. All these tools that you're learning will also come in handy as you branch out and start designing your own 3D models.

Up Next...

In Chapter 11, "A Super Project to Test Out Your New Skills," you're going to learn how to add a really cool effect to your futuristic city—a glass dome that covers and protects it from rain and enemies. But before you can do that, there are still a number of basic Tinkercad skills you must learn. Chapter 10 will introduce you to a few more Tinkercad features that will allow you to create even more unique models of your own for use with Tinkercad.

Custom Creations, Part 2

What You'll Be Doing

■ Learn about more Tinkercad tools

As you saw in Chapter 9, "Custom Creations, Part 1," Tinkercad can do a lot more than just import 3D models from Thingiverse. With Tinkercad's assortment of tools, you can create custom 3D models for anything you want to add to Minecraft—vehicles, buildings, animals, and much more. As you continue to use Tinkercad and learn about its great features, you'll start to think about building more complicated and unusual objects.

With CAD applications such as Tinkercad, it's usually not the tools that are the limit, but your imagination. If you can picture something in your mind, there's a good chance you can re-create it in Tinkercad. The trick is to learn as many techniques as possible and push your CAD application to the limits to turn your ideas into 3D models. And once you've got a 3D model on the screen, you already know how easy it is to take it into a Minecraft world.

In Chapter 9, you learned how to use some of the very basic tools of Tinkercad—to drop objects on the workplane, resize them, and merge and group them. This chapter builds on what you learned in Chapter 9 and shows you some additional Tinkercad capabilities. You'll learn some new ways to manipulate objects on the screen as well as how to eliminate parts of a model that you don't want. This comes in handy, for example, when you want only half of a sphere.

So, once again, you need to open up a web browser, point it to Tinkercad.com, and log in to your account. Once there, click on the Create New Design button and open up a blank workplane.

Rotating, Twisting, and Turning

In order to create really fun models in Tinkercad, you're going to have to frequently modify Box, Hexagonal Prism, Pyramid, and other objects. You may need to shrink them or grow them, or you might merge them with other objects. You also may need to rotate objects. For example, take a look at the Box object sitting on the workplane in Figure 10.1.

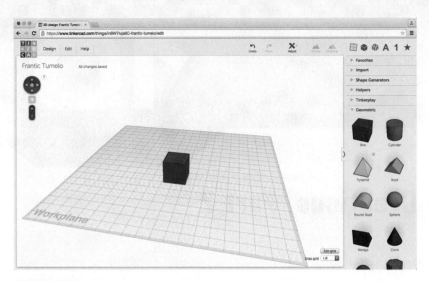

FIGURE 10.1 A Box sits, waiting to be modified.

Look carefully, and you'll notice that the box has been dropped on the workplane so that it's perfectly lined up with the grid. In this case, I've rotated the view a bit so you're looking at the box from an angle. (To rotate the view, hold down the mouse scroll button or tap-and-hold two fingers on a touchpad or hold down the Control key while moving the mouse.) But take a look at Figure 10.2, and you'll see that the view is changed so you're looking at the box directly from the front and slightly above; you can't see the box's sides at all, but you can see part of the top.

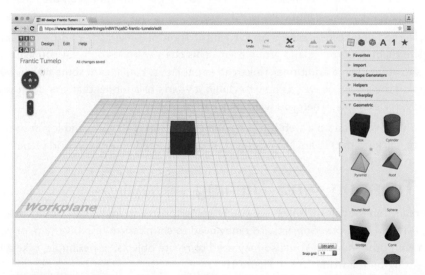

FIGURE 10.2 A Box object, viewed from the front and slightly above.

You can rotate the view all you want in order to see the box from different angles, but this isn't the same as rotating the box itself. To do that, you need to use the rotation controls that are visible when you select an object. Figure 10.3 shows the view rotated again and the box selected; notice the three curved double-arrows that appear near the box.

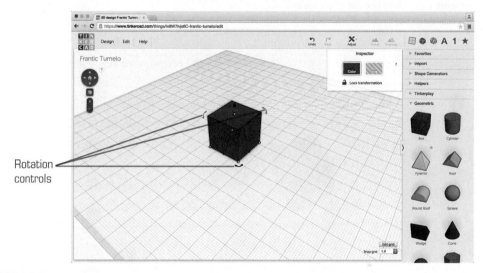

Rotation controls

FIGURE 10.3 The rotation controls appear when you select an object.

Sometimes it's easier to try using a tool than to read an explanation of it. So move your mouse pointer over one of the rotation controls (but don't click on it). When you do, you'll see an image appear that looks like the face of a clock, as shown in Figure 10.4; this is called the rotation meter.

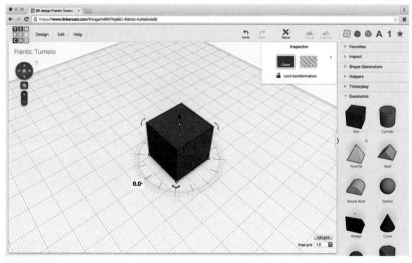

FIGURE 10.4 The rotation meter appears.

Move your mouse pointer over the other two rotation controls, and you see similar images appear. These rotation meters show you how many degrees an object has been rotated when you click-and-hold a rotation control and move the mouse. Try it. You can undo anything you do by clicking the Undo button on the top toolbar. Figure 10.5 shows the box rotated 22.5 degrees on the workplane.

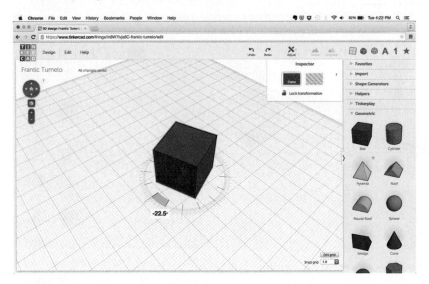

FIGURE 10.5 Rotating an object using the rotation controls.

Figure 10.6 shows the box rotated an additional 22.5 degrees, for a total of 45 degrees from its original orientation. To do this, simply continue to hold down the rotation control while moving the mouse in the direction you want to rotate the Box object.

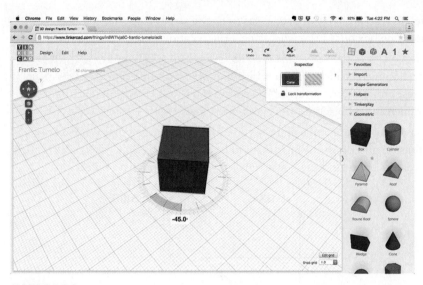

FIGURE 10.6   The box continues to rotate as long as the rotation control is pressed.

If you keep the mouse pointer very near or touching the rotation meter, the rotation will move in 22.5-degree increments. To rotate an object in 1-degree increments, move the mouse pointer off (and outside) the rotation meter and move the mouse. As you can see in Figure 10.7, the rotation meter counts in 1-degree increments, allowing you to rotate your object in very small amounts.

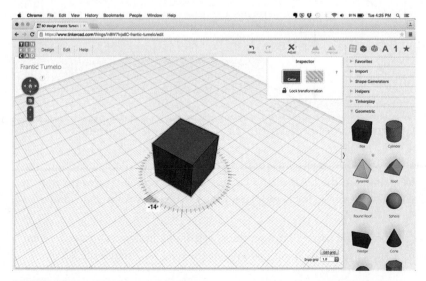

FIGURE 10.7   Rotations can be done in single-digit increments.

In the previous figures, you probably noticed I was using the same rotation meter that corresponds to rotating the box on the flat workplane. (This rotation looks similar to placing a cube on a tabletop and just rotating it while keeping the cube's bottom face flat on the table.)

The other two rotation meters allow you to rotate your object around different axes. (The plural of axis is axes, pronounced "ax-eeze.") There are three axes when you talk about rotating a three-dimensional object: X-axis, Y-axis, and Z-axis.

Figure 10.8 shows a drawing of a cube and the three axes. You can see that the Z-axis is like a thin wire that runs up and down through the middle of an object. The Y-axis runs through the object from front to back. And the X-axis runs left to right through an object.

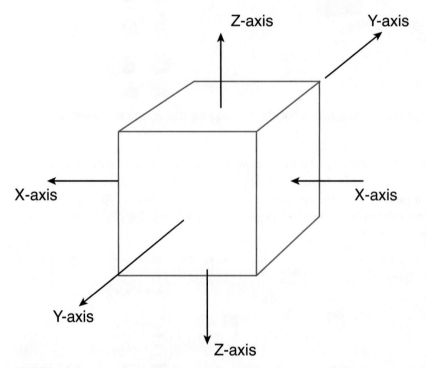

FIGURE 10.8 Three-dimensional objects can be rotated on three axes.

In the last few rotations, the Box object was rotated around the Z-axis. Imagine a thin wire cutting into the box, going into the bottom and coming out the top. The box was rotating on this "wire" (clockwise or counterclockwise), so we say the Box was rotated around the Z-axis.

Figure 10.9 shows the box being rotated around the Y-axis. If you imagine another wire cutting through the front (face) of the Box and coming out the backside, that's the Y-axis.

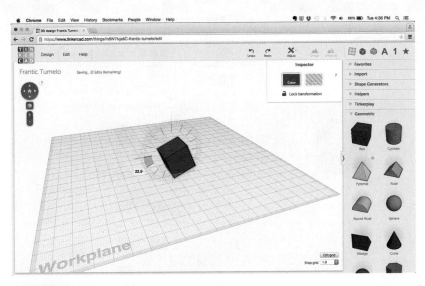

FIGURE 10.9 Rotating around the Y-axis.

NOTE

Finding the front of a 3D model

How do you know what is the "front" and "back" of an 3D model? If you can't easily look at an object and tell which side is the front and which is the back (as you can with a person or robot, where the face is considered the front), look for what Tinkercad thinks of as the "front"—the side facing the word "Workplane" on the grid that makes up your workspace.

If you look carefully at Figure 10.9, you can see that the word "Workplane" is visible, so that's considered the "front" of the box. If that's the front, than a thin (imaginary) wire that runs through the box's face and comes out the back is the Y-axis. You can even see that the rotation meter appears behind the cube and is standing up, with its own center matching up to that imaginary wire running through the front and back of the box.

The third and final rotation control rotates the box around the X-axis. Take a look at Figure 10.10, and you'll see that the rotation meter that appears is "standing up" and has its center matched up to an imaginary wire running through the box from left to right.

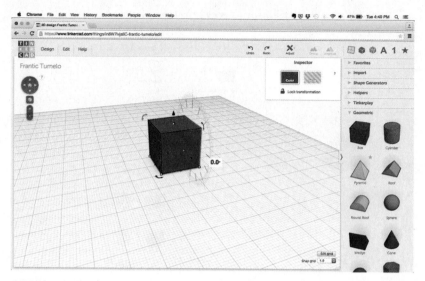

FIGURE 10.10 Rotating around the X-axis.

Now, let's get back to the plain box sitting on the workplane. You're going to use it to create a very unique building for your futuristic city by rotating the cube so it's actually "standing" on a corner.

To do this, you start by rotating the Box object on the Y-axis 45 degrees. Figure 10.11 shows what this rotation looks like.

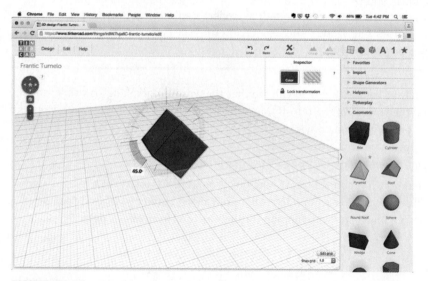

FIGURE 10.11 Rotate on the Y-axis to get halfway to the final object.

Before continuing, rotate the view a little to the left or right, and you'll notice that the rotation of the Box object sends a small portion of the box "below" the workplane (see Figure 10.12). The workplane surface isn't solid, and you saw in Chapter 9 that you can use the small black cone that appears above a selected object to raise and lower it. If you lower an object too far, it dips beneath the workplane.

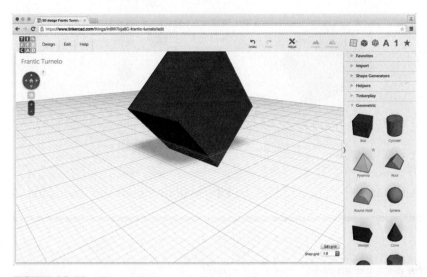

FIGURE 10.12 Sometimes rotating an object moves a portion of the object beneath the workplane.

This isn't a big deal. Any part of a 3D model that appears beneath the workplane still exists. It's not deleted. But if it bothers you visually, all you need to do is select the box, click on the black cone, and raise it up until the measurement indicates a value of 0.0, as shown in Figure 10.13.

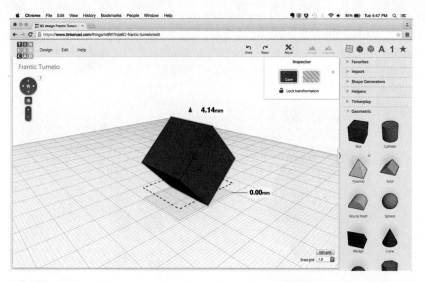

FIGURE 10.13 Raise an object up until it's no longer underneath the workplane.

NOTE

Determining the distance an object has been raised

You may have noticed the other number up near the black cone. That's a measurement of how far the object was raised. In the case of the box, Figure 10.13 shows that value as 4.14mm.

With the box raised up above the workplane, you may have noticed another problem with the object: One of its edges is now touching the workplane. To create the new object, you want the object to only be touching the workplane at a single point—where three edges touch. That means you need one more rotation.

You already rotated on the Y-axis, so now it's time to rotate on the X-axis. As shown in Figure 10.14, move the mouse pointer over the rotation control that corresponds to the rotation meter that will be centered on an imaginary line running through the left and right sides of the object.

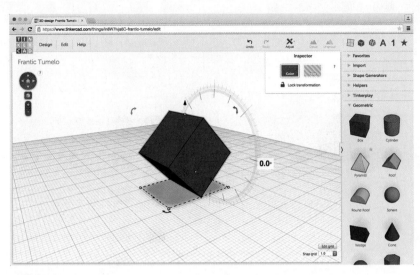

FIGURE 10.14   Preparing to rotate on the X-axis.

To make the new object, you need another rotation on the X-axis—about 30 degrees—as shown in Figure 10.15.

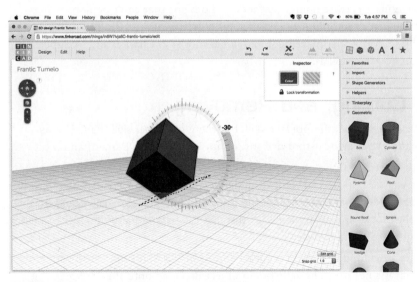

FIGURE 10.15   A final 30-degree rotation.

After this last rotation, however, a portion of the object is once again beneath the work-plane. Just click on the black cone and move the mouse up slightly, and you end up with a box that's been rotated so it's balancing on a single point, as shown in Figure 10.16.

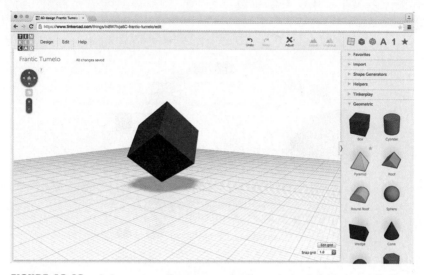

FIGURE 10.16   A box standing on a single point, defying gravity!

Rotating objects is one of those skills you'll have to practice and develop over time. Eventually, it does get easier. Being able to properly rotate objects will allow you to merge rotated objects together to create unique surfaces and designs that can't be done using the basic shapes you just drop on the workplane. (As a matter of fact, you'll see an example of rotating objects for proper placement in a larger model in Chapter 11, "A Super Project to Test Out Your New Skills.")

Deleting, Cutting, and Removing

Being able to rotate objects is an important skill, but there's another skill that's just as important for creating your own custom designs: removing (deleting) parts of an object.

When you want to create windows and doorways in buildings, for example, you need to make holes in the walls. Suppose you want to design a pyramid for a Minecraft world, but you'd like a passage added that cuts through the front and out the back. You could do this by just "mining" the blocks and creating a path through the pyramid after it's been added to your world...but there's a faster way.

Figure 10.17 shows a pyramid you might want to import into a Minecraft world with MCEdit. Notice that it's not just a basic Pyramid object dropped onto the workplane—it's got some additional features, which you add by using the black cone, rotation controls, and the Group function.

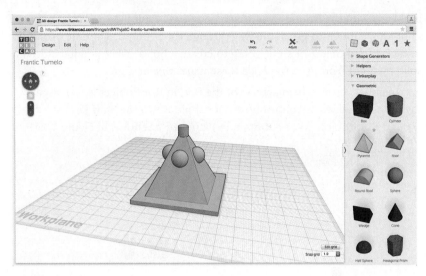

FIGURE 10.17 A solid futuristic pyramid.

It would be nice to have a pathway cut into the pyramid that runs from the front to the back—a semi-circular tunnel shape would be perfect. But you might have noticed that Tinkercad doesn't have a tool that lets you "cut" or "mine" out parts of an object that you don't like. So how can you create a semi-circular tunnel through the pyramid? It starts by creating the shape of the path you want to create.

As shown in Figure 10.18, drop a Round Roof object on the workplane.

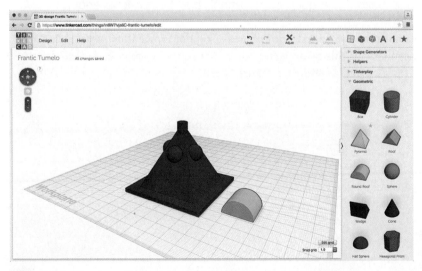

FIGURE 10.18 The Round Roof object has the basic shape needed for the tunnel.

There are a few problems with the Round Roof object, however. First, it's too large in diameter. Second, it's not long enough to go all the way through the pyramid. Third, it's solid. If you merge it with the Pyramid object, it's not going to create a hole; rather, it'll just add its solid self to the solid pyramid. You need to tackle these issues one at a time.

The first problem, remember, is that the diameter of the Round Roof object is too large. This is easy to fix with the small white control boxes. Just hold down the Shift key as you shrink down the Round Roof object to about 6mm in diameter, as shown in Figure 10.19.

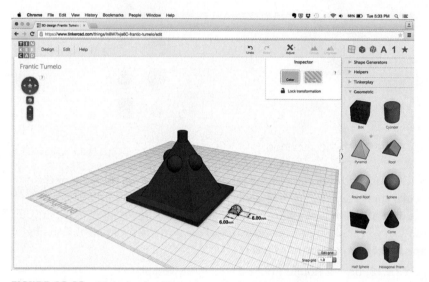

FIGURE 10.19 This looks like a good-sized tunnel, but it's not long enough.

The second problem is that the Round Roof object is still not long enough to run through the pyramid. You can change this by dragging one of the corner white control boxes to create a long Round Roof object, as shown in Figure 10.20.

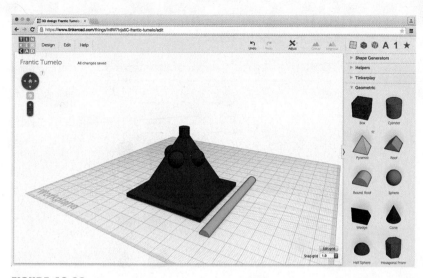

FIGURE 10.20   Lengthening the Round Roof object so it's longer than the pyramid.

Notice in Figure 10.20 that the pyramid sits on a square base that has a little bit of height to it. To create the tunnel through the pyramid, select the Round Roof object, raise it up with the black cone, and then drag it so it merges with the pyramid, above the square base, as shown in Figure 10.21.

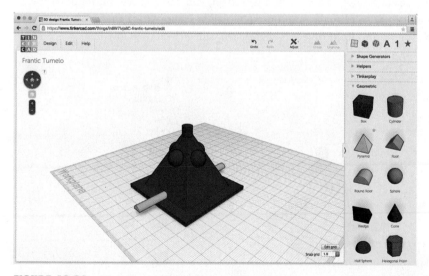

FIGURE 10.21   The Round Roof cuts through the pyramid completely.

Although the Round Roof object goes into the front of the pyramid and exits out the back, it's still solid but should be a hole. So it's time to solve the third problem: You need to turn the Round Roof object into a hole, and to do that you select only the Round Roof object and click on the Hole button, shown in Figure 10.22.

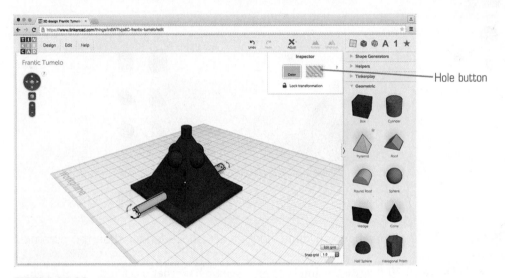

FIGURE 10.22 The Hole button turns an object into a hole.

The Hole button turns any selected object (or objects) into "negative" space—or a Hole object. When you select an object and click this button, you can still see the shape of the object, but you erase any solid space you touch. Notice in Figure 10.22 that after you click the Hole button, the Round Roof object is slightly translucent—almost invisible.

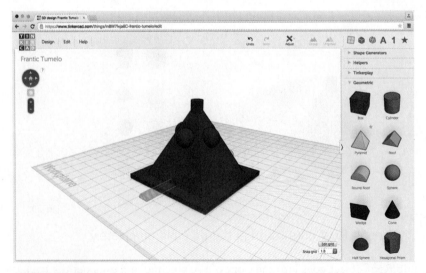

FIGURE 10.23 An object converted into a Hole object is almost invisible.

Recall from Chapter 9 that using the Group feature allows you to merge two or more selected objects. Group basically joins the objects and makes them behave as a single object.

Well, when you click on a solid object and a Hole object and then click the Group button, the Hole object removes any portion of the solid object that it touches. Figure 10.24 shows what happens after you select the (solid) Pyramid and the (Hole) Round Roof object.

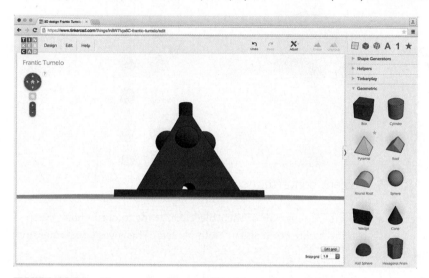

FIGURE 10.24 Group the Round Roof and Pyramid objects.

You now have a tunnel through the pyramid!

You can do a lot with the Hole button, and it's an essential tool for creating more advanced 3D models. For example, one of the most basic uses for the Hole button is cutting objects in half. One way to do this is to drop a Box object on the workplane, enlarge it so it's bigger than the object you wish to cut in half, and then convert the Box to a hole object.

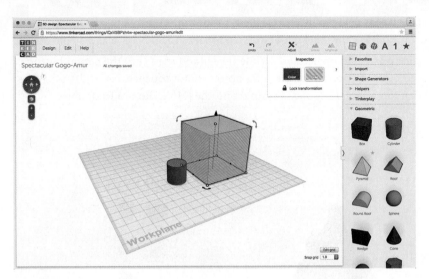

FIGURE 10.25 A big Box object converted to a Hole object.

Next, you drag the box so it overlaps only half of the object you want to cut in half. (Keep in mind that you can also use the rotate controls on Hole objects. This gives you some very interesting editing abilities.)

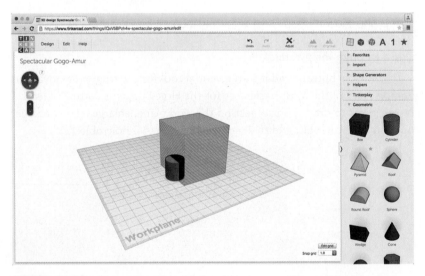

FIGURE 10.26 Drag the Box Hole object over the solid object.

You know the rest: Select the two objects (solid and Hole) and group them. What is left over is half of the original solid object, as shown in Figure 10.27.

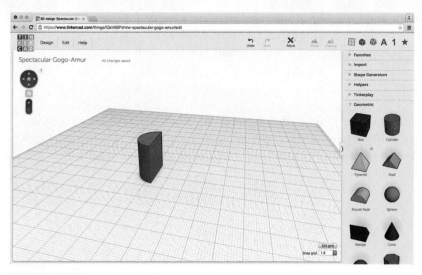

FIGURE 10.27   Half of a Cylinder object.

NOTE

Often more than one way to create an object

You could also create a half Cylinder object by dragging a Round Roof object onto the workplane and then rotating it on the X-axis. Try it to prove that it works.

As mentioned in Chapter 9, Tinkercad has enough features and tools to fill a book. I don't have the space in this book to show you every little tool, feature, and trick that's available. But you already know how to do a lot of things in Tinkercad:

- Place and move objects around on the workplane
- Resize objects
- Merge and group objects
- Rotate objects around three axes (X, Y, and Z)
- Convert objects into Hole objects
- Rename objects and share them or keep them private
- Export objects for use in Minecraft

This is plenty to get you started making your own custom objects. However, in Chapter 11 you'll learn a few more ways to use Tinkercad that you might not have considered. What you'll learn there involves importing preexisting 3D models (from sites like Thingiverse.com) and merging them with objects you create using the basic Tinkercad categories, such as

Geometric, Numbers, and Letter. By combining objects, copying and rotating some, adding hollow areas (using the Hole button), and resizing, you'll be able to create some of the strangest, craziest, and most useful objects imaginable in a Minecraft world.

Up Next...

You've learned quite a number of skills when it comes to Tinkercad, and it's time to start putting them together to create your own designs. Up next in Chapter 11, you'll get a look at a few final Tinkercad tools as well as see how to add a fun glass dome to the futuristic city you created in Chapter 9.

11

A Super Project To Test Out Your New Skills

What You'll Be Doing

- Watch as Coolcrafter10 gets an invitation at the ocean
- Inventory your Tinkercad skills and tools
- Learn all about custom objects found in the Shape Generator
- Line objects up with the Align tool
- Cover your futuristic city with glass domes

Coolcrafter10 sat on the cliff's edge with Didgee, PackRat, and Prism and watched the sun dip beneath the horizon. It had been a full day of exploration, and the four friends had come up with many ideas for how to expand their new city.

"I think using some track and adding a rail system that goes all around the city would be useful," said PackRat. "That way we could get from place to place quickly, without having to run."

Prism nodded and pointed at a constellation that had appeared overhead. "Is that the Big Crafter?"

"Yep," said Didgee as she pointed to another constellation to the left. "And there's the Little Crafter."

Coolcrafter10 stared up at the stars and then down at the city floating in the middle of the ocean. Over the past few days, he had learned more about creating and crafting than he'd picked up in three months before that. A few months ago, Coolcrafter10 would have been building a castle or statue block-by-block, and it would have taken weeks or months to complete some of his big plans. He smiled at Didgee. "You know, if you hadn't come walking by my field that day, we would have never met, and I would never have known about any of these great tools you've shown me."

Didgee shook her head. "I doubt it. The secret about Minecraft and the worlds we visit is how fast information travels. I show you, you show your neighbor, and your neighbor shows someone else. And so on and so on. What you've learned today might have just taken a bit longer to reach you."

"She's right," said Prism. "Since Didgee left on her last exploration, I've shown about a dozen neighbors and visitors how to use MCEdit and Tinkercad, and these are people who have their own neighbors and friends in other worlds. They'll spread the news, and many more crafters will gain the knowledge to do what we do."

Didgee nodded in PackRat's direction. "Would you believe that PackRat didn't even know how to use a crafting table a few weeks ago?"

PackRat's face turned red. "Didgee!"

"I'm not making fun of you. We all started out knowing very little about Minecraft. I'm just saying that we are all capable of learning new skills really fast," said Didgee. "You've gone from a newbie crafter who couldn't use a crafting table to creating 3D models of the amazing sculptures you've imported with MCEdit!"

PackRat grinned. "That's true. I could never have imagined I'd be building these huge structures in such a short time."

"And now Coolcrafter10 here has learned how to do this stuff and can help spread the word when he heads back to his home," said Didgee.

Coolcrafter10 thought about returning home soon. His little corner of the world was ready for whatever he could create and add to it, with plenty of flat areas and hills and even a nearby lake. But as he thought about leaving Didgee and the others, he grew sad.

Prism looked at Coolcrafter10 and shook her head. "I don't think he likes the idea of heading home."

"I don't," said Coolcrafter10. "I've had so much fun with all of you that the idea of returning to my big empty castle isn't very appealing."

"Then don't go back," said PackRat. "Look around you. Look at that brand-new city floating over the ocean. Do we look like we don't have room for you to join us?"

Didgee laughed. "I'm sorry, Cool. I had no idea. I figured you'd want to go back to your own castle, but I guess it would be pretty lonely. I'm with PackRat...Don't go. Stay with us!"

Prism nodded. "Yes, please do!"

"Are you serious?" asked Coolcrafter10. "You've only known me for a short while."

"It's already a done deal," said Didgee. "You're staying. And since you already have the skills that we're all using, you'll be a valuable addition to the team. And with that city over there, we'll probably meet some new crafters who will want to stick around and explore and learn and try to find new ways to do things."

Coolcrafter10 looked up at the stars and smiled. "The skills are great, but add that to having three new friends, and I just don't know what to say right now."

"Say you'll stay, dude," said PackRat.

"Yes, please stay," said Prism.

Didgee smiled and nodded. "Just nod and say okay."

"Okay," said Coolcrafter10 with a nod.

The three friends clapped and patted him on the back, and everyone smiled and laughed as they slowly turned their attention back to the water. Far out across the water, they could see the light from a lighthouse. Someone out there was providing a light for explorers visiting a different shoreline.

"I'm going to find out who that is," said Didgee. "I'll be leaving again in a few days. Want to come with me, Cool?"

Coolcrafter10 nodded. "Sure. Do you know how long we'll be gone?"

"A few days or so. We'll visit and see if the lighthouse owner has anything we can learn, and we'll share what we've learned. Then we'll come back and see if Prism and PackRat have anything new to share."

"You know we will," said Prism. "As a matter of fact, now that I've figured out this rotation thing in Tinkercad, I've got a few new ideas to test out." Prism opened up her laptop but then looked at her friends and closed the lid. "It can wait until tomorrow, though."

Coolcrafter10 pointed up in the sky. "Hey, that's Builder's Belt!"

The stars twinkled a bit brighter in the sky, and the four friends talked all night about their plans.

You've Got Skills!

You've picked up quite a few new skills in Tinkercad. By now, you should be getting quite comfortable dragging and dropping shapes, rotating and merging, shrinking and enlarging, and creating holes through solids. You use these basic skills to turn take simple objects (such as boxes and spheres) into more complex objects.

But don't forget that Tinkercad and other CAD applications allow you to import objects created by other people. And you can shrink, stretch, rotate, and group together those imported objects with other objects. I hope you're beginning to understand that you have most of the skills you need to create some incredible 3D models for importing into your Minecraft worlds. But there are still a few more secrets I need to reveal.

In this chapter, I show you a few more features that Tinkercad offers when it comes to creating 3D models for your Minecraft worlds. Once you've finished this chapter, you will have learned the skills that are most useful and popular, but there's plenty more to learn about Tinkercad. It's up to you to dig a little deeper to discover the rest of Tinkercad. And keep in mind that the Tinkercad team is always working to add new features and tools, so there's always going to be something new to learn.

So, let's jump right to it and take a look at two additional features that you'll want to try out: Shape Generator and Align. The Shape Generator lets you take pre-created shapes (made by the Tinkercad community) and fine-tune them with a control window. The Align feature lets you center objects around either a shared axis or an edge.

The Shape Generator

You can find the Shape Generators tab on the right side of the Tinkercad screen, just below the Import tab. When you open it, by clicking on the small triangle to the left of its name, it looks as shown in Figure 11.1.

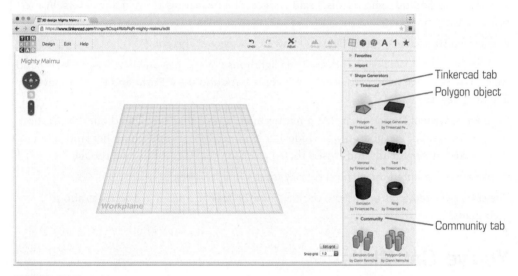

FIGURE 11.1 The Shape Generator is full of useful (and customizable) objects.

Inside the Shape Generators tab are three subtabs, labeled Tinkercad, Community, and Your Shape Generators. The Tinkercad tab currently offers six objects that you can customize by using a control window.

As an example, in Figure 11.2 I've dragged a Polygon object onto the workspace. You can see a control window to the right of the object.

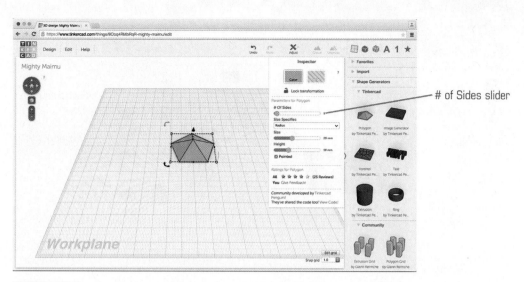

# of Sides slider

FIGURE 11.2 A control window lets you modify a Shape Generator object.

In Figure 11.2, the Polygon has five sides, but in Figure 11.3 you can see that I've increased the number of sides to eight by using the # of Sides slider. If I want to shrink or enlarge the object, I can either use the white control squares or move the Size and Height sliders in the control window.

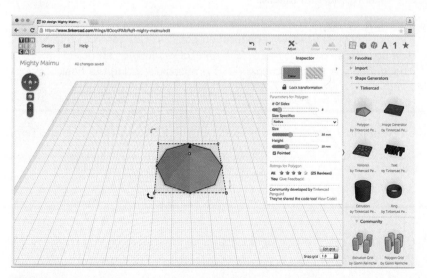

FIGURE 11.3 Modify the object by making changes in the control window.

Objects in the Shape Generators tab don't all have the same configuration settings in their respective control windows. For example, Figure 11.4 shows what the window looks like for a Text object.

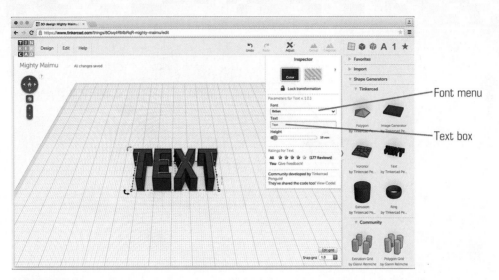

FIGURE 11.4 The Text object's control window has a completely different set of options.

NOTE

Custom objects behave like normal objects

Shape Generator objects behave like any other objects you create in Minecraft, and they aren't limited to the control window configuration options. You can rotate them, turn them into Hole objects, and much more. The control window for an object typically offers up options that are difficult to change (or impossible) using the basic Tinkercad tools.

After dropping the Text object, I can change the text to anything I like by clicking in the Text box and typing in different text. Figure 11.5 shows that I've changed it to my first name, modified the font with the Font drop-down menu, and decreased the height a bit.

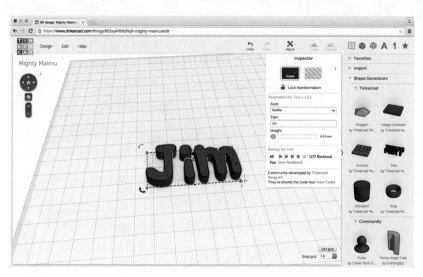

FIGURE 11.5 You can change the font and the text easily on a Text object.

The Text and Polygon objects you've seen so far in this chapter are available on the Shape Generators tab under the Tinkercad tab, but you aren't limited to the options on this tab. Dozens and dozens of other objects have been created by the community of Tinkercad users and made available for your use. You find them logically enough on the Community tab.

NOTE

Custom shapes require more learning

You can create your own custom shapes and submit them for inclusion in the Community tab, but keep in mind that creating custom shapes requires some programming skills that are beyond what I can cover in this book. To begin creating a custom shape, scroll down below the Community tab and click on the New Shape Generator button on the Your Shape Generator tab and read the simple instructions provided there. For more help on creating your own custom shapes, check out the following site: https://api.tinkercad.com.

The Community tab displays eight custom objects at a time. To view more, you can move forward or backward through the library by clicking on the small arrows at the bottom right in Figure 11.6. You can also click on a number in the bottom right of the screen to jump to a particular page. In Figure 11.6, you can see that I'm on page 12 because the 12 is darker gray than the other page numbers.

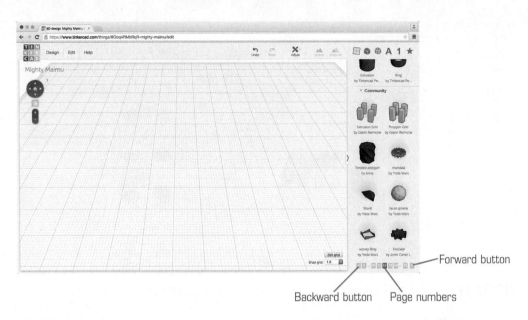

———Forward button

———Backward button   Page numbers

FIGURE 11.6 Scroll through the community objects to see what's available.

If you've ever been to a popular tourist attraction in Florida, you may recognize the shape I've dropped onto the workplane in Figure 11.7. It's a custom object, and the only thing I can change about it in the control window is the radius.

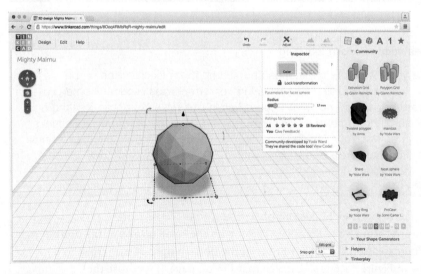

FIGURE 11.7 The Facet Sphere object has been added to the workplane.

I like a lot of the shapes I'm seeing on the Community tab. Once again, a futuristic city is beginning to take shape, as you can see in Figure 11.8.

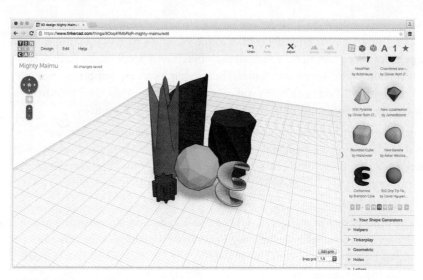

FIGURE 11.8 Another futuristic city consisting of custom shapes.

Each of these objects has a control window with unique configuration options. The most complex control window is for the ProGear object, shown in Figure 11.9. Look at all the configuration options!

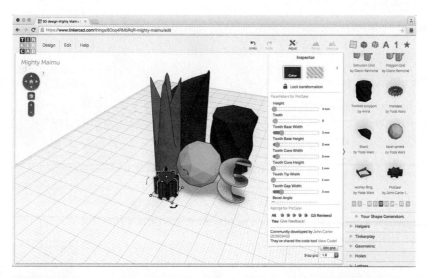

FIGURE 11.9 The ProGear object has a lot of settings that can be modified.

The Shape Generators tab is a fun tool to use. You can make all kinds of crazy shapes and designs with the objects it holds. You can then combine your special objects with basic objects (such as a Box object or a Sphere object) to make larger and more diverse 3D models.

I'm quite happy with my new little city, but before I move on to the next Tinkercad tool, I'd like to point out something for your consideration. Notice in Figure 11.8 that all the various shapes have unique colors. You can easily select all the objects and group them so they can be resized together (making them larger or smaller), but anytime you are importing multiple objects into Minecraft with MCEdit, one thing you might want to think about is whether or not you intend to change the materials of your imported objects to other materials.

For example, if you import a red sphere with MCEdit, that sphere will be pulled in and assigned a material that is close to its original color. When I imported just a red sphere with MCEdit, the sphere ended up being made of brick block. Remember that you can select an object (or multiple objects) in MCEdit and use the Fill and Replace button to change one material to another.

If I were to group the objects shown in Figure 11.8, they would end up all consisting of the same material in Minecraft. This might not be a big deal in some cases, but for this city, I'd like each building to be a unique material. This will not only provide a nice colorful city to explore but will also make it easier to select a single building and change its material if I wish to do so.

Knowing how to carefully select the colors of imported objects is going to be important later in this chapter, when I import this city into a Minecraft world. But before I show you why this will be important, let me show you one final tool that can be helpful for making sure objects line up or stack symmetrically.

NOTE

Get in the habit of saving your work

I'll return to the futuristic city in Figure 11.8 shortly, so be sure to save it if you are following along with my instructions and then create a new project before you try out what I show in the next section.

The Align Tool

Take a look at the two objects in Figure 11.10. I've placed a Box object (flattened a bit) and a Pyramid object on the workplane.

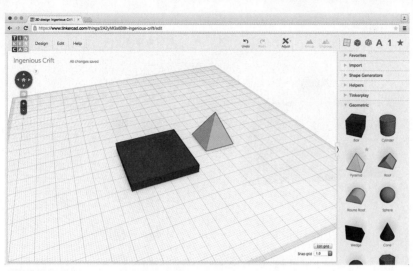

FIGURE 11.10 Two objects with different shapes.

I'd like to stack the pyramid on top of the box object and center it so there's an equal amount of space on the left and right sides as well as the front and back. In Figure 11.11 you can see that I've raised up the pyramid a bit and dragged it onto the box.

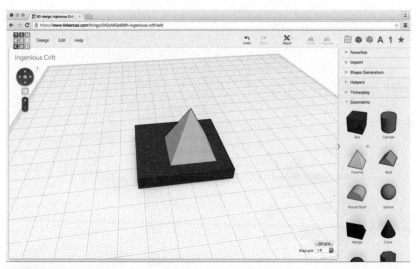

FIGURE 11.11 The objects are stacked but not centered.

There's a bit more space to the left of the pyramid than there is on the right. Also, the pyramid is a bit closer to the front edge of the box than it is to the back. The workplane is gridded, so I can use the grid lines and the mouse to move the pyramid until an equal number of grid squares are on the left and right (and in the front and the back), as shown in Figure 11.12.

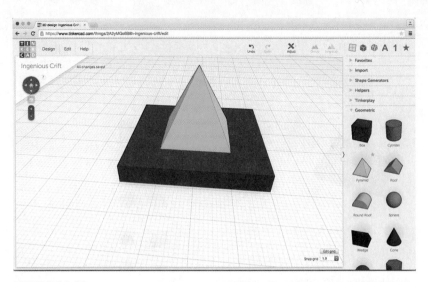

FIGURE 11.12   Use the grid lines to center an object visually.

Using the grid lines to center two or more objects, however, won't always work, and it can be a bit frustrating to count grid lines and try to drag objects carefully. Of course there's a better way.

In Figure 11.13, you can see that I've dragged the pyramid to the front-right corner of the box so you can easily see that the two objects are not even close to being centered with each other.

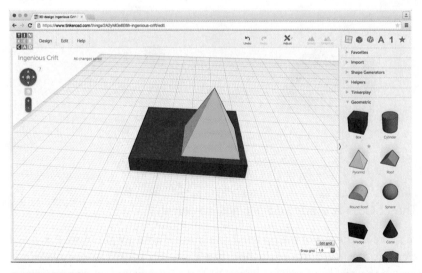

FIGURE 11.13   The pyramid is not perfectly centered on the box.

Tinkercad makes it easy to center objects left to right and also to center objects front to back. And it lets you easily do both. Also, it helps you align objects so they share an edge. Let's take a look at how to do all of these operations.

First, I'll walk you through how to center these two objects left to right. To do this, you must select all the objects you wish to center left to right. After selecting the box and pyramid, click on the Adjust menu shown in Figure 11.14 and select the Align option.

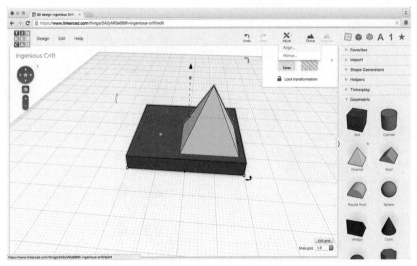

FIGURE 11.14 Use the Adjust menu and choose Align.

After you choose the Align option, a bunch of dots appear around the objects, as shown in Figure 11.15.

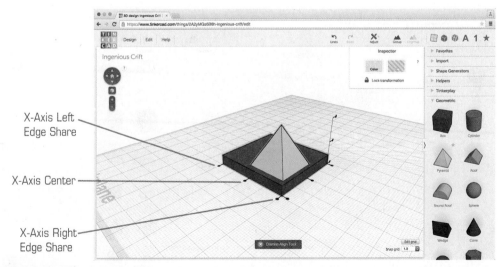

FIGURE 11.15 These alignment dots are extremely helpful tools.

These are alignment dots, and you can see that there are nine of them in all. Three dots are used for the X-axis, three for the Y-axis, and three for the Z-axis.

Centering left to right corresponds to the X-axis, so you need to use the three dots that run along the front of the object. If you click on the X-Axis Left Edge Share dot, both the pyramid and box will share the leftmost edge, as shown in Figure 11.16. You even see the word "Aligned" on the workplane so you know that the action is done.

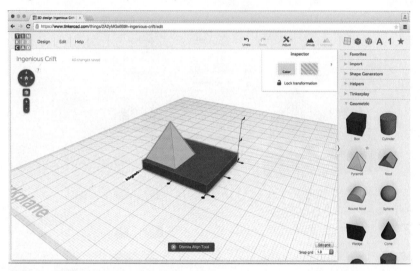

FIGURE 11.16 Aligning the two objects along the left edge.

Likewise, you can click on the X-Axis Right Edge Share dot to align the two objects along the right edge, as shown in Figure 11.17.

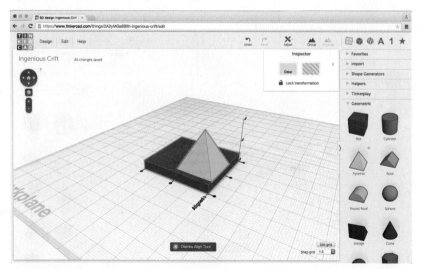

FIGURE 11.17 The two objects are now aligned along the right edge.

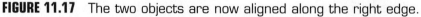

To center left to right, click on the X-Axis Center dot, and Tinkercad centers the pyramid on the box, from left to right, as shown in Figure 11.18.

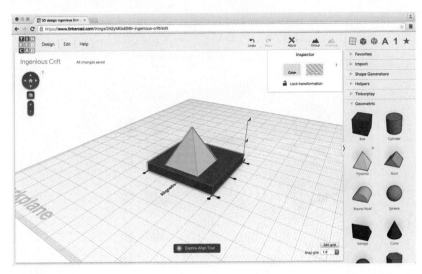

FIGURE 11.18 The pyramid is centered left-to-right on the box.

Now that the pyramid is centered on the box from left to right, what about front-to-back? You just click on the Y-axis dots to align on the front edge, back edge, or centered. Figure 11.19 shows when happens when you use the Y-Axis Center dot to center the pyramid on the box front-to-back.

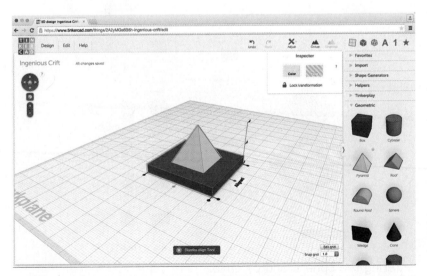

FIGURE 11.19 The pyramid is completely centered on the top of the box.

Just for fun and to see how the Align tool can be used, take a look at Figure 11.20, where I'm trying to "balance" a sphere on top of the pyramid.

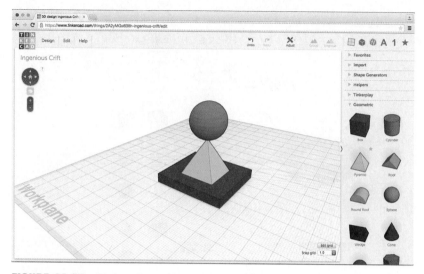

FIGURE 11.20 Balancing a sphere on top of a pyramid.

It looks centered, but the only way to be certain is to use the Align tool. To do this, select only the pyramid and the sphere and then click on the Adjust menu and select Align. Once again, you get the alignment dots, as shown in Figure 11.21.

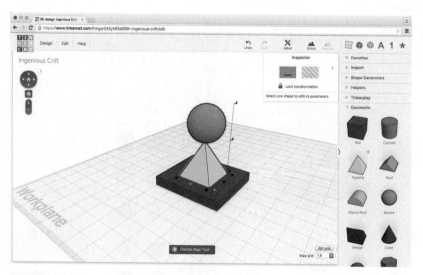

FIGURE 11.21 Centering the sphere and pyramid.

Then click on the X-Axis Center dot and the Y-Axis Center dot, and you end up with the sphere perfectly balancing on the sharp tip of the pyramid.

Although you haven't yet seen the Z-axis alignment dots in action, you can probably figure out how to use them. If you need two or more objects to share their bottom or top edges, you click on the Z-Axis Top dot or the Z-Axis Bottom dot. The Z-Axis Center dot simply matches up two or more objects so they are perfectly centered from top to bottom. Using a combination of the X-Axis Center, Y-Axis Center, and Z-Axis Center dots, you can center a sphere inside a box, as shown in Figure 11.22.

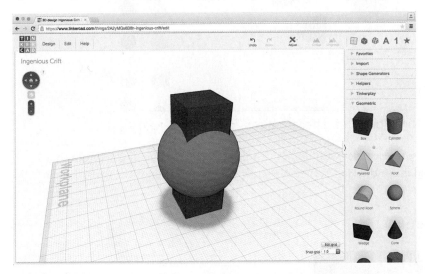

FIGURE 11.22 Centering two objects around all three axes.

Dome Cities

Now it's time to return to that futuristic city I teased you with back in Figure 11.8. Recently I watched an old science fiction movie where a bunch of cities were covered by clear domes with walkways and tunnels that allowed movement between cities. Such a setup might be fun to create using all the various Tinkercad skills you've learned so far.

To start, make a bunch of copies of the city, as shown in Figure 11.23. You might want to shrink one and enlarge one so you have three different sizes as shown here.

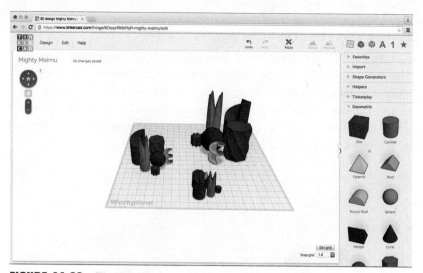

FIGURE 11.23   Three cities of different sizes.

The plan is to cover these cities with domes. Domes are hollow, but all you've got to do to make one solid is use the Half Sphere object, shown dropped onto the workplane in Figure 11.24.

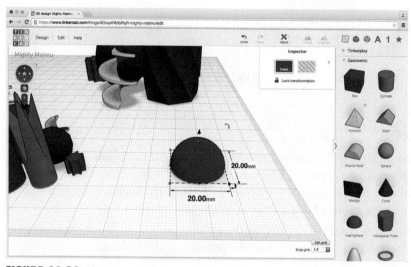

FIGURE 11.24   This Half Sphere object is solid, not hollow.

You need the domes to be extremely thin. This dome is 20mm in diameter and is solid. Making it 1mm thick (or 1 block in Minecraft) means hollowing it out so it has a 1mm thick shell. To do this, you need to create a copy of the dome and reduce it in size to 19mm. By holding down the Shift key while reducing the size, you can keep the perfect half-sphere shape, as shown in Figure 11.25.

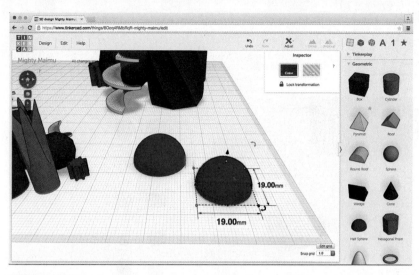

FIGURE 11.25   Create a half sphere that is 1mm smaller in diameter than the first one.

The next step is to make the 19mm diameter half sphere a Hole object, so select the 19mm half sphere and click the Hole button. You're left with the "invisible" version shown in Figure 11.26.

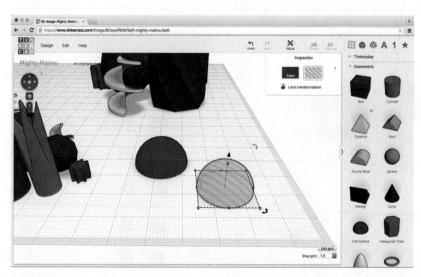

FIGURE 11.26   A Hole object is created with the 19mm half sphere.

I'm hoping you can see why the Align tool you learned about in the previous section is so useful. Here, you'll be using it to "stack" the solid half sphere on top of the Hole object half sphere and centering them on the X-axis and Y-axis. First, you merge them. In Figure

11.27 I've left a little of the Hole object visible so you can see that it's "underneath" the solid version.

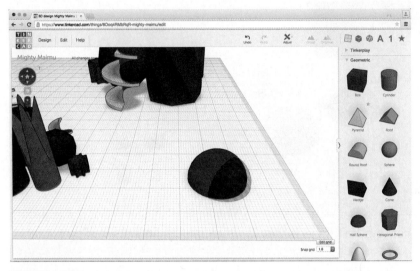

FIGURE 11.27 Merge the solid half sphere and Hole object half sphere.

Then select both objects, click on the Adjust menu, and select Align. Next, click on the X-Axis Center dot and the Y-Axis Center dot. With the Hole object centered, it's no longer visible in Figure 11.28.

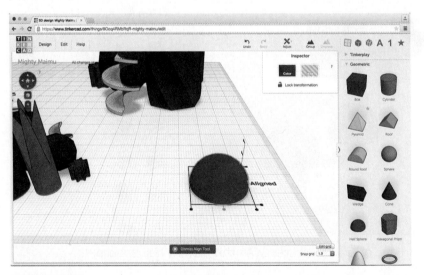

FIGURE 11.28 Align both objects on the X-axis and Y-axis.

Now group the two objects by using the Group button. Just by looking at the object, you can't tell that the grouping is successful, but if you change the view by going "underneath" the workplane, you can see that the 20mm half sphere is indeed hollow, as shown in Figure 11.29.

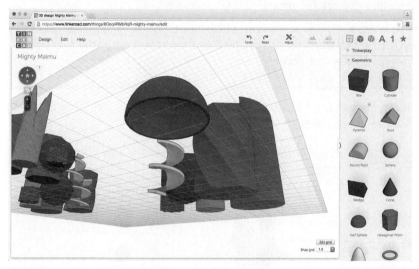

FIGURE 11.29 The half sphere is now hollow.

You need to make three copies of this sphere (and change their sizes so they'll fit over the three cities), but before you do that, you need to change the color of the half sphere to white, as shown in Figure 11.30. As mentioned earlier, choosing the color you want now will make it easier later, in MCEdit, to select only the Dome objects because they will be made of different materials than the cities. (Just make sure you don't have any white buildings.)

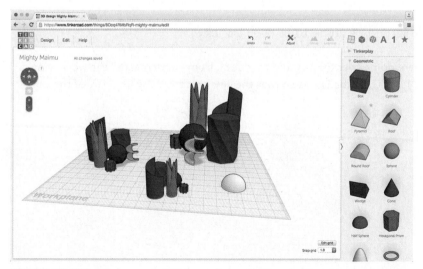

FIGURE 11.30 Change the color of the hollow half sphere to white.

NOTE

Provide space between objects for proper dome placement

You might need to select each city and drag it out a bit so you can fit a dome over each one of them. Start with the smallest city first and then drag the other two cities further away if they touch the first dome.

You need to hold down Shift as you increase the size of the hollow half sphere so it'll fit over the smallest city. You can see this in Figure 11.31.

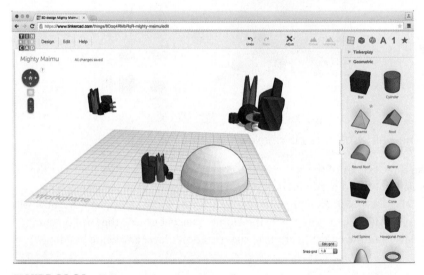

FIGURE 11.31   Enlarge the dome to fit over the city.

Drag the half sphere dome over the city and then look from "underneath" the workplane, as shown in Figure 11.32. Drag the Dome so that the city isn't touching any part of the dome.

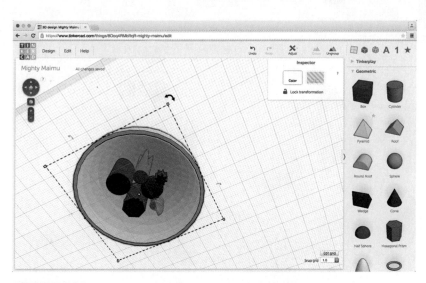

FIGURE 11.32   Move the dome over the buildings.

NOTE

Don't forget to group the city objects first

You might be wondering if you can use the Align tool to center the dome directly over the city. You can, but only if the city is grouped (and thus the same color). If the city isn't grouped, when you align along the X-axis and Y-axis, all the various (ungrouped) buildings will be centered, too...causing them to all merge together and form one very strange-looking object. Try it if you need confirmation and then use the Undo button to return your city to its original layout.

Make two copies of the dome and enlarge them and place them over the remaining two cities. Once the domes are in place, you can select a city/dome pair and drag them so all three cities are close together (but not touching), as shown in Figure 11.33.

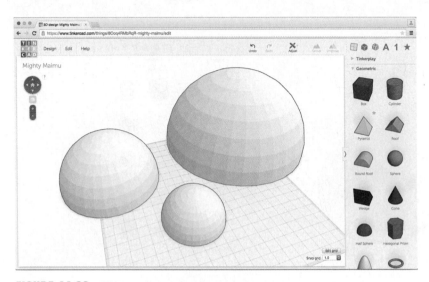

FIGURE 11.33 Three domed cities.

You can click the Design menu and choose Download for Minecraft to export your domed cities, but first you might consider adding some tunnels or walkways so you can travel from one dome to another without going outside the protection of the city domes. This isn't difficult to do: Simply create three rectangular Box objects, make them hollow (shrink down a copy of the tunnel, make it a Hole object, and center it around all three axes inside the larger Box object before using the Group button), make them white, and then use the Black Cone and Rotate controls to place them so one Box object connects two domes. Figure 11.34 shows such walkways added.

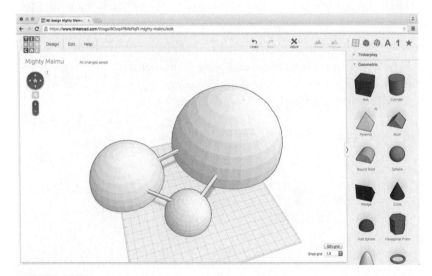

FIGURE 11.34 Add walkways to allow travel between domes.

With the cities and domes created, all that's left is to import them into a Minecraft world with MCEdit. You'll need a very large piece of flat (or semi-flat) terrain to place the domes and cities, but if you don't have that, you can always use MCEdit to clear away a nice plot of land. Take a look at Figure 11.35, where you can see that I've dropped the three domes into one of my worlds.

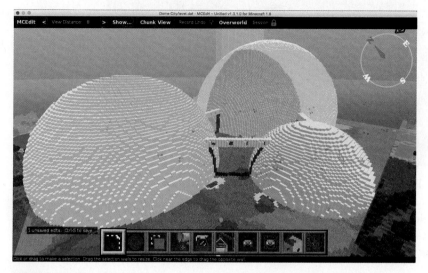

FIGURE 11.35 The domed cities are placed with MCEdit.

You could stop here, but the domes are solid, so they won't let any sunlight or starlight in. You probably want to change that!

To start, you need to find out what material the white domes are made from. To do that, you can simply select a small bit of a dome (click on the Select button on the far left if it's not already chosen). Click the Analyze button on the small window that appears on the left side of the screen, shown in Figure 11.36. An Analyze window appears in the center of the screen—here you can see that a bunch of air blocks and a bunch of quartz blocks are selected, so you know the domes are made of quartz!

FIGURE 11.36 Find out what material makes up the domes.

Next, use the Select tool again but this time select all three domes, as well as the walkways, as shown in Figure 11.37. Use the WASD keys to confirm that the selection box goes around all three domes.

FIGURE 11.37 Select all three domes.

Next, click on the Fill and Replace tool (fourth from the left), and the Fill With window appears on the left, as shown in Figure 11.38. Click on the Replace button.

FIGURE 11.38 Choose the Fill and Replace tool.

After clicking the Replace button, you get two options in the Fill With window: one is the material to search for and the other is the material to use instead of what's already there. Start with the material to be replaced: Double-click on the Stone material in the Fill With window and type Quartz in the Search window in the center of the screen (see Figure 11.39).

FIGURE 11.39 The Fill and Replace window lets you search for materials.

Click the OK button, and the quartz block appears in the Fill With window. Next, click on the material that appears in the Replace With section (the air block is the default), search for Glass in the Search window in the center of the screen (see Figure 11.40), and click the OK button.

FIGURE 11.40   Choose the material that will replace the quartz block.

Confirm your selections and click the yellow Replace button, as shown in Figure 11.41.

FIGURE 11.41   Click the Replace button to start the replacement process.

If your selections are accurate, you'll end up with semi-transparent domes, as shown in Figure 11.42. But what will this look like inside an actual Minecraft world? To find out, save your changes, exit MCEdit, and open up the world in Minecraft.

FIGURE 11.42 The quartz blocks have been replaced with glass blocks.

Figure 11.43 shows the final results. You can see the cities through the clear domes!

FIGURE 11.43 Clear domes with cities tucked inside.

Of course, here you're looking from outside the domes. You'll need to break the glass to get inside and then seal up the hole. (Instead, you could move into a dome while you're in MCEdit, and after you save the edit, you'll find yourself inside the dome when you open up and play in the world.)

The creation of the domes and the cities inside may seem like a lot of work in Tinkercad, but consider for a moment how long it would take you to build those buildings and then construct the domes over them (and glass is fragile!) using block-by-block assembly inside Minecraft!

CAD applications such as Tinkercad are a secret Minecraft weapon. With them, you can make your ideas reality much more quickly and easily than you can by using the block-by-block building technique that most Minecraft users think they're stuck with. And this means less time building and more time exploring and enjoying your creations.

Up Next...

You've finished up learning the most popular and useful Tinkercad tools and skills, but MCEdit has some additional features that you're going to want to learn before you're done with the book. In the next (and final) chapter, I'm going to show you a few final tricks that MCEDit offers to Minecraft engineers looking to push their building skills even further.

12

Discover More MCEdit Tools

What You'll Be Doing

- Learn the Copy and Paste commands
- Make a mirror image of an object
- Use the Clone tool for precise copy placements

MCEdit Mastery

As you've discovered in the previous chapters, MCEdit is a tool that Minecraft engineers can rely on when it comes to creating some truly out-of-this-world...uh...worlds. From importing and placing models that you've found online (from sites such as Thingiverse.com) to landscaping the perfect little corner of a world and preparing it for a maze or castle or a giant statue of yourself, MCEdit can take you from idea to final creation much faster than the traditional block-by-block building method.

Throughout the book, you've seen a number of projects that have used MCEdit, and hopefully you've gotten plenty of practice using this amazing tool. You may be so fast at using MCEdit, however, that you might have overlooked a few of the useful tools it offers. This chapter finishes up the book by looking at a few more uses for MCEdit that you'll hopefully find helpful with your future Minecraft projects.

Keep in mind that MCEdit is constantly being updated. I've used MCEdit 1.0 for all the projects in this book, but MCEdit 2.0 is in development. Once that version is released as an official version, you'll want to install it and test all the features you already know from 1.0 as well as take a look at what new features it brings to the table.

For now, however, let's take a look together at a few more ways that MCEdit can assist you when it comes to engineering your perfect world.

NOTE

MCEdit 2.0 information

You can read more details about MCEdit 2.0 and even test the early version by visiting the official website, at http://www.mcedit.net.

Copy and Paste

Did you just drop a nice big tyrannosaurus rex in your world? I did, and you can see it trying to find a way into the domed cities in Figure 12.1.

FIGURE 12.1 Attack of the T-rex!

NOTE

Grab your own T-rex

You can find this T-rex (created by user Hurtzmyhead) at Thingiverse.com. Go to http://www.thingiverse.com/thing:12088.

You know what's better than one tyrannosaurus rex? You might have answered "two," but the best answer is "as many as you can squeeze in"!

Fortunately, MCEdit doesn't require you to import a new tyrannosaurus rex because there's a copy feature built in that makes it super-easy to just select what you want to copy and then paste another one…and another one…and another one.

Before you can make a copy in MCEdit, you need to have the object selected. It could be an animal, a building, or even just a bit of interesting terrain that you like and want to replicate.

As shown in Figure 12.2, you click on the Select tool and drag a box around the tyranno-saurus rex. You can use the blue Nudge and yellow Nudge buttons to fine-tune the selection area and reduce it to the smallest area possible that still contains the entire dinosaur.

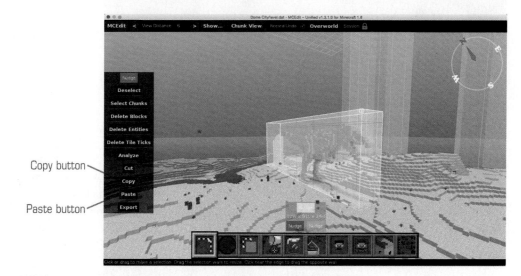

Copy button

Paste button

FIGURE 12.2 Use the Select tool to surround the dinosaur.

After selecting the dinosaur, you next click on the Copy button. A copy of the dinosaur is made available for pasting wherever you like and for however many copies you'd like to place. To place a copy, click on the Paste button and then move your mouse pointer to the desired location. As shown in Figure 12.3, a green selection area indicates where the copy will be placed.

FIGURE 12.3 Move the green selection area where you want to place the copy.

Click to lock in the location of the copy. You can use the Rotate and Roll buttons to make changes to the orientation. For example, in Figure 12.4 I've clicked on the Rotate button once to turn the dinosaur 90 degrees, so it's facing its partner. You can also click and hold on the green Nudge button and tap the WASD keys to move the location one block at a time in the direction of the tapped key.

FIGURE 12.4 Paste the copy and rotate and nudge it to place it where you want it.

NOTE

Change a copy's size easily

Keep in mind that not only can you place copies but you can also use the Scale Factor box to change the size of a copy. The value 1.0 corresponds to the original size of the object, so selecting 0.5 will change it to half of its original size. A value of 2.0 will change it to two times its original size.

To place the copy permanently, don't forget to click on the Import button. After that copy is placed, select Paste again if you want to add another. You can use the Paste button over and over again (or press Ctrl+V in Windows or Command+V on a Mac), and you can make changes to the orientation (with the Rotate button) and size (with Scale Factor) as needed.

After just a few clicks of the Paste button, the citizens of the domed cities are probably wondering just how durable those glass domes are against the gang of T-rexes shown in Figure 12.5.

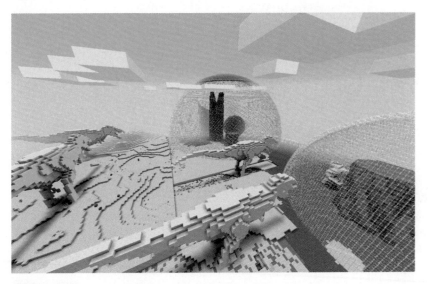

FIGURE 12.5 Attack of the T-rexes (the sequel).

Mirror, Mirror

Just as two (or a dozen) T-rexes are better than one, it's always a good idea to have an extra castle or two around for visiting friends to explore and modify. You just saw how easy it is to make a copy of any selected object. Next you'll see how you can add an extra step to what you've just learned to make something truly unique.

I'm going to start this demonstration by dropping into Tinkercad a castle that isn't symmetrical. In Figure 12.6, you're looking down on a castle from above, and you can see that the left side isn't an exact mirror of the right.

NOTE

Grab a copy of a great castle

You can download your own version of this castle (created by user smcameron) from http://www.thingiverse.com/thing:59581.

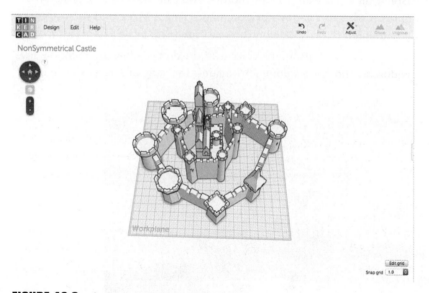

FIGURE 12.6   A nonsymmetrical castle.

If you make a copy of the castle and paste the copy and rotate it 180 degrees, you end up with something like what Figure 12.7 shows.

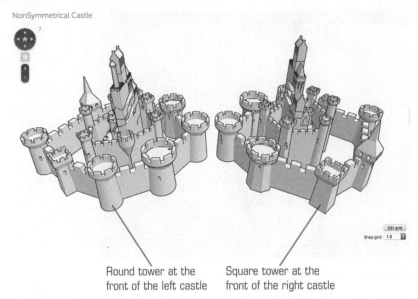

NonSymmetrical Castle

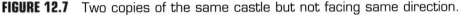

Round tower at the
front of the left castle

Square tower at the
front of the right castle

FIGURE 12.7   Two copies of the same castle but not facing same direction.

If you examine Figure 12.7 carefully, you'll notice that while the two side-by-side castles look similar, there are some differences. Look at the towers that are closest to the front of the image, and you'll see a round tower closest to the front on the left castle and a square tower closest to the front on the right castle.

I'd like a truly symmetrical castle, and while I can easily make a copy of this castle in Tinkercad and use the Mirror tool to create an exact mirror, I can also get the effect I want in MCEdit. Someday you might want to create a mirror image of something in Minecraft (as opposed to Tinkercad), so I'm going to show you how easy that is to do.

In Figure 12.8 you can see the nonsymmetrical castle placed in one of my worlds, and I'm viewing it in MCEdit.

FIGURE 12.8 This nonsymmetrical castle needs a mirror image.

Select the castle, as shown in Figure 12.9, and click Copy—just as you did in the previous section.

FIGURE 12.9 Select the castle and make a copy of it.

Now here's the tricky part: Before you place the castle in its final resting place, you need to press the G key or click Mirror. If you look at the control panel on the far left side of the screen (where the Rotate button is located), you'll notice an option called Mirror. You can click the Mirror button or just press the G key, and the copy instantly becomes a mirror image of the original.

Drag one of the round towers on the copy so it overlaps its mirror image on the castle on the right, as shown in Figure 12.10. (Use the Nudge button to get it as close as possible to overlapping, but it might not be perfect.)

Mirror button

FIGURE 12.10   Overlapping the same tower on the two castles.

When you're done with the overlapping, click the Import button, save your work, and then open up the world in Minecraft to see how it looks. As you can see in Figure 12.11, the two castles are perfect mirror images, and they share a single round tower.

FIGURE 12.11   One mega castle from two "smaller" castles!

The Mirror option is perfect when you have two objects that you want to share orientation. The Mirror tool is especially useful when copying and rotating one object 180 degrees would result in one of the objects facing backward.

Clone Clone Clone Clone

MCEdit gives you the ability to copy an object and paste as many copies as you like, but it can be a bit finicky when it comes to placing your copies exactly where you want them. That's why you're sure to find the Clone tool useful, especially if you're looking at creating something that repeats a specific number of times and you need the repeated copies to be placed carefully.

For this example, you're going to be building a bridge. Take a look at Figure 12.12, and you'll find a small section of a bridge span. You're going to use this single span to create a longer bridge with the Clone tool.

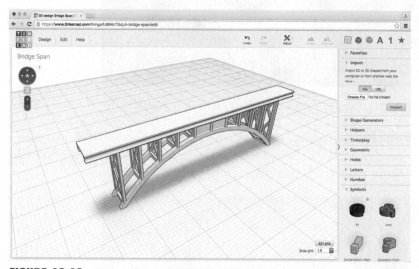

FIGURE 12.12   This little bridge can easily become one long bridge.

> ## NOTE
>
> **Grab a copy of the bridge**
>
> You can download your own version of this bridge span (created by user wolverineboat) from http://www.thingiverse.com/thing:272773.

You need to import the bridge section into a Minecraft world. (For this example, I'm using a flat world so you'll be able to easily see how this works, but the concept works just as well with mountains, lakes, and all other terrain.) Figure 12.13 shows the single section of bridge been imported with MCEdit.

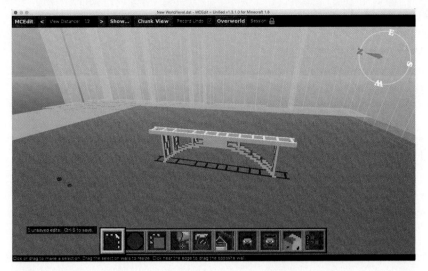

FIGURE 12.13 Import the single section of the bridge to get started.

After importing the bridge and placing it where you like (and pointed in the direction you want), use the Select tool and carefully use the Nudge buttons to reduce the selection box so it surrounds the bridge and maybe just a little bit of space around the structure. Figure 12.14 shows the bridge surrounded with the Select tool.

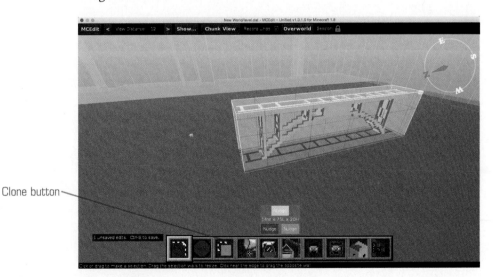

Clone button

FIGURE 12.14 Use the Select tool on the bridge section.

Next, you click on the Clone button. After clicking on the Clone button, a new window like the one in Figure 12.15 appears.

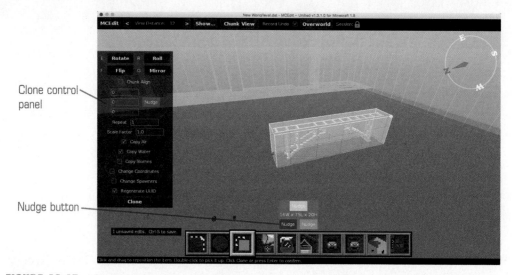

Clone control panel

Nudge button

FIGURE 12.15 Clicking the Clone button brings up the Clone control panel.

It's hard to tell from the figure, but there's an exact copy (a clone) of the selected bridge, sharing space with the original. To see the cloned copy, click on the single Nudge button and use the WASD keys to move it. The clone will appear in a green selection box. In Figure 12.16, I've used the A key to move the clone bridge to the left so you can see it.

FIGURE 12.16 The clone object will appear in a green selection box.

If you want the little bridge sections to be connected, keep pressing the A key while holding down the Nudge button. As you can see in Figure 12.17, you can stop when the end of the clone copy is still overlapping the original bridge section.

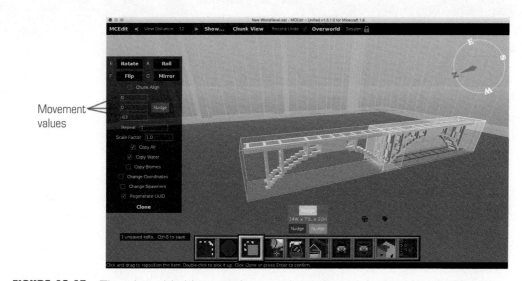

Movement values

FIGURE 12.17   The cloned bridge section overlaps the original bridge section.

Take a look at the Clone control panel, and you'll notice a text box with the value -63 in it. This means I moved the cloned bridge section 63 block lengths to the left. (If I'd moved the clone section to the right, it would have been 63, indicating that the copy moved 63 block lengths in the other direction.)

You can enter values in this box to get very specific placement, but keep in mind that the values are measured from the original object. Feel free to experiment with the WASD keys and see how a clone can be nudged forward, backward, left and right, and even up and down. The middle text box (just above the on that shows -63 in Figure 12.17) controls the up/down movement (Z-axis); a positive (+) value raises the cloned object that number of block lengths above the surface, while a negative (-) value lowers it.

Say that you're satisfied with the -63 block length movement to the left. While you could easily click the Clone button, you're not done yet. You want to connect a bunch of bridge lengths—say, 20 of them.

Because you've already defined how far the cloned object should be from the original, all you need to do now is specify how many clones should be added. For that, you type 19 in the Repeat box (not 20; the original bridge counts as 1, so you only need 19 "repeats"), and MCEdit shows the direction and length that many clones will occupy, as you can see in Figure 12.18.

Repeat box

Clone button

FIGURE 12.18 Specify how many clones will be created.

In Figure 12.18 you can see the green frame heading off into the distance. All that's left to do is to click the Clone button and let MCEdit do the hard work. As you can see in Figure 12.19, the bridge now looks like a real bridge! (Note that it can take a while to make and place a large number of copies, so be patient.)

FIGURE 12.19 The bridge disappears into the distance!

Conclusion

It is my sincere hope that during your adventures in this book, you learned something new and useful to do in Minecraft. If you learned a lot of new things, that's even better.

I've discovered over the years that when someone tells me that you "can't do that in the game/program," it lights a fire for me to go and find a way. Often, someone else has already found a solution, and all I have to do is a quick search online to find a video or set of instructions. But sometimes I have to experiment and try new things to figure out how to make things work. (The perfect example is when I was told that there was no way to view my Minecraft worlds in 3D without an Oculus Rift device. I think Chapter 7, "Seeing Your World In 3D," proved that wrong, huh?)

With Minecraft, your imagination is really your only limit. If you want something in your world, go find a 3D model on Thingiverse or some other model library. If it doesn't exist, create it with Tinkercad or another CAD application. Instead of creating something one block at a time, you can take an idea that's in your head and make it real in far less time.

I hope you've found a lot of inspiration for your Minecraft worlds, and hopefully the skills you picked up in this book will help you refine your worlds and impress your friends and family. Better yet, you may have discovered a skill you enjoy that could help you in school and maybe even a future career. You're now an official Minecraft engineer, and there is no limit to what you can learn and create for a Minecraft world and the real world.

Have fun!

MCEdit for Tablets

Throughout the book, you've seen how MCEdit can open worlds on Windows and Mac computers, and import .schematic files directly into those worlds. With Minecraft Pocket Edition (PE), fans of Minecraft can also create worlds on iOS and Android tablets. However, MCEdit cannot access the files that hold Minecraft PE worlds while the files are stored on the tablet. (MCEdit can also access Pocket Editions files from your mobile phone and the process you'll read about next works the same.)

Fans of Minecraft PE don't need to worry, however: There's always a way. There's a simple method (using a free piece of software for iOS devices) to copy a world file from an iOS tablet and getting it on a Mac or Windows computer. Once the file is on the Mac or Windows computer, you use MCEdit as normal to import objects, resize them, move them around, and more.

There is a catch, however. Right now MCEdit can only open Minecraft PE worlds created in version 0.8 and earlier. The current version of Minecraft PE is 0.11.1, and this new version is not compatible (at this writing) with MCEdit 1.0 or MCEdit 2.0.

If you're running version 0.8 of Minecraft PE, however, you can use the same MCEdit features you've seen in this book. After you make the changes to the level.dat file (which contains the information on any world you create with Minecraft PE), you simply copy the world file back to the tablet. The steps for this process are described in the next section.

Introducing iFunbox for Mac and Windows

An application that lets you move your Minecraft PE files back and forth between iOS devices and computers is called iFunbox—it's installed on a computer and then communicates with an attached phone or tablet. There are versions for both Windows and Mac, so visit http://www.i-funbox.com and download the free version for your operating system and follow the instructions to install it. I'll be using the Windows version of iFunbox; the Mac version looks a bit different but works the same. Figure A.1 shows the Windows version on the left and the Mac version on the right.

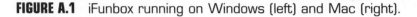

FIGURE A.1 iFunbox running on Windows (left) and Mac (right).

In Figure A.2, you can see a world I've created on my iPad using Minecraft PE. If you have an Android tablet running Minecraft PE version 0.8 or earlier, you can also follow the process described here.

FIGURE A.2 A Minecraft world created with Minecraft PE on iPad.

After installing iFunbox, save your world and close out of Minecraft PE on your tablet. You'll need to know the name of your world, so make a note of it if you have multiple worlds created. My sample world, which has a nice river running through two high canyon walls, is called Canyon.

Connecting a Tablet to iFunbox

Connect your tablet to your computer with a USB cable. iFunbox will detect when the tablet is connected, and you should see your tablet appear in the device listing when you click on the File Browser tab, as shown in Figure A.3.

File Browser tab

Managing
App Data tab

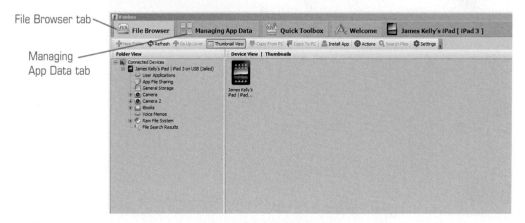

FIGURE A.3   iFunbox detects when a tablet is connected.

Click on the Managing App Data tab, and you'll see a list of all the apps on your tablet, as shown in Figure A.4. (As you can see, my sons have a lot of games installed on their dad's iPad.)

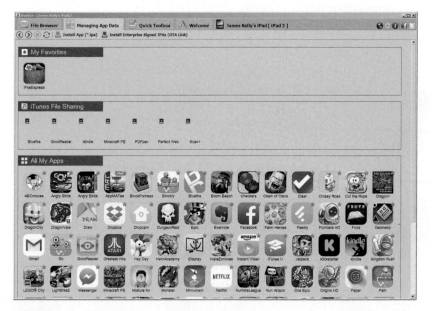

FIGURE A.4   Thumbnails of the various apps on your tablet are displayed.

Find the Minecraft PE app icon and double-click it. A new window opens, like the one shown in Figure A.5.

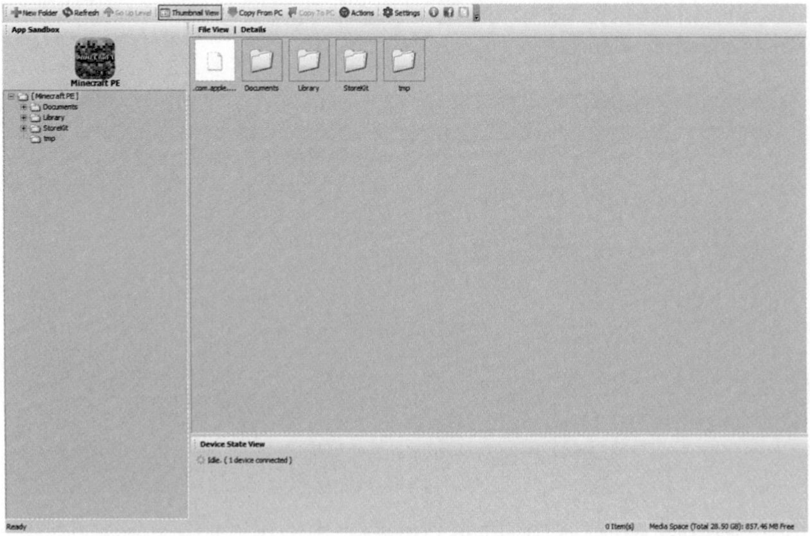

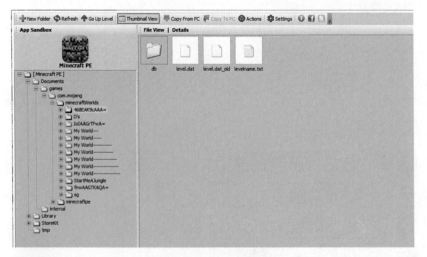

FIGURE A.5   The App Sandbox window opens and lets you explore Minecraft PE.

Click on the + symbol next to Documents and continue opening up the folders inside, as shown in Figure A.6. As you can see in the figure, the path to your game files is Documents, games, com.mojang, minecraftWorlds.

FIGURE A.6   Expand the Documents folder until you locate the minecraftWorlds folder.

Sometimes the name of your world matches a folder (such as the StartMeAJungle folder shown in Figure A.6) and other times it can be hard to find. If you click on a folder inside the minecraftWorlds folder, you'll see a text file called levelname.txt. If you double-click that, it opens up a document, as shown in Figure A.7, that lists the name of the world so you can confirm which folder matches the world you want to edit.

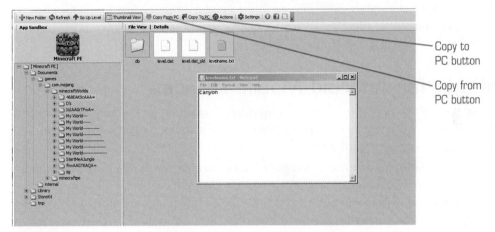

Copy to PC button

Copy from PC button

FIGURE A.7 Find the folder for the game world you want to edit.

Create a folder on your desktop to hold the Minecraft PE files that you'll be editing with MCEdit. I've created one called Minecraft PE Levels. Click once on the folder that holds the Minecraft PE game world you want to edit and then click the Copy to PC button. In the window that opens, browse to the folder you created to hold the world files and click the Save button, as shown in Figure A.8.

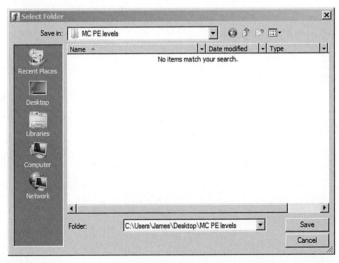

FIGURE A.8 Save the world's folder to your computer.

Once the folder is saved to your computer, you can use MCEdit to make changes, import .schematic files, and use pretty much any of the other features that MCEdit offers.

Save your changes in MCEdit and then open up iFunbox again. This time, however, open up the minecraftWorlds folder once again (after connecting your tablet), click on the Copy from PC button, and browse to the saved folder on your computer. Replace the original folder (still on your tablet) with the new folder (stored on your computer). Open up Minecraft PE, and if everything worked correctly, you should see your Minecraft PE world modified with whatever you did using MCEdit.

MCEdit for Android Mobile Devices

Android phones and tablets don't need software like iFunbox for you to transfer files to and from a computer—connect an Android mobile device to a computer and it shows up as a basic storage device like a hard drive.

Double-click your Android device's storage device and browse to the following directory: My Files > Games > com.mojang > minecraft worlds. Locate the level.dat file associated with the world you wish to edit and copy that file to your computer and open and edit with MCEdit. When done, overwrite the level.dat file on your phone or tablet with the one you edited on your computer.

Adding Interactive Elements With Redstone

Redstone is a standard block found in Minecraft that allows you to create automated objects. Buttons to open doors, vending machines for potions, and triggers for traps are popular items, but because redstone allows you to "wire up" creations, there's not a lot you can't do with a redstone block. Imagine adding controlled lighting to your castle or maybe an automatic arrow firing system to anyone who triggers a pressure plate when enemies approach your home.

This appendix provides a basic description of how to use redstone along with how to create a simple mechanism. (You might also hunt down a copy of Stephen O'Brien's Minecraft books as he goes into a bit more detail about Redstone than I can in this appendix.)

Redstone Basics

The redstone block can be found in both Creative mode and Survival. Keep in mind that when you're in Survival mode, redstone may be difficult to find at first and later it may be difficult to obtain in large quantities. For this reason, many of the redstone creations you'll find online are done in Creative mode, where redstone quantities are of no concern.

Redstone blocks can be mined for redstone dust (see Figure B.1). With redstone dust and other basic items (such as a stick or an iron ingot), you can create objects like a redstone torch, a redstone repeater, or a piston. Then you can send "current" (Minecraft's version of electricity) along a line of redstone dust to these items to power traps, doors, lights, and other features.

FIGURE B.1 You can mine redstone block for redstone dust or use it as a power supply.

For more information on redstone components, visit http://minecraft.gamepedia.com/ Redstone_components. To view more details, including a recipe for creating a particular redstone device, click on an individual component (such as a redstone piston).

A Simple Circuit

For one of the best online sources of information on redstone circuits, visit http://minecraft. gamepedia.com/Redstone_circuit and examine the various examples of contraptions. There are some amazing designs that can add fun capabilities to your creations. Imagine putting a lamp in each window of a castle and turning them all on at the same time with the push of a single button. Or, to prepare for a castle invasion, you can easily power a pressure plate that, when stepped on, will unleash arrows from a nearby dispenser. With redstone, you can do these things and much more.

In a nutshell, using redstone is all about moving current from one place to another. You can drop redstone dust on top of other blocks to create a path where the current can flow. Current flowing in redstone dust can go a maximum of 15 block lengths (any combination of straight paths and 90-degree turns). Also, you can use redstone components such as torches and repeaters to extend how far the dust can carry current.

Take a look at Figure B.2, and you'll see that I've placed a line of redstone dust that runs 10 block lengths. At this point, the redstone dust is unpowered.

FIGURE B.2 A line of unpowered redstone dust.

At the end of the redstone dust, I drop in a simple lever. Notice in Figure B.3 what happens when the lever is flipped: The redstone dust lights up, and little red bursts of energy are visible to indicate that current is flowing. There isn't yet anything at the end of the line, however, so let's change that.

FIGURE B.3 The redstone dust lights up when the lever is flipped.

After flipping the lever back to the off position, I've added a door to the end of the redstone line, as shown in Figure B.4. (This door is framed by sandstone blocks, but it could easily be placed between brick or quartz or any other material to act as a doorway.)

FIGURE B.4 Add a door on the other end of the redstone dust.

A flip of the lever causes the door to open, as shown in Figure B.5.

FIGURE B.5 The door opens when the lever is pulled.

This is a very simple example, but I hope it's helping you understand the value of redstone. It's handy to be able to turn objects on and off in a Minecraft world by using redstone dust and other objects that are powered (such as doors and dispensers). Imagine hollowing out a T-rex statue and placing glowing red torches powered by redstone dust in the dinosaur's eyes. If you created a castle in Chapter 1, "Taking Over a Castle," and placed it in a world, consider using pistons to create a large door that opens and closes, protecting you from creepers, giant spiders, and zombies.

The uses of redstone are really only limited by your skill and imagination, so get started using redstone and see what kinds of automation you can bring to your worlds.

Advanced Redstone

Much has been written—even entire books—about redstone. If you find the subject interesting, look online, and you'll find hours and hours of examples in videos and tutorials. Minecraft fans have built some amazing things; large computers, clocks, video games, and roller coaster parks are just a few of the crazy (and fully functional) items that people have powered with redstone.

A few resources on redstone are available in Appendix C, "Resources," but here are a couple more for those of you who can't wait to get started using this incredible tool:

- *Minecraft Crafting Guide* (http://www.minecraft-craftingguide.com/mechanisms.html)— This is a great list of things you can build with redstone, complete with recipes and descriptions of how the items work.

- *Minecraft Redstone Handbook* (http://www.amazon.com/Minecraft-Redstone-Handbook-Official-Mojang/dp/054568515X)—This is the official Mojang book on using redstone, and it contains excellent tutorials as well as a number of examples of using redstone to create impressive games and structures.

Resources

There are so many Minecraft-related resources out there that it would be almost impossible to list them all. New books, new videos, and new websites appear so frequently (videos are posted almost hourly) that compiling a comprehensive source list isn't possible for an appendix like this one. Instead, this appendix provides you with a list of books, videos, and websites that I've found useful over the years. Some of these resources are related to Minecraft directly, while others offer skills that you may find useful outside of playing Minecraft.

Keep in mind that resources come and go. A video listed here could easily be taken down at any time, books go out of print, and websites sometimes go out of date or get shut down. If one of the resources listed here is no longer available, look around, and you're likely to find something similar.

If you find something useful or interesting that you believe other Minecraft fans will find useful, please consider posting the information to this book's Facebook page. If it's relevant and useful or interesting, I'll add it to my Minecraft Engineer Resource List with a nod of thanks to you for submitting it! You can find the book's Facebook page at https://www.facebook.com/engineeringminecraft.

Books

The following are some of the books currently available related to Minecraft, computer-aided design (CAD), and similar topics:

- *The Ultimate Guide to Minecraft Server* (http://www.amazon.com/ dp/0789754576/)—This book, written by fellow writer and friend Tim Warner, will teach you everything you need to know about setting up your own Minecraft server and customizing it to fit you and your friends' exact requirements.

- *The Ultimate Player's Guide to Minecraft* (http://www.amazon.com/dp/078975357X)—For both beginners and experts, this book explains all the ins and outs of living and surviving in a Minecraft world. In addition to discussing Minecraft basics, it also covers many rather complex features explained in easy-to-understand language. It's a great all-in-one-book guide.

- *3D Modeling and Printing with Tinkercad* (http://www.amazon.com/3D-Modeling-Print-ing-Tinkercad-Create/dp/0789754908)—This book goes deeper into the bells and whis-tles that Tinkercad offers. It offers plenty of hands-on exercises and projects to expand your Tinkercad skills and apply them to Minecraft.

- *Minecraft: The Complete Handbook Collection* (http://www.amazon.com/dp/0545685192)—These four books cover topics from building to survival to combat to using redstone. It is widely considered one of the best Minecraft book series for beginners.

- *Adventures in Minecraft* (http://www.amazon.com/dp/111894691X)—With this book, you will learn how to modify Minecraft worlds by programming your own tweaks and objects. It's not so much a how-to book for creating Minecraft structures. Rather, it's a great introductory book to the field of programming that introduces the Python pro-gramming language.

Videos

There are just too many videos for me to ever hope to review and share them all with you, but I've listed here a handful that stand out. As always, parents and teachers should try their best to view the videos first to ensure that a helpful video hasn't been replaced with something that's not "kid-friendly" and not suitable for viewing. Everything listed here was safe when I checked:

- **"How to Make a" series** (https://www.youtube.com/user/MagmaMusen)—With silly music and text-based instructions included, these videos are fun to watch. You'll be amazed at how quickly and easily MagmaMusen creates some amazing little creations—from a pinball machine to a secret passage to a dishwasher.

- **Awesome Redstone Minecraft House** (https://www.youtube.com/watch?v=IHfJgPB3b48)—This video presents working elevators, push-button controls, and hidden passages. You'll get an idea of just how powerful a working knowledge of the Minecraft redstone block can be for your own structures. (See Appendix B, "Redstone Tutorial," for more information on redstone.)

- **Minecraft: Redstone for Dummies – A Basic Guide** (https://www.youtube.com/watch?v=XN_MIX7M460)—This video provides a short and easy introduction to red-stone and how it works. It doesn't go super deep, but it will help even novices build some very simple automated features using redstone.

- **Autodesk Tinkercad tutorials** (https://www.youtube.com/user/Tinkercad)—From the company that owns Tinkercad, you'll find dozens of helpful how-to videos on using

Tinkercad. These are the "official" videos from Autodesk, but a quick search of YouTube for "Tinkercad tutorial" will yield hundreds more.

- **MCEdit Tutorial** (https://www.youtube.com/watch?v=Bpuq2LIUy1E)—User SethBling does a great job of introducing the basics of MCEdit. He also has a four-part redstone tutorial that's worth watching.

Websites

Websites come and go, but a few have managed to stand the test of time and offer up some good information and tutorials. Here is a list of some websites I've found useful and relevant to the projects and skills you've read about in this book:

- **Minecraft Wiki's Tutorials page** (http://minecraft.gamepedia.com/Tutorials)—There are many websites devoted to helping novice Minecrafters, and Minecraft Wiki stands out as one of the best kid-friendly and useful sites, with dozens of guides (complete with full-color images) and reference lists. Minecraft is always being updated, and this site is very good at keeping up-to-date tutorials and archiving out-of-date content. This is one of the best places to start for all Minecraft novices with questions.

- **How-to Geek's Engineering with Redstone lesson** (http://www.howtogeek.com/ school/htg-guide-to-minecraft/lesson11/)—The HowToGeek.com website has some great articles on a large variety of topics, not just Minecraft. But it also has some outstanding single-page tutorials related to Minecraft topics. This redstone lesson is excellent, but be sure to check out the other lessons that the site offers.

- **Stereoscopy** (https://en.wikipedia.org/?title=Stereoscopy)—If you enjoyed seeing your Minecraft worlds in 3D (Chapter 7, "Seeing Your World in 3D"), you might be interested in learning more about how your eyes work and some additional methods you might use to create some fun 3D Minecraft images.

- **Making a 3D Print of a Real Object Using 123D Catch and Meshmixer** (http://www. instructables.com/id/Making-a-3D-print-of-a-real-object-using-123D-Catc/)—You learned in Chapter 8, "A Full 360!" how to use the 123D Catch app to create a 3D video of a Minecraft world object (in that case, an Easter Island–like monolith). This article shows you how to print an object like that one in plastic, using a 3D printer.

INDEX

Symbols

A

Z

Other Books
YOU MIGHT LIKE!

ISBN: 9780789755742

ISBN: 9780789755735

ISBN: 9780789754578

ISBN: 9780134037646

ISBN: 9780789754769

ISBN: 9780789754349

SAVE 30%
Use discount code MINECRAFT

Visit Quepublishing.com
to learn more!

REGISTER THIS PRODUCT
SAVE 35%*
ON YOUR NEXT PURCHASE!

How to Register Your Product

- Go to quepublishing.com/register
- Sign in or create an account
- Enter ISBN: 10- or 13-digit ISBN that appears on the back cover of your product

Benefits of Registering

- Ability to download product updates
- Access to bonus chapters and workshop files
- A 35% coupon to be used on your next purchase – valid for 30 days
  To obtain your coupon, click on "Manage Codes" in the right column of your Account page
- Receive special offers on new editions and related Que products

Please note that the benefits for registering may vary by product. Benefits will be listed on your Account page under Registered Products.

We value and respect your privacy. Your email address will not be sold to any third party company.

* 35% discount code presented after product registration is valid on most print books, eBooks, and full-course videos sold on QuePublishing.com. Discount may not be combined with any other offer and is not redeemable for cash. Discount code expires after 30 days from the time of product registration. Offer subject to change.

quepublishing.com